A DIP INTO THE BATH CLUB.

CHRISTIE'S REVIEW
OF THE SEASON 1982

CHRISTIE'S REVIEW OF THE SEASON 1982

Edited by John Herbert

PHAIDON · CHRISTIE'S
OXFORD

Distributed through Phaidon · Christie's Ltd
Littlegate House, St Ebbe's Street, Oxford OX1 1SQ

British Library Cataloguing in Publication Data

Christie's review of the season.—1982
   1. Art—Periodicals
   705   N9

ISBN 0-7148-8002-7

Design and layout by Norman Ball
Phototypeset in CRTronic Baskerville by
Logos Design, Datchet, Berkshire

Printed and bound in The Netherlands by
Drukkerij Onkenhout b.v., Hilversum

ENDPAPERS: Henry Mays Bateman: *A Dip into the Bath Club*
Signed and inscribed. Pen, ink and watercolour
77.5 x 47 cm. Sold 17 and 18.9.81 for £2,100 ($3,843)

FRONTISPIECE: Queen Anne black japanned bureau bookcase
Early 18th century
99 cm wide; 237.5 cm high
Sold 17.10.81 in New York for $946,000 (£516,939)
Record auction price for a piece of English furniture
From the collection of The Pierpont Morgan Library.
Formerly owned by H.R.H. the late Duke of Windsor, K.G., and subsequently by Merle Oberon

All prices include the buyer's premium where applicable. The currency equivalents given throughout the book are based on the rate of exchange ruling at the time of the sale

4

CONTENTS

Ivory netsuke of
standing Dutchman
holding a wild pig
across his back
Unsigned
Kyoto school
18th century
Sold 28.10.81 in
London for £7,590
($13,889)

The Hon. Patrick Lindsay at an early stage in the bidding for Turner's *Temple of Jupiter Panellenius Restored* which sold for £648,000 ($1,121,040)

Chalcedony scent bottle in the form of a
cat with rose-cut diamond collar signed by
Boucheron
Sold 19.11.81 in Geneva for
Sw.fr.30,000 ($8,928)

Foreword

BRENDAN GILL

The 1981-1982 season was economically a vexatious one on both sides of the Atlantic; it is therefore not unreasonable of Christie's to feel a measure of modest jubilation at having survived so satisfactorily the current hard times – a feat accomplished in part thanks to the fiscal prudence practised by management in earlier, easier times. The firm pressed vigorously forward in sale after sale, against a tide of almost universally dolorous expectations. One favourable omen during the course of the season was the silencing of the objections voiced by British art-dealers to Christie's imposition, several years ago, of a buyer's premium of 10 per cent. Early in the autumn common sense prevailed, and a number of dealers withdrew the legal action they had proposed to take against Christie's and their Bond Street rivals on the grounds of alleged collusion over the introduction of the premium. As a reciprocal gesture of goodwill the auction houses undertook to review independently amongst other matters the buyer's premium. In December Christie's announced they would be reducing it to 8 per cent as from January 1st. Following the withdrawal of dealers' action, Her Majesty's Government's Office of Fair Trading asked the Fine Art Trade organizations for evidence which they claimed they had of collusion over the introduction of the premium. The Director-General of the Office of Fair Trading decided categorically that there was no case to answer.

It remains only for dealers and auction houses to resume their habitual stance as friendly rivals, which will be to the benefit not only of London as an art market but also New York and European auction centres.

Another favourable omen was the repeated evidence that even in periods of comparative hardship, articles of the highest quality continued to draw staggeringly impressive prices. If there were fewer sales than usual at Christie's this season, the percentage of items sold at each auction was reassuringly high – that is to say often in the nineties and a stunning 100 per cent in the case of an auction of musical manuscripts. Moreover, the rarity of the items offered was as remarkable as ever, and this has led to notably happy consequences for the vendors. In an auction house, a breaking sound is welcome only when the thing being broken isn't a rosy morsel of Meissen but a record price; and record-breaking amounted to a commonplace at Christie's throughout the year. Among artists achieving their highest auction prices were Copley, Tait, Sargent, Cassatt, Munnings, Kandinsky, Rothko, Motherwell and Stella. New price levels were attained in photography as well: Edward Weston's *Nautilus* brought $28,000 (£15,052), a record for a 20th century photograph.

Some record-breaking figures are more astonishing than others, either because of the enormous increase in price that has been reached since the item first appeared at a sale, or because the price it brings is so much greater than any informal pre-auction appraisal of its

Viewing room at Christie's Park Avenue prior to the sale of Contemporary Art on 5.5.82

value had led the public to expect. In the first instance, we have the example of a Tissot painting, *The Bunch of Lilacs*, that sold in 1887 for 150 guineas; for 7,000 guineas ($16,170) in 1975 and this year at Christie's brought £81,000 ($148,230); and the still more exceptional example of a pair of George III marquetry commodes which sold at Christie's in 1931 for 15 guineas and this year brought £88,000 ($168,080).

In the second instance, we have the example of a Queen Anne black japanned bureau bookcase that Christie's sold in New York in October for $946,000 (£516,939). The bookcase had once belonged to Queen Mary who gave it to her son, the Duke of Windsor, by whom it was sold at auction in 1957 for just over 1,500 guineas. It came into the possession of the actress Merle Oberon and was sold at auction by her estate in 1973 for $95,000 (£39,583). The purchaser presented it to The Pierpont Morgan Library a few years ago, with the understanding that the Library would be free to dispose of it whenever it chose to do so. Charles Ryskamp, the

1967 Morris Minor 1000 four-door saloon
Price new in England: £642
Sold 20.7.82 at Beaulieu for £1,300 ($2,275)

The historic Morris Minor was supplied new in 1967 to Lambeth Palace for the use of the
Archbishops of Canterbury. In August 1980, when it had done only 18,000 miles (28,800km) it was
presented by the present Archbishop, Dr Robert Runcie, for entry in the Air India Himalayas Rally as
a fund-raising gesture for the Gunnar Nilsson Cancer Charity. It was driven in this event by the well
known ex-BMC rallyist, the Rev. Rupert Jones, and successfully completed the 3,000 mile (5,000km)
marathon in fifteenth place. Since completion of this event, it has returned into the hands of Lord
Montagu, the sponsor, and has been on display in the National Motor Museum

distinguished director of the Library, whenever he hastened past the bookcase in a corridor of
the Library, began to suspect that its gilt was flaking off; alarmed, he consigned it to Christie's
where the general expectation was that it would bring between $300,000 and $400,000. As
things turned out, a number of bidders pushed the price quickly to about half a million dollars;
from that point on, a fierce duel of dollars was waged between two collectors, neither of whom
was willing to yield until at last the hammer was brought down at a price three or four times as
great as the estimate.

To a layman, what is perennially startling about the world of auctions is not how high prices may go, even in a recession, or how great a variety of rarities are subject to the disciplined extravagance of the true collector – some shrunken human heads from Peru were sold at Christie's this year, at what was surely a good price for shrunken human heads, and so was a 1934 Packard sport phaeton (at $350,000 [£184,210], a record for any American car); no, what startles us is how vast a treasure-house of beautiful objects the world possesses and is able to buy and sell with undiminished ardour, generation after generation.

Throughout history, it has been a small privileged class that has produced – or has provided the incentive for others to produce – the exquisite creations, whether in the form of gems, ceramics, paintings, sculpture, manuscripts, or printed books – that make up so much of the cultural inheritance of the human race. In early times, that privileged class must have numbered in the thousands, and by the 18th century, if one includes all of the civilizations that had risen, flourished and declined by that date, perhaps it could have been numbered in the hundreds of thousands. And yet what an astounding assortment of ancient, lovely objects are offered to us daily, with nothing more lofty and inaccessible than money being needed to make them our own!

The following pages show what a wealthy new collector might have gathered up this very year, simply by keeping awake at all of the Christie's auctions this season in New York, London, Geneva and elsewhere. Our imaginary collector would have been accused, of course, of cultivating a taste as indiscriminate as that of the American robber-barons of the 19th century, to say nothing of their counterparts in Renaissance Italy, but no matter. With an effort, we bear in mind that this Review, both in length and variety, is but a tiny fraction of the heaped-up assortment of wonders that have passed through Christie's auction rooms in the course of *a single season*. We shake our heads incredulously; at the same time, we must take care to avoid superlatives, for nothing is more likely than that fresh cornucopias of wonders will go on tirelessly pouring themselves out under the insouciant gaze of James Christie's ghost and in the presence of his industrious professional descendants. The melodrama of acquisition and disposal is an inveterately thrilling one; we are lucky indeed to have Christie's serving us as a stage upon which that melodrama has been enacted for well over two centuries now and, so every portent declares, will continue to be enacted for centuries to come.

Listen! At the front of the auction room, a voice strikes a note of confident high spirits. "We have here," the voice says, "an 18th-century British chronometer with an unusually interesting provenance..." Eagerly, we lean forward; the plot has begun to unfold and nobody present can predict its ending.

Negotiated Sales

CHRISTOPHER R. PONTER LL.B

Prudent rearrangement of a family's financial position often occasions a charge to Capital Transfer Tax which can be satisfied in part by the transfer of pre-eminent works of art, or by a direct sale by private treaty to a national institution. Opportunity then arises for the local gallery or museum to acquire objects long associated with a particular family or historic house in their area, utilizing the "douceur" arrangements.

Following the death of Lord Leigh in 1979, his Trustees decided to take advantage of the heritage provisions of the 1975 legislation to refurbish Stoneleigh Abbey in Warwickshire. Prior to the sale of items not considered to be essential to the house, Warwick Museum expressed interest in two flintlock guns made by the celebrated local gunmaker, Nicholas Paris of Warwick, and a gross price of £40,000 ($74,000) was agreed. Subsequently an important mahogany side table by William Gomm was purchased by the nation to be placed on display in the Chapel at Stoneleigh for which it was commissioned in 1764.

Since the family of the Dukes of Newcastle left Clumber Park in Nottingham, their archives, comprising the personal and political papers of the Pelham family and the early Dukes of Newcastle, have been carefully stored and catalogued in the University Library. By negotiating a satisfactory transfer in lieu of taxes, this position has been made permanent. Three family portraits, and three Dutch paintings, from the Newcastle collection totalling nearly £200,000 ($370,000) await allocation.

The links between the Sefton family and the Walker Art Gallery, Liverpool, were strengthened with the negotiated transfer during the year of a group of family paintings by the local artist Richard Ansdel in lieu of the C.T.T. payable on the death of the Countess of Sefton. The gross value involved was £125,000 ($231,250).

Many visitors to The Royal Pavilion, Brighton, will have admired the stunning display of silver-gilt in the Banqueting Room, much of which comprised items on loan from the Londonderry family since 1955. Christie's were pleased to negotiate a private treaty sale to Brighton Corporation of a representative group of the Ambassadorial plate ordered by the 3rd Marquess of Londonderry following the Treaties of Vienna in 1813/15. The overall gross value was in the region of £250,000 ($462,500).

As reported elsewhere, the unique Mostyn Tompion clock was sold privately to the British Museum for a net sum, including the "douceur", of £500,000 ($925,000).

The Londonderry Silver: one of a pair
of silver-gilt soup-tureens, covers and
stands
By Paul Storr
1813; the stands 1814
Stands 50.8 cm long

Silver-gilt seven light candelabrum
By Paul Storr
1814; 87.6 cm high

These two illustrated items come from
a large collection of silver-gilt and silver
assembled by Charles, 3rd Marquess of
Londonderry (1778-1854), including
certain plate issued to him as British
Ambassador to the Emperor of Austria
in 1814. This Ambassadorial Plate is
among the most imposing services of
Regency silver gilt to remain intact.
Acquired by The Royal Pavilion,
Brighton

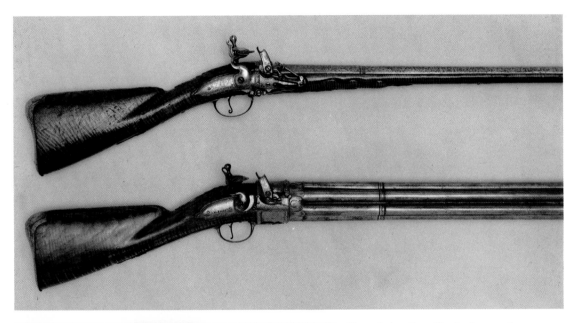

Breech-loading flintlock sporting gun
By Nicholas Paris of Warwick
Late 17th century
30 in. barrel
Now in The Warwick Museum,
Warwick

GEORGE SEURAT: *Nu Assis*
Charcoal on paper
Drawn 1883/4
31.4 x 24.1 cm
Study for the central figure
in *La Baignade à Asnières*
in The National Gallery, London
Now in The National Gallery
of Scotland, Edinburgh

PICTURES, DRAWINGS AND PRINTS

ALEXANDRE FRANCOIS DESPORTES:
Cassowary, a Great Crested Grebe, a Lesser Sulphur-crested Cockatoo, a Roseate Spoonbill, with other Birds and an Armadillo, in an Exotic Landscape
Signed
113 x 133.4 cm
Sold 23.4.82 in London for £48,600 ($86,994)
From the collection of Major Sir William Pennington-Ramsden, Bt.
It is known that Desportes made studies of exotic fauna in the royal menagerie of King Louis XIV

ALESSANDRO BONVICINO, called MORETTO DA BRESCIA: *The Madonna and Child with Saint Roch*
85.6 x 112.2 cm
Sold 9.7.82 in London for £48,600 ($84,078)
Previously sold at Christie's 16 February 1940 for 40gns

GUIDO CAGNACCI: *The Redemption of Mary Magdalen*
229.4 x 265.5 cm
Sold 11.12.81 in London for £209,000 ($401,280)
This hitherto unpublished picture is first recorded in the 1809 Bulstrode Inventory

Carlone's Ceiling Painting

WILLIAM MOSTYN-OWEN

The succession in 1723 of the young Clemens-August of the Bavarian house of Wittelsbach to the position of Archbishop-Elector of Cologne marked the start of a brilliant era in the patronage of the arts in that city. Thanks to his enormous revenues, Clemens-August was able to undertake the complete rebuilding of his summer palace Schloss Brühl, and in 1728 he appointed François de Cuvilliés as his architect. This remarkable man, who started as Court dwarf in Munich, had risen to be the greatest exponent of the Rococo style in Germany. But for his ambitious scheme for the staircase, the Elector called on the still more audacious Balthasar Neumann who had already produced the staircases at Würzburg and at Bruchsal and who took as his theme of decoration the power, the munificence and the good taste of Clemens - August. The breathtaking height of the stair is enhanced by the bravura of the stucco-work by Artari, the ingenuity of the ironwork by Sandteuer and the crowning glory of the oval ceiling by Carlo Carlone.

Born in 1686 into a family of *stuccatori*, Carlone must be considered as one of the great exponents of 18th century rococo. Leaving Italy at the age of 24 he embarked on a career that took him in the next 15 years throughout Germany and Austria, and his work is to be found at Linz, Wagram, Passau, Vienna, Ludwigsburg and Breslau. In 1725 and 1726 he was in Italy and then returned northwards, working at Prague and Ansbach. Between 1737 and 1740 he decorated the Cathedral at Monza and carried out schemes of decoration in no less than five Lombard villas.

At the age of 54 he once again returned to Germany but his work at Schloss Brühl started about 10 years later when he frescoed not only the ceiling over the staircase but also those of the *Gardensaal* and the *Musiksaal*, an astonishing feat for a man of his age and the culmination of a great career.

CARLO INNOCENZO CARLONE: *Magnanimity and Magnificence as Benefactresses of the Arts*
139.7 x 125.7 cm
Sold 9.7.82 in London for £226,800 ($392,364)

ANTONIO CANAL, IL CANALETTO: *The Grand Canal, Venice, looking East from the Campo di San Vio*
60 x 97 cm
Sold 18.6.82 in New York for $220,000 (£124,293)

ANTONIO CANAL, IL CANALETTO: *Extensive View of Piazza San Marco, Venice*
126.4 x 202.5 cm
Sold 11.12.81 in London for £60,500 ($116,160)
From the collection of the Bath Club
Previously sold at Christie's 7 May 1898 for 165gns

The Diana and Cupid of Batoni

FRANCIS RUSSELL

It was as a portrait painter that Pompeo Batoni was most assiduously employed by the English, and this summer's exhibition at Kenwood House showed how responsive the painter was to the aspirations of his sitters, for whom the Grand Tour marked the final, and most extravagant, stage of an education that was overwhelmingly classical in emphasis. Sir Humphry Morice, of whom Batoni supplied three portraits, was a traveller of a rather different kind. He was in his late thirties when in 1760 his health led him to set out for Italy; a connoisseur of discernment he had inherited both the means and the collection of his 2nd Cousin, Sir William Morice, 3rd Bt. of Werrington, who himself had sat to Rosalba and purchased a number of distinguished Venetian pictures. Morice reached Rome in the spring of 1761 and must then have commissioned the *Diana and Cupid*; the inscription on it implies that it was finished in that year, although Batoni's receipt for 300 zechins was not signed until 1 April 1762.

The picture, like so many by the artist, is conspicuously well preserved, its brilliance of colour – the apricot of Diana's robes is particularly memorable – scarcely impaired by an old varnish. Such details as the wings of Cupid, the hounds, of whose appeal to the English Batoni had long been in no doubt, and the landscape mark this as a masterpiece of his full maturity. It is indeed a key work in that sequence of historical pictures in which the painter anticipates the more rigorous neoclassicism of the following generation without departing from the essential canons of the Grand Manner which had dominated the Roman School for so long. It is of additional interest as one of less than half a dozen pictures of the kind ordered by British patrons.

Batoni's portraits are almost all of standard sizes, and it is thus of particular interest that the two of Sir Humphry reclining with his hounds, the signed and dated example of 1762 (or 3) at Norton Conyers and the better-known picture in the Ford Collection, which are otherwise unique in this respect, are of exactly the same size as the *Diana and Cupid*. That Morice is presented as a sportsman, with his gun, his hounds and the trophies these have retrieved, strengthens my conviction that the composition was conceived, however loosely, as a pendant to the *Diana*: its place as the predecessor of such reclining portraits in *plein air* settings as Wright of Derby's *Sir Brook Boothby* is thus even more intriguing than has hitherto been realized.

The *Diana and Cupid* was housed not at Werrington, the house inherited from his cousin and to which Morice owed his control of the borough of Launceston for which he sat in Parliament for 30 years, but at The Grove, near Chiswick, where his collection of landscapes by such masters as Claude, Poussin and Gaspar, Rosa and Orizzonte was admired by Horace Walpole and others. Sir Humphry died unmarried in 1785, leaving the considerable sum of £600 a year for the maintenance of his horses and dogs, descendants perhaps of those Batoni observed so carefully. A year later his collection was sold *en bloc* for £4,000 to Lord Ashburnham, who was advised by an agent that the *Diana and Cupid* "was painted under the direction of Sir William Hamilton...It was thought at Rome to be the best picture he ever made, which perhaps is not saying a great deal". The picture remained in the Ashburnham collection until it was sent to Christie's, 18 June 1824. That it fetched 50 guineas shows how far Batoni's reputation had by then been eclipsed. Over a century later, on 31 March 1933, it returned to Christie's and was sold for 195 guineas.

POMPEO GIROLAMO BATONI: *Diana Breaking Cupid's Bow*
Signed and dated Roma 1761
124.5 x 172.7 cm
Sold 9.7.82 in London for £140,040 ($242,269)

PIETER BRUEGEL THE YOUNGER: *Summer: Harvesters Working and Eating in a Cornfield*
Signed and dated 1624
On panel
72.4 x 104.8 cm
Sold 11.12.81 in London for £242,000 ($464,640)
One of two renderings of *Summer* by Pieter Bruegel the Younger which combine motifs created by his father in the *Summer* or *Corn Harvest*, Metropolitan Museum of Art, New York, and in the engraving of *Summer*

PIETER BRUEGEL THE YOUNGER: *The Adoration of the Magi*
On panel
40.5 x 57 cm
Sold 9.7.82 in London for £70,200 ($121,446)
From the collection of Lord Trevor

MARTIN RYCKAERT: *Extensive Wooded River Landscape with Travellers on a Path and Shipping on a River below*
Signed
On copper
34.3 x 50.8 cm
Sold 23.4.82 in London for £43,200 ($77,328)

DAVID TENIERS THE YOUNGER: *Peasants Feasting and Dancing outside an Inn*
Signed
On panel
25 x 35 cm
Sold 18.6.82 in New York for $55,000 (£31,073)

MOSES VAN UYTTENBROECK: *The Nurture of Bacchus*
Signed with initials and dated 1629 (?)
On panel
56 x 87 cm
Sold 23.4.82 in London for £64,800 ($115,992)
Now in the National Gallery, London

JACOB ISAACKSZ. VAN RUISDAEL: *Wooded River Landscape with Houses and a Church on a Hill to the Right, a Town in the Distance to the Left*
Signed
78.6 x 98.5 cm
Sold 9.7.82 in London for £172,800 ($298,944)
Previously sold at Christie's 10 March 1851 for 355gns, and 30 June 1894 for 1,600gns

AMBROSIUS BOSSCHAERT THE ELDER:
Still Life of Roses, Lilies, a Tulip and other Flowers
Signed with monogram and dated 1605
On copper
18.4 x 14.6 cm
Sold 23.4.82 in London for £59,400 ($106,326)
The earliest dated work by the artist

JAN DAVIDSZ. DE HEEM: *Peaches, Grapes, Red Currants and other Fruit in a Blue and White China Bowl*
Signed (?)
On panel
33 x 48.9 cm
Sold 23.4.82 in London for £43,200 ($77,328)

LOUIS GABRIEL
BLANCHET: *Portrait of
Prince Charles Edward
Louis Philip Casimir
Stuart, "The Young
Pretender", aged 18*
Signed and dated 1738
190.5 x 141.6 cm
Sold 16.7.82 in
London for £43,200
($79,920)
Now in the National
Portrait Gallery,
London

NICOLAS TOURNIER: *The Denial of Saint Peter*
159.3 x 240 cm
Sold 23.4.82 in London for £28,080 ($50,263)

Brunel's Chardin

LAURA LINDSAY

For over 100 years, a small panel by Chardin remained unknown to the art world. It emerged at Christie's and was sold at auction last April. Because of the recent reappraisal of his *oeuvre*, the discovery was greeted with some excitement. The French art connoisseur Théophile Thoré, who took the pen-name William Bürger when he was banished from France for his republican views during the 1848 revolution, saw the picture exhibited in the Manchester Art Treasures Exhibition of 1857. The small panel had been discreetly hung between pieces of furniture in the ornamental section, but Thoré singled it out and commented on its fine quality. He had been the first of his contemporaries to recognize the greatness of Vermeer and later of Carel Fabritius; it was perhaps inevitable that he should find this work by Chardin, with its Vermeer-like charm, particularly appealing.

The owner of the picture at that time, was Isambard Kingdom Brunel, the celebrated engineer. His success had increased his fortune, enabling him to indulge in a taste for collecting. During his various trips abroad, he acquired a fine collection of works of art, with which he furnished his London house in Duke Street. Family tradition had it that he purchased the Chardin during a visit to Paris in 1848, the same year Thoré had been forced to flee the city.

Chardin was born in Paris in 1699. Although he worked for a time with the artists, Pierre Jacques Cazes and Nicholas Noel Coypel, he was largely self-taught. In 1728, he was admitted to the Académie Royale as a still-life painter of animals and fruit. He exhibited regularly at the Salon and was greatly admired by critics and collectors of the day.

In the 1730s, Chardin began to paint genre subjects, thus much enhancing his reputation. To satisfy demands of collectors and patrons not content with the numerous engravings that were being made of his paintings, he frequently painted replicas. The *Young Draughtsman* exists in several versions, the prime one being in the Nationalmuseum, Stockholm. It had been exhibited in the Salon of 1738. Chardin's greatness does not lie in the flamboyant appeal of his subject matter, but in his straightforward approach to everyday themes, as – in this case – a young artist studying. Like the Le Nains and the Netherlandish artists before him, Chardin found beauty in the commonplace and expressed it with a new poetic sensitivity.

By choosing a banal subject, drawn from his direct experience, and not complicating it needlessly with detail, he unobtrusively captures the sense of concentration and tranquillity.

JEAN BAPTISTE SIMEON CHARDIN: *'Un Jeune Ecolier qui Dessine': A Young Draughtsman Seated Copying an Academy Study*
Signed (?)
On panel
21 x 17.1 cm
Sold 23.4.82 in London for £178,200 ($318,978)

Brunel's Chardin

Chardin conveys the young student's total absorption in his task by skilfully placing him with his back turned and face averted, excluding any facial expression. The youth studiously bends over his drawing. No movement intrudes. The torn, untidy coat, and the humble position on the floor of the uncluttered studio, highlight the impoverished status of a young but dedicated student. Chardin's work, with its simple grace and honest vision, provides a striking contrast to the rococo brilliance of the courtly art of his contemporaries. With subtle control he creates soft gradations of tone. The mellow yellows and browns, with touches of red, executed with a characteristically gritty texture, help to convey a mood of stillness and intimacy, which together constitute the beauty of this work of art.

JEAN HONORE
FRAGONARD:
*Mademoiselle Marie
Catherine Colombe en
Vénus Glorieuse*
55 x 45 cm
Sold 18.6.82 in New
York for $104,000
(£58,757)
Mademoiselle
Colombe (1754-1837),
who was also painted
by Fragonard as
Cupid, was an actress
in the Comédie-
Italienne, Paris

A Masterpiece Rediscovered: Turner's 'The Temple of Jupiter Panellenius Restored'

MARTIN BUTLIN
Keeper of the Historic British Collection, The Tate Gallery

The reappearance after more than a 100 years of a major work by a great artist is always cause for excitement, but perhaps also for a certain degree of apprehension. Will the work live up to expectations? In the case of J.M.W. Turner's *The Temple of Jupiter Panellenius Restored* anxiety was increased by the doubts expressed about the picture's authenticity on the last occasion it appeared in the salerooms, in 1876, together with the considerable adverse criticism it had received both from the Press when it was first exhibited at the Royal Academy in 1816 and from that ardent but by no means uncritical Turner lover, John Ruskin.

The early history of the painting, before its disappearance from view in 1876, had its unusual features. It failed to find a purchaser at the Royal Academy in 1816 and was eventually bought some seven years later by the engravers Messrs Hurst & Robinson. They would have bought the picture with its copyright, giving them the right to issue prints of the composition. In fact it was not until after the business had passed in 1827 to the firm of Moon, Boys and Graves that an engraving did appear, by John Pye, in 1828. Ten years later the painting was sold to the private collector Wynn Ellis. It was at his sale at Christie's on 6 May 1876 that Henry Graves, the previous owner, cast doubts on whether the picture was in fact the original or a copy that Ellis had had made, but as Graves was the underbidder when the picture was sold to the dealer Goupil his objections ring somewhat false. At this point the picture disappeared from view, having in fact been bought for an ancestor of the vendor at Christie's this year. The composition was known, however, from Pye's engraving, though this, lacking the colour of Turner's original and, inevitably, many of his other qualities, also left some doubt about the merits of the original.

The picture was exhibited in 1816 as a companion to *View of the Temple of Jupiter Panellenius, in the Island of Aegina, with the Greek National Dance of the Romaika: the Acropolis of Athens in the Distance. Painted from a sketch taken by H. Gally Knight Esq. in 1810;* this is now in the possession of the Duke of Northumberland. The critics were on the whole agreed on the superior merits of the picture showing the temple restored, but there was disagreement over the quality of the two works as a whole. The critic of *The Sun* said that "These two pictures are like two new guineas, fresh from the Mint, yellow, shining, gorgeous, and sterling; but, unlike the said coins, they will be improved in worth by age, and be more valuable in 1916 than in 1816." *The Repository of Arts* stated that "These are two very fine pictures by this eminent artist." However, William Hazlitt, in *The Champion*, was unsparing in his criticism, beginning by saying that "Claude did not acquire his established fame, by employing such meritricious means of attraction, as are to be found in Mr Turner's two landscapes", and writing them off as "a combination of gaudy hues." Here then was further cause for worry when we first heard that the picture had reappeared last summer.

John Ruskin, in the first volume of *Modern Painters*, published in 1843, included the two *Temple of Jupiter Panellenius* pictures in a list of "nonsense pictures". This term he explained a few years later in his *Notes on the Turner gallery at Marlborough House*, 1856: Turner "spoiled his most careful works by the very richness of invention they contained, and concentrated the material for 20 noble pictures into a single failure". Today it is difficult to take this criticism altogether seriously. Other pictures condemned by Ruskin under the same heading include *Dido building Carthage* (which Turner specially singled out to be bequeathed to the National Gallery and hung next to one of their paintings by Claude), *The*

JOSEPH MALLORD WILLIAM TURNER, R.A.: *The Temple of Jupiter Panellenius Restored*
116.8 x 177.8 cm
Sold 16.7.82 in London for £648,000 ($1,121,040)

Decline of the Carthaginian Empire, Bay of Baiae; Regulus and *Caligula's Palace and Bridge*; even *Crossing the Brook* was damned with faint praise.

One of the first things that was noticeable when the picture re-emerged was indeed its richness of incident. In a way it did contain material enough for "twenty noble pictures". For instance, the glimpse of sea on the horizon on the left, framed by trees, would make a picture in itself, rather like the second version of *Lake Avernus: Aeneas and the Cumaean Sibyl* of 1814-15, now in the Yale Center for British Art. The composition of the picture uses not one but three different ways of leading the eye into space. On the left the progression is by planes parallel to the picture surface, followed by two diagonal coulisses. On the right a larger triangular wedge leads us back towards a second glimpse of the sea. In the centre we are led into the picture and up to the temple by a number of directional devices: the diagonal at the edge of the pool in the foreground; the figure whose arm stretches up from the pool and acts as a pointer towards the procession of further figures above; the arms of those figures themselves which lead us up past the trees to the succession of buildings that culminate in the great temple. The sky too is enriched by a great variety of cloud forms, a variety only exceeded by the sky in *Entrance of the Meuse: Orange-merchant on the Bar, going to pieces*, exhibited in 1819 and now in The Tate Gallery. A "nonsense picture" indeed! But what a magnificent piece of nonsense!

What saves the picture from falling apart is the strength of the composition and of the foreground forms. The various devices leading into depth have already been mentioned. These are countered by the strong horizontals and verticals that give the work a classical repose based on Turner's study of the works of Poussin. The firm modelling of the forms is enhanced by the fall of the dawn light across the picture, picking out vital parts of the composition and also enriching the surface. The actual quality of Turner's brushwork is also of the highest quality. Any fears, therefore, that the comparative dryness of the engraving might be repeated in the painting were unfounded.

One of the critics in 1816, from the *Annals of the Fine Arts*, summed up Turner's accomplishment in this picture as "A clear, well-painted picture of the British Claude, that embraces the beauties of a first-rate landscape painter, with the knowledge of a professed architect." "The knowledge of a professed architect" is in fact the subject of this picture, the restoration of the ruined temple on Aegina, thought in the early 19th century to be dedicated to Jupiter, or rather Zeus, Panellenius. The temple was in fact dedicated to Aphaia, the local title for a Cretan goddess named Britomartis, assimilated in classical times to Athena; the confusion may have arisen over the existence of another temple dedicated to Zeus Panellenius further south on the same island. The companion picture of the temple as it was in Turner's day was, as the title shows, based on a drawing by Henry Gally Knight, made on the spot in 1810. The next year the first thorough excavations of the site began under a joint German and British team and, as John Gage has pointed out in an article in the second number of *Turner Studies*, the reconstruction of the temple by one of those involved, the architect C.R. Cockerell, had probably been made known to Turner through his fellow architect, Thomas Allason. However, just as it is difficult to reconcile Turner's view of the temple as it was in the 19th century with the site as it is at present (admittedly after further excavations), it is difficult to see Turner's picture as more than the freest of reconstructions. The façade of the temple has the right number of columns and is correctly raised on an artificial base, but the placing of the ancillary buildings is completely arbitrary, and the detail of the pediment sculpture lacks the archaic forms and the prominent round shields of the actual sculptures, restored by Thorvaldsen in Rome and now in the Glyptothek in Munich. Similarly the Greek inscription and relief on the left-hand side of the picture are not altogether convincing. As John Gage points out, the two Greek words seem to read "The Unconquered Charioteer" but it is difficult to see why the upper word should be larger than the lower and the relief shows the chariot if not actually destroyed, then at least in a condition that gives rise to considerable anxiety: one horse is down, a figure is being dragged along the ground, and the charioteer himself seems to be precariously striving to retain his balance. However, a Nike or victory is poised above him, and there may well be some subtlety here which has not yet been explained.

Turner fails to match his Greek subject in another respect. In 1816, when the picture was exhibited, he had been no further south than the Alps, let alone to Greece where in fact he never visited. His knowledge of Mediterranean light was derived from the pictures of Claude, and he was able to give a passable impression of the warm, glowing light of the Campagna in his Italian pictures even before he first travelled to Rome and Naples in 1819. But what neither Gally Knight nor Thomas Allason told him was that the light of Greece and the colour of the soil is very different from that of Italy, cold, sharp, brilliant, anything but the lush overall warmth of Turner's picture. On the frame of this work, too, George Jones could have written the words "splendide mendax"; as Turner said on the occasion when Jones used these words to criticise *The Bay of Baiae*, "all poets are liars". In this picture, probably in part inspired by Byron's *Childe Harold's Pilgrimage*, Turner shows himself the greatest poet of painting ever to turn his eye towards Greece.

JOHN CONSTABLE, R.A.: *Wooded Landscape outside the Park Pales of Old Hall, East Bergholt, with a Ploughman (A Summerland)*
51.4 x 76.8 cm
Sold 16.7.82 in London for £324,000 ($560,520)
Record auction price for a work by the artist
This picture was exhibited at the Royal Academy in 1814 and was purchased, probably in the following year, by John Allnutt, Lawrence's portrait of whom is illustrated on page 46

JOSEPH WRIGHT OF DERBY, A.R.A.: *Moonlit Wooded Lake with a Castle*
Signed with initials and dated 1788 (?)
58 x 76.2 cm
Sold 16.7.82 in London for £59,400 ($102,762)
by order of the Trustees of the R.C.A. Palmer Morewood Will Trust
This is apparently the picture which the artist sold to a Mr Bird of Liverpool for 30 gns. Its pendant, *A Cottage on Fire*, was sold
for £58,320 ($100,893)

SIR JOSHUA REYNOLDS, P.R.A.: *Portrait of Jane, Countess of Eglinton*
Bears inscription
238.6 x 137 cm
Sold 16.7.82 in London for £259,200
($448,416)
Record auction price for a work by the artist
This picture was painted in 1777 and cost 150 gns. With the Hoppner, the Raeburn and the Lawrence, illustrated on pages 45, 44 and 46, it formed part of the outstanding series of English portraits acquired at the beginning of the century by Sir George A. Cooper, Bt., for Hursley

SIR HENRY RAEBURN, R.A.: *Portrait of Mrs Margaret Stewart of Physgill and Glasserton, Wigtonshire*
238.6 x 152.3 cm
Sold 16.7.82 in London for £162,000 ($280,260)
Record auction price for a late work by the artist painted in 1823

Opposite

JOHN HOPPNER, R.A.: *Portrait of H.R.H. Frederica Charlotte Ulrica, Princess Royal of Prussia and Duchess of York*
271.7 x 210.7 cm
Sold 16.7.82 in London for £162,000 ($280,260)
Record auction price for a work by the artist
This is one of the painter's most ambitious portraits. It and its companion portrait of the Duke of York, which was sold for £59,400 ($106,920), were exhibited at the Royal Academy in 1792

SIR THOMAS LAWRENCE, P.R.A.: *Portrait of John Allnutt*
236.2 x 144.6 cm
Sold 16.4.82 in London for £108,000 ($190,000)
This portrait aroused considerable interest when it was exhibited at the Royal Academy in 1799. John Allnutt (1773-1863) was a wine merchant. He was a close friend of the artist and also a patron of Constable from whom he purchased the *Wooded Landscape outside the Park Pales of Old Hall, East Bergholt, with a Ploughman*, illustrated on page 41

SIR THOMAS LAWRENCE, P.R.A.: *Portrait of Miss Julia Beatrice Peel*
142.1 x 111.7 cm
Sold 16.7.82 in London for £216,000 ($373,680)
Record auction price for a work by the artist
Sold by order of the Trustees of the Hursley Settlement
Sold at Christie's 6 June 1907 for 8000 gns.
This portrait of his daughter was one of the major series commissioned by Sir Robert Peel, the politician, in the late 1820s

GEORGE CHINNERY: *Group Portrait of Lady Harriet Paget with Five of her Children*
53.2 x 60.2 cm
Sold 16.4.82 in London for £41,040 ($72,230)
From the collection of Clarence A.E. Paget, great-grandson of Lady Harriet Paget

BEN MARSHALL: *Group
Portrait of the Corbet
Family of Ynys y
Maengyn*
90.1 x 69.8 cm
Sold 20.11.81 in
London for £52,800
($100,848)

JOHN FREDERICK HERRING, SEN.: *"Memnon", a Chestnut Racehorse with William Scott up, Wearing the Colours of Richard Watt on Doncaster Racecourse*
Signed and dated 1825
70 x 86.2 cm
Sold 16.4.82 in London for £86,400 ($152,064)

JOHN E. FERNELEY, SEN.: *"Pussy", a Dark Brown Racehorse with his Trainer, "Old John" Day, Mr T. Crosby, and W.B. Day at Epsom*
Signed and dated Melton Mowbray 1834
81.2 x 107.2 cm
Sold 16.4.82 in London for £48,600 ($85,536)

FREDERICK WILLIAM WATTS: *Dedham Vale, Suffolk*
96 x 127 cm
Sold 28.10.81 in New York for $57,200 (£31,602)

ARTHUR HUGHES: *The Lady of Shalott*
Signed and dated 1873
92.7 x 158.1 cm
Sold 16.10.81 in London for £50,600 ($95,128)

STANHOPE ALEXANDER
FORBES, R.A.: *The Slip*
Signed
Painted July 1885
106 x 85 cm
Sold 4.6.82 in London
for £24,840 ($44,960)
Previously sold at
Christie's 1 May 1913
as *The Slip at Newlyn*
for 94gns

JAMES JACQUES JOSEPH TISSOT:
The Bunch of Lilacs
Signed
54 x 37.5 cm
Sold 26.3.82 in London for
£81,000 ($148,230)
Record auction price for a
work by the artist
Previously sold at Christie's
28 April 1877 for 330gns;
26 February 1887 for 155gns;
7 December 1895 for 48gns

JOHN ARCHIBALD WOODSIDE: *Pennsylvania Country Fair*
Signed and dated 1824
50.5 x 66 cm
Sold 3.6.82 in New York for $286,000 (£158,011)
Record auction price for a work by the artist

Opposite

JOHN SINGLETON COPLEY, R.A.: *Mr Joshua Henshaw II*
One of a pair of portraits with *Mrs Joshua
Henshaw II (Catherine Hill)*
76.8 x 64.1 cm and 76.8 x 64.8 cm
The pair sold 11.12.81 in New York for $385,000
(£203,703)

ARTHUR FITZWILLIAM TAIT: *The Buffalo Hunt*
Signed and dated 1861
62.2 x 92.7 cm
Sold 4.6.82 in New York for $275,000 (£151,930)
From the collection of the late Harry T. Peters, jun.

ARTHUR FITZWILLIAM TAIT: *Duck Shooting*
Inscribed on the reverse
96.5 x 127 cm
Sold 4.6.82 in New York for $275,000 (£151,930)
From the collection of the late Harry T. Peters, jun.

WINSLOW HOMER: *The Red Canoe*
Signed and dated 1889
Watercolour
34.9 x 49.8 cm
Sold 3.6.82 in New York for $286,000 (£158,011)
From the collection of the late
Doris Warner Vidor

Opposite

ROBERT FREDERICK BLUM: *The Flower Market, Tokyo*
Signed
c. 1891
80.5 x 64.3 cm
Sold 3.6.82 in New York for $473,000 (£261,325)
Record auction price for a work by the artist

JOHN SINGER SARGENT, R.A.: *Women at Work*
Signed
56.4 x 71.2 cm
Sold 11.12.81 in New York for $605,000 (£320,106)
Record auction price for a work by the artist

WILLIAM HENRY RINEHART: *"Thetis", a Marble Group of a Nereid and a Fish*
Signed and dated 1862
116.8 cm high
Sold 3.6.82 in New York for $35,200 (£19,447)

FREDERIC REMINGTON: *"The Bronco Buster": Bronze Equestrian Group of a Cowboy*
Inscribed © Frederic Remington and stamped Roman Bronze Works N.Y.; underside inscribed N82
Rich blackish green patina
61.3 cm high
Sold 3.6.82 in New York for $99,000 (£54,696)

SOLON HANNIBAL BORGLUM: *"Lassooing Wild Horses": a Bronze Equestrian Group of a Roundup*
Inscribed and © Solon H. Borglum and – cire perdue cast – Roman Bronze Works N.Y. 1902
78.8 cm high
Sold 11.12.81 in New York for $88,000 (£46,560)
Record auction price for a work by the artist
From the collection of Mr Stanley Carlson

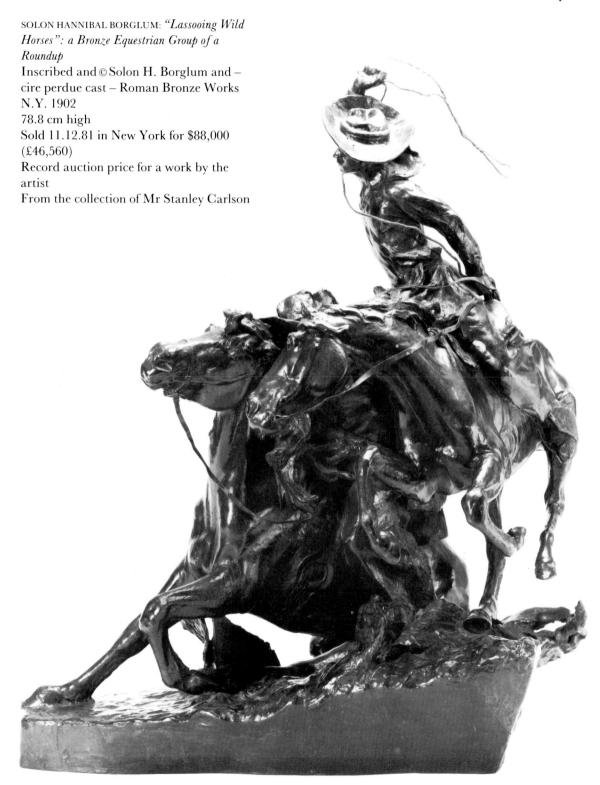

JOHN GLOVER: *Near Launceston, Tasmania*
On panel
29.2 x 39.3 cm
Sold 12.5.82 in London at Christie's South
Kensington for £17,000 ($30,600)
Previously sold 1 October 1974 at
Christie's in Sydney for A$17,000 (£9,444)

CORNELIUS KRIEGHOFF: *Huntsmen Shooting
Moose in Winter*
Signed and dated 1854
45.2 x 67.8 cm
Sold 28.10.81 in London at Christie's
South Kensington for £85,000 ($155,550)
From the collection of
Lady May Abel-Smith

FEDERICO MADRAZO: *Portrait of the Duchess of Alba, Full Length, Standing before a Fireplace*
Signed with initials
195 x 124.5 cm
Sold 27.11.81 in London for £30,800 ($56,056)

Angelo Morbelli and Italian Divisionism

PROFESSOR A.P. QUINSAC,
Professor of Art History at the University of South Carolina

A 19th century masterpiece, *Alba Domenicale*, was sold on the 27th November 1981. Its author, Angelo Morbelli (1854-1919) is, together with Giovanni Segantini, Giuseppe Pellizza, Gaetano Previati, Emilio Longoni and Vittore Grubicy, one of the six major protagonists of Italian Divisionism, a school of painting which until recently was erroneously considered a poor and inglorious imitation of French Neo-Impressionism. Since the late 1960s, extensive studies have been conducted and a full grasp of the importance of this movement in Italy has been achieved. The section dedicated to the Italian group in the exhibition "Post-Impressionism", organized by the Royal Academy and presented in London and Washington in 1979, reflected this new understanding. In reality, Italian Divisionism and French Neo-Impressionism (also called Pointillism) developed independently from each other in the late 1880s, in two cultural contexts as different as were Milan and Paris. Both schools nonetheless have in common an allegiance to the principle of colour as an optical element. This principle eliminates previous mixings on the palette and achieves a freshness of tonality and luminous intensity as a result of the interaction on the canvas of chemically "pure" colours (colours divided according to the prism).

Alba Domenicale was painted in 1891, a transitional moment in Morbelli's life when he was beginning to experiment on his own with the new technique. The Italian Divisionists very often worked in quasi-isolation, unaware of each other's efforts, and by this time Segantini and Previati had already achieved paintings fully based upon the new principle. *Alba Domenicale* on the other hand is not yet fully subordinated to it: the tones have been obtained mostly by previous mixings. However, the vibrance of the dawn light of this region of Piedmont – the hills of the Monferrato where Morbelli had his country estate – could not have been rendered with such a convincing intensity, had the artist not already fully understood the relationship between light and colour through his studies of optics.

Twenty-five years later, at the request of a patron, and probably also because he was particularly fond of this composition and subject matter, Morbelli produced a second version, now in the Ricci Oddi Museum in Piacenze. The replica (1915) is an entirely divisionist painting. The brushwork, long filaments of pure colour, extremely thin and linear, in tonalities of purples, greens and browns evocative of dusk rather than dawn, creates a sense of stillness, reinforced by the reduced focus on the landscape. Morbelli seems the most systematic of all the Italian Divisionists, at least in his paintings executed after 1900, because he does not allow for any spontaneity of execution, but applies the paint in a rigorously graphical manner, using metal brushes specifically designed by him for this purpose.

The first version of *Alba Domenicale*, in contrast, is more impressionistic in its texture and chromatism. Even though it is not a study from nature but a re-elaboration in the studio of sketches taken out of doors, it carries a feeling of immediacy in the observation of a moment in the daily life of Piedmontese peasants that the second version no longer conveys. Unlike Morbelli's later work, when his choice of subject matter was often influenced by an increasing interest in socialist theories, this painting contains no social message. The four figures, on their way to early Sunday mass on a spring morning, are presented from the rear. The avoidance of facial representation, combined with the minute description of their costume, makes no concessions to pathos and elevates the picture beyond mere anecdotal genre. As a result, the landscape in its openness and startling luminosity suggests a sense of serenity. It is likely that Morbelli viewed this work as a celebration of the harmony between man and nature, the representation of a moment of grace in

ANGELO MORBELLI: *Alba Domenicale*
Signed and dated 1890
75 x 112 cm
Sold 27.11.81 in London for £57,200 ($111,540)

which the acceptance of one's fate overcomes any fatigue or consciousness of social deprivation. There remains a lingering feeling of loneliness, however, and this loneliness is omnipresent in Morbelli's work. It corresponds to his own isolation. Morbelli was almost totally deaf by the age of 40, a man caught between the solid bourgeois tradition of the Piedmontese gentry and a strong sense of guilt about social injustice.

FERENCZ EISENHUT: *Arab Slave Market*
Signed and dated München 1888
136 x 224 cm
Sold 25.6.82 in London for £32,400 ($55,080)

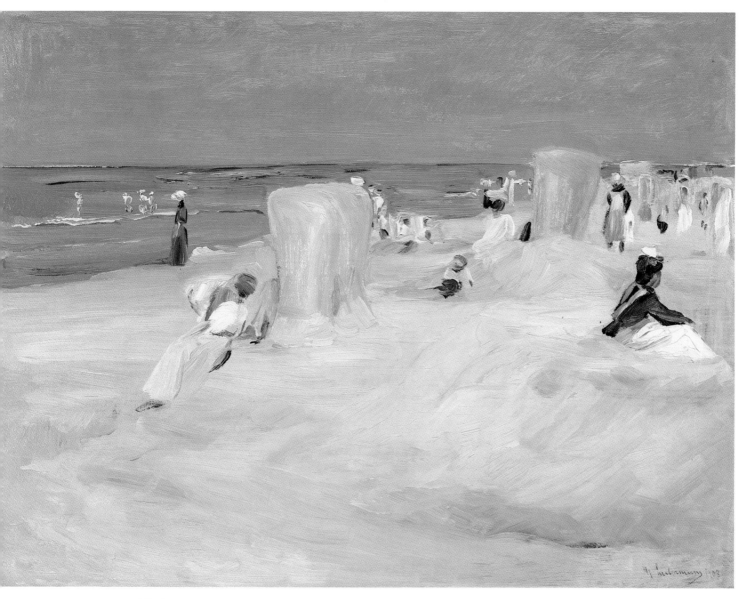

MAX LIEBERMANN: *The Beach at Noordwyk*
Signed and dated 1908
On panel
54.5 x 75.5 cm
Sold 26.3.82 in London for £43,200 ($78,624)

CARL LARSSON: *Young Girl at a Grand Piano*
Signed with initials and dated 1908
Watercolour, bodycolour and charcoal
97 x 63 cm
Sold 26.3.82 in London for £28,080
($51,105)

ALBERT ANKER: *Portrait of the Artist's Son Ruedi, Eating at a Table*
16 x 22 cm
Sold 27.11.81 in London for £29,700 ($57,915)

DON SILVESTRO DEI GHERARDUCCI: *Saint Stephen Enthroned: Initial O from a Choir Book*
Floriated border, bodycolour and gold on vellum, silhouetted
23.1 x 22.8 cm
Sold 8.12.81 in London for £11,000 ($21,560)
With the rediscovery of this illumination, all the cuttings from the celebrated choir books decorated by Don Silvestro for the Convent of Santa Maria degli Angeli that were brought to England in the early 19th century by William Young Ottley are accounted for. Executed in the 1390s the miniatures are the artist's masterpieces, and Vasari records that at the time of the Siege of Florence in 1524 their fame was such that the Republican party in the city considered using them as a bribe to secure the support of King Francis I of France

Attributed to
GIOVANNI BADILE:
*Portrait Head of a Boy in
Profile to the Left*
Inscribed 'joane
badille qual fu prete'
Pen and brown ink
20.7 x 15.3 cm
Sold 6.7.82 in London
for £32,400 ($56,700)
This is one of two
profile portraits with
attributions to
Giovanni II Badile
from an album
arranged by Antonio
Badile in 1500 which
was later in the
Moscardo collection.
The Badile were a
family of Veronese
painters whose
activity spread over
two centuries. This
drawing and its
erstwhile companion,
now in the Art
Institute of Chicago,
possibly date from the
1430s

RAFFAELLO SANZIO, called RAPHAEL:
The Head of a Horse
Metalpoint heightened with white (slightly oxidized) and black chalk on lilac preparation
14.4 x 10.8 cm
Sold 6.7.82 in London for £37,800 ($66,150)

This drawing was owned in the 18th century by the Hon. Edward Bouverie, by whom it was apparently attributed to Van Dyck. It was only after it was brought to Christie's that it was recognized as being by Raphael, no other wholly unrecorded drawing by whom has come to light for many years.

Raphael was interested in the horse at various stages of his career. In 1503, at the age of 20, he helped Pinturicchio to devise the great fresco of *The Departure of Enea Silvio Piccolomini for Basle* at Siena, in which a cavalcade appears; in the following years he painted two panels of Saint George and the Dragon in which horses play a dominant role in the composition. This study, although reminiscent of these earlier works, was drawn in preparation for the fresco of the *Meeting of Pope Leo I and Attila* in the Stanza d'Eliodoro of the Vatican, which dates from about 1513: in this the lower section of the horse's head is partly concealed by that of the foremost of the two soldiers who stand before the Pope.

Raphael was one of the last artists to employ the traditional medium of metalpoint, and this study is of particular technical interest as one of the few in which he used black chalk to rework and amplify his initial sketch. Despite its small dimensions the new drawing may be compared with the celebrated black chalk cartoon of a horse's head in the Ashmolean Museum, which is notably similar in conception. It evinces a liveliness not always apparent in the fresco itself, in which Raphael relied extensively on the workshop.

GIROLAMO FRANCESCO MARIA MAZZOLA, IL PARMIGIANINO:
Study of a Youth Standing, his Left Arm Akimbo, his Right Outstretched,
with a Subsidiary Study of a Leg
Red chalk
On two rejoined sections of a single sheet, two small
sections made up
30.3 x 12.3 cm
Sold 23.5.82 in London for £11,880 ($21,503)
This previously unknown drawing comes from the collections of
Sir Peter Lely, Jonathan Richardson, sen., Sir Joshua Reynolds and
Dr Wellesley, at whose sale in 1866 it fetched 11 shillings. The sheet
was cut across the middle by Parmigianino himself, who then
reused it for a further study on the reverse: it was apparently
reassembled by Reynolds

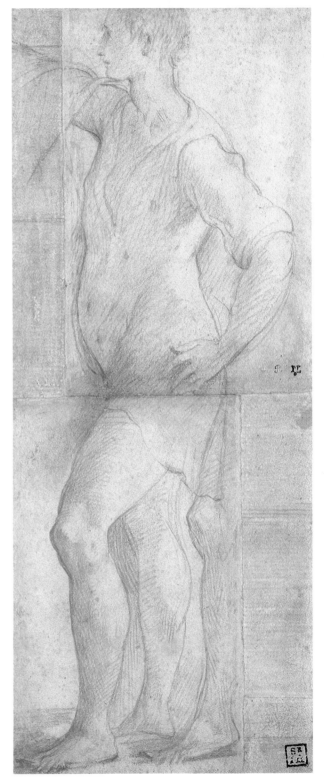

GIOVANNI BATTISTA TIEPOLO:
*Winged Deity Holding a
Dagger, with Magicians and
other Figures on Clouds*
Black chalk, pen and brown
ink, brown wash
26.2 x 21.4 cm
Sold 8.12.81 in London for
£16,500 ($32,340)
Formerly in the collection of
Tomás Harris, the drawing
is of about 1740

THE MONOGRAMMIST A S: *The Idolatry of Solomon*
Pen and brown ink, watermark a high crown
21.2 x 32 cm
Sold 6.7.82 in London for £9,180 ($16,065)
Sold at Christie's 12 July 1887, for £1.10s., this is by the same hand as a drawing at Munich which is dated 1530

A Watercolour attributed to Dürer

NOËL ANNESLEY

No photographic reproduction could adequately convey the impact of this beautiful study. It formerly belonged to William Esdaile, and when his collection of prints and drawings, one of the finest ever formed, was sold at Christie's in June 1840, it appeared as part of lot 511, described as "a parroquet, and a wing of the same; a pair on vellum, brilliantly coloured; dated 1524". A certain Mr Smith acquired it, with the preceding lot, for 11 gns. Subsequently, it entered the collection of Alfred Morrison (1821-1897) of Fonthill, himself a distinguished connoisseur, and remained in the family until auctioned by his grandson this July.

In subject, technique and brilliance of colour, the closest parallel in Dürer's *oeuvre* is afforded by a watercolour in the Albertina (Winkler 614), also on vellum, and of similar dimensions, with a monogram and date 1512. Nature studies by Dürer, or in his style, form a large and diverse group and raise complex problems of attribution. Curiously enough, the British Museum Printroom, with its magnificent holding of the artist's drawings (based on the bequest of Sir Hans Sloane in the 18th century), has no nature studies that can be seriously associated with him. We were, therefore, particularly grateful to the authorities at the Albertina for allowing us to make a side-by-side comparison of the two watercolours, as well as with others from the unrivalled series of nature studies in their charge. While it was not possible to endorse the traditional attribution to Dürer of the Margadale watercolour without qualification, the two works under discussion seemed at the very least to have been executed in the same studio.

The Margadale *Wing* is ornithologically the more precise. The slightly worn and ragged Vs at the ends of the primary feathers suggest an older bird. The Albertina *Wing*, seen from a different viewpoint, though without doubt from the same species of Roller, is that of a first-year bird with plumage in pristine condition. Unlike the Margadale watercolour, it exists in other versions. At least six are recorded of which that at Bayonne, on paper, is probably the earliest and the best.

Dürer would have had frequent opportunities to observe the European Roller around Nuremberg, and to be struck by its exotic colouring and behaviour. It is the northern representative of a large family of birds ranging from Africa into Asia. The name derives from the habit of rolling or tumbling in flight. While a familiar sight on the continent, it is an extremely rare visitor to Britain; some excuse, perhaps, for the 1840 cataloguer's misidentification.

Attributed to ALBRECHT DÜRER: *The Left Wing of a European Roller (Coracias Garrulus), Apparently Life-size, with Scapular Feathers*
With a monogram and date 1524 in pen and black ink
Watercolour and bodycolour on vellum
18.9 x 23.8 cm
Sold 6.7.82 in London for £75,600 ($132,300)
From the collection of Lord Margadale of Islay, T.D.

JOHANN WILHELM BAUR: *Mediterranean Seaport with Company and Carriages before a Row of Palazzi*
18.2 x 26 cm
Sold 23.3.82 in London for £7,020 ($12,706)
From the collection of Eva, Countess of Rosebery, D.B.E.
One of a series of Italian seaport *capricci* executed by this German born artist in the 1640s

FLEMISH SCHOOL, *c.* 1610: *The Spanish Armada, with the Burning of the Boats at Calais in the Left Background*
Inscribed 'Armee Navale Despaigne/Surnommee Invincible Vaincue par Les Anglois le 22 Juillet 1588' on the cartouche above and with the arms of King James I below, with the letters 'I' and 'R'
Bodycolour and gold on vellum
13.3 x 31.8 cm
Sold 23.3.82 in London for £11,880 ($21,503)
A related gouache is in an English private collection: in this Queen Elizabeth and the Earl of Leicester are shown on the shore on the right. The English flagship in the present work is the Ark Royal
Now in the National Maritime Museum
From the collection of Eva, Countess of Rosebery, D.B.E.

Both gouaches on this page are from the celebrated collection formed in the mid-19th century by Baron Meyer de Rothschild of Mentmore

AELBERT CUYP: *View of Papendrecht from Dordrecht*
Black chalk, grey wash, watermark a foolscap
18 x 30.9 cm
Sold 16.11.81 in Amsterdam for D.fl.62,700 (£13,749)
From the collection of the late D.G. van Beuningen, removed from 'Noorderheide', Vierhouten
One of a surprisingly small number of drawings of specific views by the great Dordrecht painter, this was the outstanding work in Christie's first sale of Dutch and Flemish drawings in our new Amsterdam saleroom, which also included a series of drawings by the Willem van de Veldes from the van Beuningen collection

JEAN BAPTISTE ISABEY: *Young Man Seated at a Desk*
Signed. The letter on the desk inscribed "Jean V…"
Black chalk, grey wash heightened with white
45.4 x 37.2 cm
Sold 6.7.82 in London for £9,504 ($16,632)

SIMON VOUET: *An Angel*
Black and white chalk on blue paper
37 x 24.5 cm
Sold 23.3.82 in London for £9,180 ($16,616)

CARLO BOSSOLI:
Extensive View of Turin
Signed and dated 1853
Bodycolour
31.5 x 48.4 cm
Sold 26.11.81 in
London for £4,180
($8,109)

PETER FENDI: *Sketchbook*
17.3 x 13.6 cm overall
Sold 26.11.81 in
London for £15,400
($29,876)
Peter Fendi was one of
the outstanding
Austrian painters of
the Biedermeier
period. This hitherto
unknown sketchbook,
begun on 28 August
1831, contains studies
for a number of
compositions,
including the *Mother's
Blessing* in the Stadt
Museum, Vienna, and
was purchased by the
reigning Prince of
Lichtenstein for whose
family the artist
worked

PAUL SANDBY, R.A.: *Lower Ward, Windsor Castle: Henry VIII Gate and Salisbury Tower*
Bodycolour
38.2 x 54.7 cm
Sold 15.6.82 in London for £22,140 ($39,852)
Record auction price for a drawing by the artist

DANIEL GARDNER: *Portrait of Rebecca, Lady Rushout (Baroness Northwick) and her Three Elder Children, Anne, Harriet and John (later 2nd Lord Northwick)*
Pastel and bodycolour, oval, on paper laid on canvas
66.4 x 83.8 cm
Sold 16.3.82 in London for £12,960 ($23,328)
Record auction price for a pastel by the artist
The 2nd Lord Northwick's collection of Old Master Pictures was among the most important of the 19th century; it was partly dispersed at Thirlestane House after his death, and more recently, in these Rooms (Northwick Park Collection, 1966)
From the collection of the late Peter Whitbread

JOSEPH MALLORD WILLIAM TURNER, R.A.: *Venice: A Storm Approaching S. Giorgio Maggiore and the Dogana*
Watercolour over a pale grey wash preparation on Whatman paper dated 1834
21.6 x 31.8 cm
Sold 16.3.82 in London for £145,800 ($262,440)
Record auction price for an English watercolour

JOSEPH MALLORD WILLIAM TURNER, R.A.: *Venice: The New Moon*
Watercolour
24.1 x 30.5 cm
Sold 15.6.82 in London for £83,160 ($149,688)
From the collection of the late Dagnall Ells

JOHN WHITE ABBOTT:
*The Erme, near
Ivybridge, Devon*
Drawn in 1800
Pen and grey ink and
watercolour
20.4 x 18 cm
Sold 15.6.82 in
London for £10,368
($18,662)
Record auction price
for a watercolour by
the artist

WILLIAM DANIELL, R.A.: *Eton College*
Signed and dated 1827
Pencil and watercolour
33 x 53.4 cm
Sold 16.3.82 in London for £14,040 ($25,272)
Record auction price for a watercolour by the artist
Windsor Castle. Now in the Brewhouse Gallery, which houses Eton College's picture collection, having been acquired with the help of the National Art-Collections Fund

MILDRED ANNE BUTLER: *Lady Sketching under a Parasol*
Watercolour heightened with white
26.6 x 17.7 cm
Sold 13.10.81 in London for £7,700 ($14,630)

Mildred Anne Butler died in 1941. For 40 years the contents of her studio, large exhibition pieces and delicate sketches alike, remained at Kilmurry, Co. Kilkenny, her family home. Stored in cases, well away from the ill-effects of sunlight and damp, they retained all the freshness, so vital to their distinctive charm, with which they had left the artist's easel or sketchbook. Last autumn her cousin's executors offered them for sale, and for the first time the full range of her achievement could be seen. Growing from an early dependence on her friends Naftel and Stanhope Forbes she developed a highly personal style perfectly suited to her favourite subjects: the woods, fields and cattle of the home farm, the house itself, and, most memorably, the flower gardens recalled in sketches of flowing colour from the earliest spring to the end of summer. English and Continental buyers responded eagerly to these delightful drawings: collectors from Ireland itself, above all, flocked to the sale. The collection fetched £181,225 ($344,327): almost half the watercolours returned to Ireland, four of them bought by the National Gallery in Dublin (in addition to two purchased by private treaty). Mildred Anne Butler now at last commands the high regard in which she was so deservedly held in her lifetime, firmly established once more in the mainstream of Edwardian watercolour painting.

DANTE GABRIEL ROSSETTI: *Arthur's Tomb: Sir Launcelot Parting from Guinevere*
Signed with monogram, inscribed and dated 1854
Pencil, pen and brown ink and watercolour with gum arabic
23.5 x 37.8 cm
Sold 4.6.82 in London for £28,080 ($50,825)
Formerly in the collection of John Ruskin, and of William Graham. Sold at Christie's 3 April 1866 for 80gns and bought by an ancestor of the vendor

LUCAS VAN LEYDEN: *The Triumph of Mordecai* (Bartsch, Hollstein 32) Engraving, first state (of three) S. 21.1 x 28.8 cm Sold 1.12.81 in London for £7,700 ($15,092)

AUGUSTIN HIRSCHVOGEL: *Landscape with the Conversion of Saint Paul* (Bartsch, Schwarz 77)
Etching
S. 10 x 25.4 cm
Sold 1.12.81 in London for £11,550 ($22,628)

Right

JUSTE DE JUSTE: *Pyramide de Six Hommes* (Zerner J2)
Etching with engraving, from the set of five Pyramides
P. 25.8 x 20.6 cm
Sold 30.6.82 in London for £4,320 ($7,430)

Far right

MARTIN SCHONGAUER: *Christ on the Cross with Four Angels*
(Bartsch VI, 25;
Lehrs V, 14)
Engraving
S. 29.1 x 19.2 cm
Sold 1.12.81 in London for £11,000 ($21,560)

Right

UGO DA CARPI: *The Descent from the Cross, after Raphael*
(Bartsch XII, 43, 22)
Chiaroscuro woodcut from three blocks, printed in black and two shades of green, first state (of two)
L. 35.6 x 27.5 cm
Sold 30.6.82 in London for £2,592 ($4,458)

Far right

HENDRIK GOLTZIUS: *Saint John the Baptist*
(Bartsch 226)
Chiaroscuro woodcut from three blocks, printed in black, lime-green and pale ochre
L. 23.8 x 14.1 cm
Sold 1.12.81 in London for £7,700 ($15,092)

REMBRANDT HARMENSZ. VAN RIJN: *Landscape with Trees, Farm Buildings and a Tower* (Bartsch, Hollstein 223)
Etching with drypoint, fourth (final) state
P. 12.2 x 32.1 cm
Sold 10.5.82 in New York for $55,000 (£30,555)

REMBRANDT HARMENSZ. VAN RIJN: *Adam and Eve* (Bartsch, Hollstein 28)
Etching, second (final) state
P. 16.4 x 11.7 cm
Sold 10.5.82 in New York for $30,800 (£17,111)

After JEAN ANTOINE WATTEAU:
Figures de Différents Caractères,
de Paysages, et d'Etudes
Dessinées d'après Nature:
Volumes I and II, by
F. Boucher and others
Etchings, the complete series
Overall S. 49 x 32 cm
Sold 1.12.81 in London for
£8,250 ($16,170)
From the collection of Eva,
Countess of Rosebery, D.B.E.
Fomerly in the collections of
the Bibliothèque Nationale,
Paris, and Archibald Philip,
Earl of Rosebery

FRANCISCO DE GOYA Y
LUCIENTES: *Los Proverbios*
(Delteil 202-19)
Etchings with burnished
aquatint and drypoint, title
and set of 18, from the First
Edition
Averaging P. 24.5 x 35.2 cm
Sold 1.12.81 in London for
£16,500 ($32,340)

EDOUARD MANET: *Les Courses*
(Guérin 72)
Lithograph, between 1865 and
1878, on greyish Chine appliqué,
a superb, rich impression before
letters and before the edition of
100 printed by Lemercier in 1884
L. 35.3 x 50.9 cm
Sold 11.5.82 in New York for
$47,300 (£26,277)

Far left

EDOUARD MANET:
Le Buveur d'Absinthe (Guérin 9)
Etching, 1861, third state (of five)
P. 28.9 x 16 cm
Sold 11.5.82 in New York for
$7,700 (£4,277)

Left

THEODORE GERICAULT:
Le Factionnaire Suisse au Louvre
(Delteil 15)
Lithograph, 1819,
second (final) state
L. 39.4 x 32.9 cm
Sold 11.5.82 in New York for
$9,900 (£5,500)

PAUL GAUGUIN: *Idole Tahitienne* (Guérin 44)
Woodcut printed in black, ochre and terracotta, *c.*1894-5, touched with violet and green top right
S. 14.7 x 11.9 cm
Sold 11.5.82 in New York for $16,500 (£9,166)
One of five or six impressions, each of which is different

Munch's Vision of Reality

JAMES ROUNDELL

In recent years Christie's Print Sales have produced a succession of remarkable prices for important graphic works by Edvard Munch. The record £63,800 ($149,930) for *Abend, Melancholie* and £60,500 ($142,175) for *Angstgefühl* in 1980 are just two examples. The sale on 1st December 1981 contained an impression of the lithograph of perhaps his most celebrated image *Das Kranke Mädchen* (The Sick Girl). The subject was to become one of the major preoccupations of his *oeuvre*. He returned to it on many occasions, either to rework the original painting or to create new versions in differing media. At its inception it represented the turning point in his art and opened the way to the future development of Munch's work.

Norwegian art in the second half of the 19th century was dominated by formal academic traditions with an emphasis on naturalistic representation of the Norwegian landscape. The leading figure of this school was Christian Krohg (1852-1925) whose style Munch emulated closely as a young man. Munch's first exhibited work was *Morgen* in 1884, a picture firmly in the Krohg tradition. However, a new group of artists and writers appeared, rebelling against the middle-class ideals of the "establishment". These radicals were based in Christiania (old Oslo) and became known as the Christiania Bohemians. Their artistic creed was to paint without beautification. Munch admired the leader of the Christiania Bohemians, Hans Jäger, who was the first significant figure in Norwegian artistic circles to praise his art. The group had little contact with international art. In 1885 Munch went to Paris for three weeks on a scholarship. The visit stimulated him to produce three key works, *Das Kranke Mädchen, Der Tag Danach* and *Pubertät*.

For the first time in his art, in *Das Kranke Mädchen* Munch depicted not only the physical reality of the sick girl but also the spiritual tragedy of the subject. It marked the beginning of Munch's obsession with his own inner feelings and personal experience, and his translation of this into themes of the greatest significance in the drama of life. In the case of *Das Kranke Mädchen* Munch looked back to his youth and the early deaths from tuberculosis of his sister and mother. This great personal tragedy was to inspire the rawest display of pictorial emotion. Munch later wrote about the first version of the subject executed in 1886: "I finally stopped, tired out – I had achieved much of that first impression, the trembling mouth – the transparent skin – the tired eyes – but the picture was not finished, in its colour – it was pale grey." Although Munch used a model for the subject (Betsy Nielsen), it is obvious this was only as a compositional guide: the real form was taken from the anguished memories of past events still burning in his mind. The application of the paint reflected the emotional involvement in its fleeting, insubstantial, rapid character. The whole took the form of a nightmare realized on canvas, the haunting tones of such an experience being reflected in the colouration. Munch himself described it as "an altogether nervously constructed and colourless picture."

Munch made an etching of the subject in 1894 (Schiefler 7), but it was the lithograph of 1896 which directly recaptured the emotions, forms and colours of the original picture. The raw application of the lithographic ink has all the force of a vision etched in the mind momentarily realized on paper. The handcolouring powerfully brings to fleeting life the transparent skin and trembling mouth of the girl in Munch's memory hovering between life and death. In this lithograph Munch has transformed an event of great personal and private tragedy into an image of relevance to all who are aware of the frailty and transience of the gift of life.

EDVARD MUNCH: *Das Kranke Mädchen* (cf. Schiefler 59)
Lithograph, 1896, extensively handcoloured in pastel (red, orange, lemon yellow, warm yellow, green, blue and white) on thin grey-toned Chine, signed and numbered 5 in blue crayon, the rare first version of this subject
L. 46.6 x 57.5 cm
Sold on 2.12.81 in London for £52,800 ($104,016)

ODILON REDON: *Béatrice* (Mellerio 168)
Lithograph, printed in yellow, grey and blue, 1897, signed in pencil
S. 56.2 x 42.6 cm
Sold 11.5.82 in New York for $23,100 (£12,833)

PIERRE AUGUSTE
RENOIR: *Le Chapeau
Epinglé, 2e Planche*
(Delteil, Stella 30;
Johnson 108)
Lithograph, *c*.1898,
printed in seven colours
L. 60.4 x 49.5 cm
Sold 21.2.82 in Tokyo
for Y.605,000
(£14,102)
An impression of this
lithograph printed in
11 colours was sold
1.7.82 in London for
£14,040 ($24,148)

PAUL CEZANNE: *Les Baigneurs,* Large Plate (Cherpin 7; Venturi 1157; Druik I; Johnson 23)
Lithograph, 1896-8, printed in black and extensively watercoloured
L. 40.7 x 50.5 cm
Sold 23.11.81 in New York for $49,500 (£26,052)

PABLO PICASSO: *Le Repas Frugal* (Bloch 1; Geiser 2 II a) Etching, 1904, on Arches, second state, a superb impression, one of very few taken before the plate was steel-faced P. 46.1 x 37.8 cm Sold 11.5.82 in New York for $112,200 (£62,333)

GEORGES ROUAULT: *Cirque de l'Etoile Filante*
Ambroise Vollard, Paris, 1938
(Chapon & Rouault 240-56)
Mixed method etchings with aquatint printed in colours, 1934-6, title, text, justification, and set of 82 wood engravings (by G. Aubert) in texte and 17 original plates hors texte
P.30.8 x 21 cm
Sold 2.12.81 in London for £12,100 ($23,837)

Opposite

PABLO PICASSO: *Buste de Femme d'après Cranach le Jeune* (Bloch 859)
Linocut, printed in colours, 1958, signed in blue crayon, numbered 41/50
L. 65.2 x 53.3 cm
Sold 11.5.82 in New York for $82,000 (£45,833)

ERICH HECKEL: *Weisse Pferde* (Dube 242b2, IV)
Woodcut printed in black, green, blue-grey, dark blue and pale ochre, 1912, signd and dated in pencil
L. 30.6 x 31.2 cm
Sold 1.7.82 in London for £10,800 ($18,576)

ERNST LUDWIG KIRCHNER: *Badende* (Dube 183)
Woodcut printed in black, 1911, extensively watercoloured in blue, green, rose and yellow, signed and inscribed in pencil
L. 30 x 45 cm
Sold 23.11.81 in New York for $22,000 (£11,578)
The only known impression, as Frau Dube has kindly confirmed

LOUIS BLEULER: *Ouvrage Représentant en 70 à 80 Feuilles les Vues les plus Pittoresques des Bords du Rhin depuis ses sources jusqu'a son Embouchure dans la Mer*, after L. Bleuler, S. Frey, F. Schmidt and others by J.J. Hurlimann, J.J. Falkeisen, F. Salathé and others
Coloured aquatints, title with etched vignette by F. Junghanns and 63 plates from the set of about 78, published by L. Bleuler, Schaffhouse,
c. 1843
Averaging P. 29 x 40 cm
Sold 25.5.82 in London for £37,800 ($68,040)

THOMAS SHOTTER BOYS: *London as it is* (Abbey, Scenery, 239)
Coloured tinted lithographs, the set of 26 plates published by T. Boys, London 1842
L. 32.2 x 44.5 cm and smaller
Sold 6.10.81 in London for £7,700 ($14,245)

CURRIER AND IVES, PUBLISHERS: *The American National Game of Baseball. Grand Match for the Championship at the Elysian Fields, Hoboken, N.J.* (Conningham 180)
Lithograph, 1866, extensively handcoloured and with touches of gum arabic
L. 49.8 x 75.9 cm
Sold 24.3.82 in New York for $12,100 (£6,722)

GEORGE BELLOWS: *A Stag at Sharkey's* (Muson 46)
Lithograph, 1917, signed, titled and inscribed 'No.61' in pencil
L. 48 x 61.1 cm
Sold 23.9.81 in New York for $26,400 (£14,270)

Above left

REGINALD MARSH: *Tattoo – Shave – Haircut* (Sasowsky 140)
Etching with engraving, 1932, tenth (final) state,
signed in pencil
P. 25.1 x 25.1 cm
Sold 24.3.82 in New York for $7,700 (£4,277)

Above

EDWARD HOPPER: *Night on the El Train* (Zigrosser 21)
Etching, 1920, signed and inscribed in pencil
P. 18.7 x 20 cm
Sold 23.9.81 in New York for $15,400 (£8,324)

JAMES ABBOTT McNEILL WHISTLER: *Nocturne* (Kennedy 184)
Etching with drypoint, 1879, fourth state (of five), signed
on the tab with the butterfly
P. 20 x 29.8 cm
Sold 10.5.82 in New York for $24,200 (£13,444)

JIM DINE: *Self Portrait (Stencil)*
(Williams College cat.14)
Lithograph printed in colours
collaged to a sheet of
Hodgkinson mould-made, 1970,
signed and dated in pencil,
numbered 8/17
S. 152.4 x 101.6 cm
Sold 14.4.82 in New York for
$12,100 (£6,722)

PAUL CÉSAR HELLEU: *Dora Hugo et la Femme de l'Artiste*
Signed
65 x 81 cm
Sold 28.6.82 in London for £51,840 ($88,128)
From the collection of the late Paul Wallraf
Record auction price for a work by the artist

HENRI FANTIN-LATOUR:
Petit Bouquet
Signed and dated 91
42.2 x 33.3 cm
Sold 19.5.82 in
New York for
$187,000 (£103,888)

Opposite

MARY CASSATT: *La Liseuse (Lydia Cassatt)*
Signed
*c.*1878
81.3 x 64.8 cm
Sold 19.5.82 in New York for $770,000 (£427,777)
Record auction price for a work by the artist
Lydia, the artist's elder sister, joined Mary Cassatt in
Paris in 1877. They both lived together until Lydia's
untimely death of Bright's disease on 7 November 1882

BERTHE MORISOT: *Femme et Enfant assis dans un Pré*
Signed
1871
Watercolour
19.5 x 24 cm
Sold 30.3.82 in London for £42,120 ($75,394)

117

CLAUDE MONET: *Peupliers au Bord de l'Epte, Automne*
Signed and dated 91
101 x 66 cm
Sold 19.5.82 in New York for
$737,000 (£409,444)
While on a walk, Monet discovered this line of poplars along the south bank of the River Epte near Limetz, a few miles upstream from Giverny. The trees were due to be sold and felled, so the artist, following an unsuccessful appeal to the Mayor for a postponement, had to pay the buyer to leave them standing while he worked on a series of, ultimately, 23 canvases

Opposite

PIERRE AUGUSTE RENOIR: *Deux Femmes aux Chapeaux Fleuris*
Signed
*c.*1915
56.2 x 52 cm
Sold 19.5.82 in New York for
$407,000 (£226,111)
From the collection of
Whitman College

PAUL SIGNAC: *Le Port de Volendam*
Signed and dated 96
65 x 81 cm
Sold 30.11.81 in London for £99,000 ($194,040)
From the collection of the late Mrs E. van Beek-van Hoorn Janssen, Rotterdam

THEO VAN RYSSELBERGHE: *Voiliers et Estuaire*
Signed with monogram
c.1890
50 x 61 cm
Sold 30.11.81 in London for £33,000 ($64,680)
Now in the Musée d'Orsay, Paris

HENRI DE TOULOUSE-LAUTREC:
Amazone
Stamped with monogram
1899
Black and coloured crayons and
pencil on paper laid down on
board
49.5 x 33 cm
Sold 20.5.82 in New York for
$176,000 (£97,777)
From the collection of the Estate
of Mrs Sydney J. Lamon

AMEDEO MODIGLIANI: *Etude de Tête*
Signed and dated 013
Gouache and oil on board
41 x 32.5 cm
Sold 20.5.81 in New York for
$110,000 (£61,797)

Salvador Dalí: *L'Enigme du Désir* or *Ma Mère, ma Mère, ma Mère*

JOHN LUMLEY

The importance of the dream is the vital link between psychology and Surrealism. The ideas of Freud became part of the language of the 1924 Surrealist manifesto written by André Breton, the leading figure around whom the Surrealist poets and painters were grouped. Less known, however, is that the influence also went the other way, and there is no better example of the debt of certain psychologists to Surrealism than in the painting *L'Enigme du Désir* by Salvador Dalí. From 1946 until our sale in March, this picture belonged to Mr Oskar Schlag, a psychoanalyst and graphologist in Zürich. Schlag first saw the picture when it was on exhibition in a local gallery. He liked it immediately and bought it in order to hang it in his consulting room. He wanted to gauge his patients' reactions to the image in the same way as Rorschach, another Swiss psychologist of an earlier generation, used his famous ink-blot test. Although now retired, Schlag has indeed found that on several occasions the picture has helped him in his work although he has admitted that even after 35 years he has never completely understood its meaning.

That puzzle will remain although there can be no dispute that *L'Enigme du Désir* is one of the finest of all Dalí's works. It was painted in 1929 at Cadaquès in the north-east of Spain near the place where the artist lives to this day. It was included in the autumn of that year in Dalí's first one-man exhibition, which immediately established his reputation in *avant-garde* circles in Paris. It was the Vicomte de Noailles who bought it then, and now, after Schlag and our sale in March, it has found a permanent home in the Staatsgemäldesammlungen, Munich.

SALVADOR DALI: *L'Enigme du Désir* or *Ma Mère, ma Mère, ma Mère*
Signed and dated 29
110 x 150 cm
Sold 29.3.82 in London for £453,600 ($816,480)

PABLO PICASSO: *Stand à la Kermesse*
Signed
c.1900
38.3 x 46.3 cm
Sold 3.11.81 in New York for $495,000 (£266,129)

PABLO PICASSO: *Bouteille
d'Anis del Mono, Compotier,
Pipe*
Signed
1915
Oil and sand on board
60.5 x 43.8 cm
Sold 3.11.81 in New York
for $550,000 (£295,698)

Opposite

WASSILY KANDINSKY: *Skizze zu Composition II (Fragment)*
Signed and dated 1910
Oil on board
61.8 x 52.3 cm
Sold 19.5.82 in New York for $1,210,000 (£672,222)
Record auction price for a work by the artist and for a German
Expressionist painting
A study for the right-hand section of *Composition II*, formerly in the
collection of Baron von Gamp, Berlin, is now lost

FRANZ MARC: *Der Rote Stier*
Signed with initial
1913
Gouache on paper
39.5 x 43.5 cm
Sold 3.11.81 in New York for $341,000
(£183,333)

ERICH HECKEL: *Unterhaltung*
Signed and dated 10
65 x 70 cm
Sold 30.11.81 in London for £162,800 ($319,088)
Record auction price for a work by the artist

ERNST LUDWIG KIRCHNER: *Negertänzerin*
Signed and dated 05
170 x 94 cm
Sold 3.11.81 in New York for $198,000 (£106,452)
From the collection of Henry Ford II

PABLO PICASSO: *Portrait de Dora Maar*
Signed and dated 31.10.37
65 x 46 cm
Sold 3.11.81 in New York for
$385,000 (£206,989)

HENRI MATISSE: *Femme aux Glaïeuls*
Signed
1922
50.2 x 61 cm
Sold 30.11.81 in London for £236,500 ($463,540)

FERNAND LEGER: *Paysage Américain*
Signed and dated 43-44
67.5 x 94.5 cm
Sold 29.3.82 in London for £70,200 ($126,360)

PAUL KLEE: *Arktische Tau* or *Polarlandschaft*
Signed
1920
Oil on board
52 x 51 cm
Sold 30.11.81 in London for £121,000 ($237,160)

GIORGIO MORANDI: *Natura Morta*
Signed on the reverse
*c.*1952
43 x 56 cm
Sold 19.5.82 in New York for $148,500 (£82,500)
Record auction price for a work by the artist

PAUL DELVAUX: *L'Aurore*
Signed and dated 2.64
Oil on panel
122 x 243.8 cm
Sold 19.5.82 in New York for $220,000 (£122,222)

CONSTANTIN BRANCUSI:
Tête de Femme
Signed
Signed again and
dated Paris 1925 on
original black stone
base
White marble
28.2 cm high
Sold 19.5.82 in
New York for
$770,000 (£427,777)

ALBERTO GIACOMETTI:
Homme qui marche
Signed, inscribed
Alexis Rudier/Fondeur.
Paris and
numbered 1/6
Painted bronze
48 cm high;
38.5 cm wide
Sold 19.5.82 in
New York for
$352,000 (£195,555)

MARINO MARINI:
Cavaliere
Stamped *MM* and
Fonderia Artistica Italia
1951
Number three of an
edition of six
Bronze with patina
partly chiselled and
painted
55 cm high, including
base
Sold 28.6.82 in
London for £54,000
($91,800)

JEAN TINGUELY: *Fontaine F*
1968
Painted iron, motor and mixed
media
270 x 140 x 70 cm
Sold 29.6.82 in London for £21,600
($36,720)

Contemporary Art Sales

MARTHA BAER

With the fall of the hammer on Lot One in our first Contemporary Art sale in New York, November 17, 1977, Christie's began a trend in New York which today has made us the leading auction house for Contemporary Art. We offer approximately four times the number of lots we had in our first season and have increased our sold total over five times. During that period we have sold beautiful works of art from outstanding collections of Contemporary Art, including Mrs Albert D. Lasker, Mr and Mrs Eugene M. Schwartz, The Harry N. Abrams Family Collection, and Janice and Clement Greenberg. We have sold for museums throughout the country and, in keeping with a 200-year-old tradition at Christie's, have sold for artists' Estates, including Franz Kline and Joseph Albers.

I think it must be true for every department head at Christie's that there are sales which are particularly special, not because of their financial success but because of the fine quality of the works we have collected and around which we can then develop a cohesive sale. I remember in particular my second sale at Christie's, November 3 1978. We had for offer three sculptures by David Smith and three early paintings by Robert Motherwell, two artists whose work was difficult to find and whom I admire immensely. With a then unheard-of estimate of $50,000 – $60,000 (£23,000 – £30,000), I chose Smith's *Jurassic Bird*, a steel sculpture from 1945, for the catalogue cover illustration and was thrilled to see it sell for $75,000 (£37,500). Indeed, we had a much larger sculpture, *7 Hours*, from 1961, which we sold for a record price of $90,000 (£45,000). With these two prices David Smith became a major auction name whose market continues to strengthen when a sculpture infrequently comes up for sale. Another special work, Robert Motherwell's *Fishes with Red Stripe*, an oil on paper from 1954, which has travelled to 11 international exhibitions, was also included in the November 1978 sale, fetching $32,000 (£16,000). Another early Motherwell painting of this quality has not been at auction until last spring when we sold *Je T'Aime, No. 111, with Loaf of Bread* (*see* page 147). The six works by these two artists, and paintings by Mark Rothko, William Baziotes, Adolph Gottlieb, Jack Tworkov, Arshile Gorky and Ad Reinhardt in the November 1978 sale, set Christie's on a course of offering top works by widely recognized "modern masters" associated with the New York School or Abstract Expressionism.

Another special sale – the one which finally broke the record for the most important sale of Contemporary Art – was held on May 16, 1980, and firmly established us as the leading auctioneers in Contemporary Art. We sold Jackson Pollock's 1953 *Four Opposites* for $550,000 (£239,130), still the top price for a Contemporary work of art at auction, a large Barnett Newman painting, *Primordial Light*, 1954, two beautiful Morris Louis paintings from the "unfurled" series and an important early de Kooning of 1945, *Study for Marshes*, together with smaller works by Frank Stella, Andy Warhol, Claes Oldenburg, Roy Lichtenstein, Milton Avery and Larry Rivers. These works were of such fine quality that they made the saleroom look like a museum of modern art. With 65 lots, we had a sold total of $2,600,000 (£1,130,430).

Our last sale on May 5 1982, broke that record and became the most successful sale of Contemporary Art ever held in any country. The most exciting aspect of the sale was the absolutely top quality of the works offered, and their rarity on the market. A "black" painting by Frank Stella, *Reichstag*, painted in 1958, belongs to a famous series of 23 paintings, most of which are in museum collections. Jackson Pollock's *Night Dancer* of 1944 is a particularly excellent example of his "pre-drip" period. The small 1958 Robert Rauschenberg "combine" painting and the early 1960s Jasper Johns *Numbers*, encaustic on paper on canvas, illustrated on the front and back covers of the catalogue, are exquisite examples

MARK ROTHKO:
No.1–1962
Signed and dated 1962
on the reverse
175.5 x 152.5 cm
Sold 5.5.82 in
New York for
$297,000 (£164,088)
Record auction price
for a work by the artist
From the collection of
Mrs Albert D. Lasker

of paintings by these two major contemporary artists. Mark Rothko, Milton Avery, Robert Motherwell and Morris Louis are just a few of the other artists who were represented by beautiful works in this sale. In an hour and a half $3.9 million (£2.2 million) was spent and record prices established for more than a dozen artists.

I have great confidence that the Contemporary Art market will continue on a strong and steady course. The art scene is extraordinarily lively and the audience is expanding, as evidenced by an attendance of more than 1,000 people in our landmark sale last May.

FRANZ KLINE: *Horizontal Rust*
Signed and dated 60 on the reverse
220 x 124.5 cm
Sold 5.5.82 in New York for $220,000
(£121,546)
From the collection of Mrs Albert D. Lasker

Opposite:
JACKSON POLLOCK: *Night Dancer (Green)*
Signed and dated 44
110 x 86.5 cm
Sold 5.5.82 in New York for $330,000
(£182,320)
From the collection of
Mr and Mrs Crawford A. Black

MORRIS LOUIS: *Aleph Series II, 1960*
Acrylic on canvas
198 x 269.5 cm
Sold 5.5.82 in New York for $220,000 (£121,546)

ROBERT MOTHERWELL:
Je t'aime, No.III, with
Loaf of Bread
Signed, inscribed with
title and dated 27 April
1955 and July 1955 on
the reverse
183 x 137.5 cm
Sold 5.5.82 in
New York for $220,000
(£121,546)
Record auction price for
a work by the artist

ROBERT RAUSCHENBERG:
Summer Rental
Signed, inscribed with
title and dated 1960
on the reverse
"Combine" painting:
oil and paper on
canvas
178 x 137 cm
Sold 18.11.81 in
New York for
$187,000 (£97,395)

FRANK STELLA: *Reichstag*
Signed, inscribed with title and dated 58 on the stretcher
Black enamel on canvas
215.5 x 309.5 cm
Sold 5.5.82 in New York for $462,000 (£255,248)
Record auction price for a work by the artist

WILIAM BAZIOTES: *Primeval Landscape*
Signed
Signed again, inscribed with title and dated 1953 on the reverse
152.5 x 183 cm
Sold 18.11.81 in New York for $143,000 (£74,479)
Record auction price for a work by the artist
From the collection of the Samuel S. Fleisher Trust

JOHN GRAHAM: *The Horse of the Apocalypse*
c.1947-1955
Oil, charcoal and graphite
on masonite
183 x 122 cm
Sold 18.11.81 in New York
for $187,000 (£97,395)

JACQUES EMILE BLANCHE: *La Promenade à l'Eléphant*
Signed
98 x 102 cm
Sold 29.6.82 in London for £12,960 ($22,032)
From the collection of the late Paul Wallraf

SIR ALFRED MUNNINGS, P.R.A.: *Before the Start, Newmarket*
Signed
52.1 x 80.7 cm
Sold 4.6.82 in New York for $357,500 (£197,573)
Record auction price for a work by the artist
From the collection of Arthur M.R. Charrington III

LAURENCE STEPHEN LOWRY, R.A.: *Football Match*
Signed and dated 1932
Oil on panel
43.1 x 53.3 cm
Sold 12.3.82 in London for £17,280 ($31,449)
Previously sold at Christie's 3 November 1967
for £1,575

PAUL NASH: *Wall against the Sea*
Signed and dated 1922
62.2 x 90.1 cm
Sold 12.3.82 in London for £18,360 ($33,415)

ALGERNON TALMAGE, R.A.: *Mrs Talmage and a Friend*
Signed and dated 1916
120.6 x 115 cm
Sold 6.11.81 in London for £3,520 ($6,652)

ROBERT BEVAN: *Cumberland Market*
Signed
*c.*1914-15
50.8 x 60.9 cm
Sold 6.11.81 in London for £30,800 ($58,212)

VICTOR PASMORE: *Chrysanthemums*
Signed
1943
60.9 x 45.7 cm
Sold 12.3.82 in London for £16,200
($29,484)
Record auction price for a work by
the artist

Opposite, far left

SIR WILLIAM ORPEN,
R.A., R.H.A.:
The Lady in Black
Signed and dated 1901
116.7 x 52.7 cm
Sold 6.11.81 in
London for £26,400
($49,896)

Opposite, left

WALTER RICHARD
SICKERT, A.R.A.:
The New Bedford
Signed
Painted c.1908-9
91.4 x 35.5 cm
Sold 12.3.82 in
London for £32,400
($58,968)
From the collection
of the late
Miss Margot
Grahame

JOHN LUKE: *Landscape Composition*
Signed and dated 47
Signed again and dated Knappagh Farm, Killylea,
Co. Armagh, Ireland, 1947
Tempera on gesso on board
42 x 43.2 cm
Sold 12.3.82 in London for £6,480 ($11,793)
Record auction price for a work by the artist

MARK GERTLER: *Self Portrait*
c.1909-11
Soft pencil
29.2 x 20.3 cm
Sold 6.11.81 in London for £4,950 ($9,355)
From the collection of the late Theodore Besterman

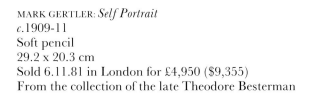

WALTER RICHARD SICKERT, A.R.A.: *Nude at a Mirror;*
Quai Voltaire
Signed and inscribed Quai Voltaire
1906
Black chalk, pen and black ink heightened with white
27.9 x 20.3 cm
Sold 6.11.81 in London for £3,740 ($7,068)
From the collection of the late Theodore Besterman

MARK GERTLER: *Vanity*
Signed and dated 1912
121.8 x 45.7 cm
Sold 6.11.81 in London for £7,150 ($13,513)

BOOKS AND MANUSCRIPTS

BOOK OF HOURS, *Latin and French*
With Calendar (use of Paris)
France, possibly Bourges
*c.*1470
Sold 25.9.81 in New York for $60,500 (£33,611)

Album of Illuminated Initials cut from an Antiphonary
Cambrai, *c.*1265, and North-Eastern France, late 14th century
Sold 9.12.81 in London for £26,400 ($51,480)

LIFE AND ACTS OF
SAINT SIMPERT:
*Illuminated manuscript on
vellum, with two full-
page miniatures by Hans
Holbein the Elder*
Augsburg 1492
Sold 23.6.82 in
London for £140,400
($238,000)
From the collection of
the late Count
Antoine Seilern

JOSEPH LYCETT: *Views in Australia or New South Wales, and Van Diemen's Land*
48 coloured aquatint views
1824
Sold 25.11.81 in London for
£20,900 ($40,128)

GEORGE FRENCH ANGAS:
South Australia Illustrated,
10 original parts
Coloured lithographed title
and 60 plates
1846-7
Sold 25.11.81 in London for
£9,900 ($18,810)

JOHN GOULD: *The Birds of Australia*
8 vols.
683 hand-finished coloured
lithograph plates
1840-69
Sold 24.3.82 in London for
£54,000 ($97,740)

CALYPTORHYNCHUS BANKSII.

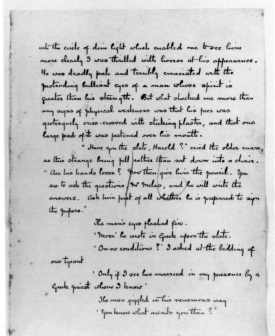

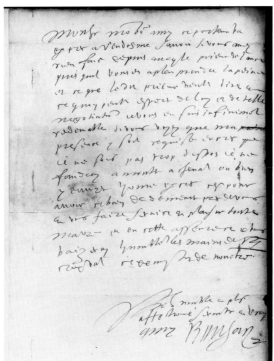

Far left

HUMPHRY REPTON
(1752-1818): *Autograph
Draft of his
Autobiography, Part 2*
Sold 4.11.81 in
London for £18,700
($34,782)

Left

SIR ARTHUR CONAN
DOYLE (1859-1930):
*'The Greek Interpreter',
the Autograph
Manuscript*
1893
Sold 5.5.82 in London
for £15,660 ($28,501)

Far left

PIERRE DE RONSARD
1524-85): *Autograph
Letter signed ('Ronsard')
to the author Florent
Chrestien*
c.1582
Sold 23.6.82 in
London for £20,520
($34,884)

Left

SIR THOMAS MORE:
*Libellus vere aureus nec
minus salutaris quam
festivus de Optimo Reip.
Statu, deq. Nova Insula
Utopia*
First edition, 1516
Sold 24.2.82 in
London for £81,000
($149,850)
Sold by the 10th Duke
of Devonshire's
Charitable Trust

Selection of French armorial bindings from the library at Chatsworth
Sold by the 10th Duke of Devonshire's Charitable Trust
A series of sales from this library totalled £677,380 ($121,928) during 1981-2

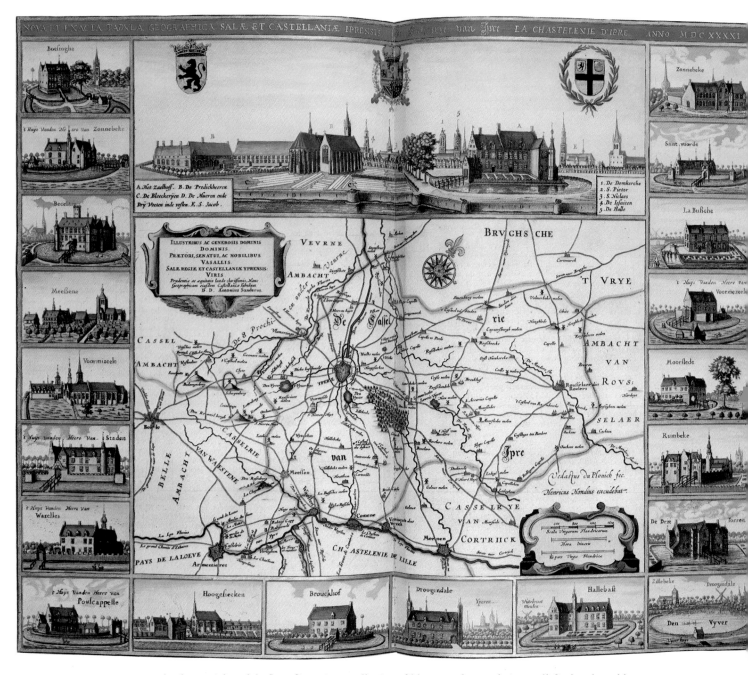

W. & J. BLAEU, N. VISSCHER and others: *Atlas of the Low Countries, a collection of 90 maps, plans and views, all finely coloured by a contemporary hand*
1664-84
Sold 14.7.82 in London for £18,360 ($31,579)

CLAUDIUS PTOLOMAEUS: *Cosmographia*
32 large woodcut maps, all finely coloured by a contemporary hand [Ulm, Johannes Reger, 21 July 1486]
Sold 14.7.82 in London for £27,000 ($46,440)

The secret correspondence of Marie Antoinette and Axel von Fersen

PAMELA WHITE

Marie Antoinette, not yet 20 and Dauphiness of France, met the young Swedish nobleman Count Axel von Fersen in 1773 or 1774. One story ascribes their first meeting to one of the masked balls in Paris which she secretly attended. She had already embarked on the career of reckless extravagance and disregard for court conventions that was to provoke an unprecedented public campaign of hostility and vilification. The Queen's passionate attachment to Fersen, which began as a part of her single-minded pursuit of pleasure, ripened into the most important relationship of her life. From about 1786 to 1789, during the aftermath of the Diamond Necklace affair and the gathering force of revolution, Fersen visited her secretly but frequently at Trianon and St Cloud. By the time of open revolution and the imprisonment of the royal family in the Tuileries, they met daily. Fersen was by then her most intimate friend and confidant, advising both her and the King on political matters, vainly trying to marshal support for her among the royal families of Europe, and carrying her smuggled correspondence. Surrounded as she was by enemies and spies, watched, intrigued and plotted against by the National Assembly, the mob, the French royal family, the National Guard and her servants, Fersen was her only ally. It was he who painstakingly arranged the flight to Varennes, that tragicomic escape turned royal progress in June 1791. After this débâcle Fersen was able to steal only one last meeting with the Queen. However he continued, in an extensive secret correspondence, to support and advise her.

During her imprisonment Marie Antoinette managed under heavy surveillance to write and receive a number of letters, often written in invisible ink or in cipher; they were conveyed by various trusted friends in boxes of chocolates, tucked into nosegays, or rolled in hatbrims. Her correspondence with Fersen was clearly her most vital emotional release, political forum, and link with the outside world; her letters are extremely free, fully discussing events in Paris, political developments, the mesh of intrigue surrounding her, plans for escape, the life of the royal family in captivity, and her abiding love for him. He not only carefully preserved these letters, noting the date of their arrival and means of conveyance, but recorded minutes of his replies – fortunately, since the Queen, whose apartments were subject to repeated searches, destroyed virtually all the letters she received. (At the storming of the Tuileries in 1792 not a single paper of Marie Antoinette's could be found.) At the same time the discretion of Fersen and then his descendants ensured that this crucial correspondence – and indeed the relationship it illuminates – remained unknown until Baron Rudolf Klinckowström published a heavily bowdlerized version of the letters in 1877-8, editing out any passages hinting at passion and perhaps others of political sensitivity. In about 1900, presumably to preserve the family honour for all time, he destroyed nearly all the originals.

The collection offered at Christie's on 5 May, and now in the Archives Nationales in Paris, contains all that remains of this most valuable archive of the French Revolution: four autograph letters from Marie Antoinette to Fersen, written from the Tuileries in 1791-2, characteristically neither signed nor naming their recipient, with a few lines in cipher and other passages irrevocably overscored, together with Fersen's transcripts of 24 other letters from Marie Antoinette to himself, 1791-2, and of 34 letters from himself to the Queen, 1788-93. Three memoranda drafted by Fersen early in 1791 recommend to Louis XVI and the Queen that the King leave Paris, and analyse the political situation in Europe; again characteristically, the annotations in the margins are in the hand of Marie Antoinette rather than the King. Several

MARIE ANTOINETTE and
AXEL VON FERSEN: *Secret correspondence:
collection of autograph letters, minutes,
notes, memoranda, documents and
transcripts of letters, comprising Marie
Antoinette's secret correspondence with
Count Axel von Fersen during the French
Revolution*
1788-94
Sold 5.5.82 in London for £15,120
($27,518)
Sold by order of the Estate of
Baroness Thyra Klinckowstroem

papers relating to the flight to Varennes include the original bill for items supplied for the berline in which they escaped.
(The French royal family were never reticent; the coach was furnished with a silver dinner service and a wine cellar.)
Signed "Louis" by the coachbuilder, the bill is dated 19 June 1791 – the day before the royal family left Paris – and is a
document of great poignance from an archive of the utmost importance.

171

Historical Americana: The Chew Family Papers

CHRISTOPHER R. COOVER

A number of families may look with justifiable pride upon the role of an ancestor in the civil and political affairs of America's colonial and revolutionary periods. Of these, a small proportion have managed to preserve the manuscripts and papers of that forebear from the depredations of the Revolutionary War and subsequent upheavals, and the normal vicissitudes of time and successive ownership. Only a very few American families, though, possess today an archive of the size, extent and historical importance of the Chew Family Papers.

The most interesting portion of this archive – an estimated 60,000 pieces occupying the equivalent of approximately 200 manuscript file boxes, and consisting of letters, drafts, affidavits, documents and memoranda – derives from the multi-faceted career of Benjamin Chew (November 29 1722 – January 20 1810). Born in the colony of Maryland, Chew journeyed to London in 1741 to complete his study of the law in the Middle Temple. He moved to Philadelphia in 1754, and in his long and distinguished public career held many important legislative and judicial posts in the government of his city and the province of Pennsylvania: member of the Philadephia Council, City recorder, Speaker of the Assembly of the Lower Counties (later the state of Delaware), and Register-General, Attorney-General of the province and, ultimately, Chief Justice of the Supreme Court of Pennsylvania.

The Penn family, Lords Proprietary of the province, found him to be a reliable and hardworking agent, and in 1750 they appointed him to serve on the crucial Pennsylvania-Maryland Boundary Commission. It was to prove an especially taxing and particularly delicate charge, one which occupied much of Chew's energies during the next 18 years.

In 1972, Cliveden, the Neo-Palladian/Middle Georgian stone house built by Benjamin Chew in Germantown outside Philadelphia, was given by the Chew family to the National Trust for Historic Preservation. It had long been the family's intention to donate the Chew Family Papers to the Historical Society of Pennsylvania, already the repository of a vast collection of manuscripts relating to the colonial period of Pennsylvania and the nation. The hindrance to this generous gift was a tax obligation. Christie's was asked by the family to examine the archive – much of it inventoried but essentially unexplored – and to select a small group of highly significant individual pieces for sale, to facilitate the bequest.

The sale, held on the evening of April 1st 1982, constituted the first single-owner auction of printed and manuscript Americana ever held by Christie's. It was an unqualified success: in a scant 38 minutes, its 25 lots realized the total of $921,140 (£511,740). The documents encompassed nearly a century of the nation's colonial history, from the inception of William Penn's "Holy Experiment" of Pennsylvania, to America's Declaration of Independence in 1776.

172

THE CHEW FAMILY
PAPERS: *Grant of
Pennsylvania from
King Charles II to
William Penn.
Pennsylvania Charter*
Document signed by
Sir Richard Pigott,
Clerk of the Patents:
Royal Charter
granting William
Penn the Proprietary
Province of
Pennsylvania.
Westminster,
4 March 1680/81
Sold 1.4.82 in
New York for
$52,800 (£29,333)

The colony of Pennsylvania was created from England's vast land-holdings in the New World on March 4th 1680-81, when William Penn received a grant from King Charles II. A Quaker, Penn objected strenuously to the name chosen for the new province by the King, even to the extent of attempting to bribe the court's secretaries to have it altered. The King's Charter was a substantial document, setting forth not only the boundaries of the new colony but defining in considerable detail the prerogatives of Penn as proprietor; he was empowered to make laws, appoint the legislature and judiciary, was granted the right to sell or rent land and levy taxes, to collect duties, incorporate towns and raise troups for the defence of the colony. Of equal importance, religious belief and practice were exempted from regulation or control.

Once the Charter's exact wording had been approved and the text officially recorded, two copies, both laboriously engrossed on vellum, were prepared. To one copy, a wax impression of the Great Seal of England was affixed, in an elaborate, highly formalized ceremony. Remarkably, both copies of this historic document are extant today: the one which originally bore the great seal (long since detached and lost) belongs, appropriately, to the state of Pennsylvania. The other, less ornate, and with a blank wax seal, but of equal official character and in considerably better condition, was found among the papers of Benjamin Chew and sold for $52,800 (£29,330).

The new territory lay between two earlier Royal grants – the Duke of York's to the north, and Maryland, the property of Lord Baltimore, to the south. The Charter, therefore, went to considerable lengths to define the colony's boundaries, but as knowledge of the New World's geography was inexact and the distances involved were enormous, it is not surprising that controversy soon erupted between Lord Baltimore and William Penn over the precise limits of their common boundary. The beginnings of what proved a complex, expensive and long-lived dispute between the proprietors is a document signed at Philadelphia by William Penn in 1683 which delegated several lieutenants (including a nephew) to "treat transact & conclude" a settlement with Lord Baltimore. Documents signed by Penn during his first residence in the colony (from October 1682 to August 1684) are of great rarity. The one-page manuscript was bought for $7,480 (£4,156) by the Chicago dealer Kenneth Nebenzahl, bidding on behalf of the Historical Society of Pennsylvania.

No substantial progress was made toward a resolution of the altercation during the lifetimes of the original proprietors, despite intermittent negotiations and appeals to Royal authority. The effects of the stalemate were considerable: collection of taxes and sale of land in the disputed territories became virtually impossible, and although the population of the colonies increased, little revenue was forthcoming to either side. On May 10th 1723, a momentous treaty was at last concluded between William Penn's sons and heirs John, Thomas and Richard, and Charles Calvert, 5th Lord Baltimore and proprietor of Maryland. These Articles of Agreement, as they were called, defined in the most explicit terms possible, by reference to landmarks and measurements in miles and degrees of latitude and longitude, the correct boundary between the colonies. A map of the region, with the lines of division carefully indicated, was produced for additional clarification. Lord Baltimore himself furnished the drawing for the map, which was engraved on copper in the Fleet Street shop of the well-known cartographer and map-seller John Senex. The Chew archive contains one of three surviving copies of this important document signed by the three Penn brothers and Lord Baltimore, with a printed impression of the Senex map. This was on a large vellum sheet, in fine condition, and sold for $9,350 (£5,194).

Not long after the signing of the Articles of Agreement, Lord Baltimore realized to his dismay that his own map, supplied by his agent in America, contained critical inaccuracies advantageous to the Penns. He repudiated the agreement. The Penns responded by appealing to the High Court of Chancery; after 15 years of legal machinations and political manoeuvrings, a decision was rendered compelling Lord Baltimore to comply with the terms of the 1732 treaty and to cooperate in a joint survey and mapping of the elusive boundary. Both sides appointed influential attornies, educators and public officials to a joint Pennsylvania-Maryland Boundary Commission. Benjamin Chew was an early Penn family appointee. The Commission held meetings at regular intervals, (meetings which were often argumentative) to plan, direct and oversee the work of the surveying teams in the field. Careful minutes of their proceedings and details of the survey costs were kept in duplicate. The Penn set of these records, four volumes of notes and accounts in neat long hand and with the individual commissioners' signatures at the end of each entry, were acquired for the Historical Society of Pennsylvania by Nebenzahl for $3,850 (£2,162).

Progress on the survey and mapping was disappointingly slow and it became clear that only the most highly qualified surveyors and mathematicians would be capable of completing the difficult and complicated task. Accordingly, the proprietors undertook to "...send over to America two persons well skilled in Astronomy, Mathematics, and Land Surveying." Their choice fell upon two young men, Charles Mason, an astronomer at the Royal Observatory, and a surveyor, Jeremiah Dixon of Cockfield, Durham. A contract, specifying the terms of their employment, was drawn up and signed by the Penn brothers, Thomas and Richard, by Lord Baltimore's attorney, and by Mason and Dixon. With the familiar engraved Senex map attached, this historical contract, signed on August 4 1763, sold for $15,400 (£8,556) to Nebenzahl for the Historical Society of Pennsylvania.

The hiring of Mason and Dixon proved a wise decision, and resulted in a definitive survey and a final resolution of the seemingly endless boundary quarrel. They arrived in America in 1763, took an oath administered by the Boundary Commission, and were soon in the field with their cumbersome and delicate astronomical instruments. Most of their large support party,

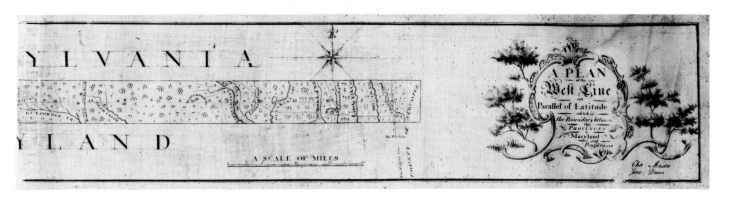

THE CHEW FAMILY PAPERS: ORIGINAL DRAWING FOR THE MASON-DIXON LINE: *Charles Mason and Jeremiah Dixon.*
A Plan of the West Line or Parallel of Latitude which is the Boundary between the Provinces of Maryland and
Pennsylvania, n.p., n.d.
Drawn at Philadelphia, 26 December 1767 – 29 February 1768
Signed below the cartouche: Cha: Mason, Jere: Dixon
16.4 to 17.2 x 192.4 cm; each of the 4 central sections approx. 35.5 cm wide; 2 outer sections approx.
23.5 and 27.5 cm wide
Sold 1.4.82 in New York for $396,000 (£220,000)
Record auction price for an Americana manuscript

which included guides, hunters, wagoners, labourers and axe-men (to clear the thick forests in a wide swathe along the line), were Indians of the Iroquois or Six Nations alliance.

The running of the lines, which ran through the thick forest of the Appalachian Mountains, traversed only by a few little-used military roads and Indian trails, required four years to complete. From their camp site in the wilderness, Charles Mason wrote occasional letters to members of the Boundary Commission, informing them of their progress.

A series of six of these first-hand reports came to light among the Chew Family Papers. On October 2 1767, from a camp site on the Monaungahela River (south of present-day Pittsburgh), Mason reported tersely that "26 of our Men left us for fear of the Shawnees and Delawares. We have still left us 15 Axmen with whom we shall continue the Line so long as they can be prevailed upon to stay with us, and the Season will permit." The refusal of the Indian members of the surveying party to continue into territory occupied by other tribes forced the termination of the survey, a mere 36 miles short of its intended terminus after 233 miles of territory had been surveyed and mapped. "We crossed a War Path (used by the Six Nations to go against their Enemies the Cheroques), there we were informed by the Cheif [sic] of our Indians that he was come to the full Extent of his Commission from the Six Nations to go with us on the Line; and that he would not proceed one step farther." The six letters sold to Kenneth Nebenzahl for the Historical Society of Pennsylvania for $13,200 (£7,333).

Upon their return to Philadelphia, the surveyors drew, from carefully noted astronomical calculations and map field observations, a meticulous map of the boundaries they had plotted. Their map was laid out in two distinct sections, one of the irregular, eastern boundary between Pennsylvania and the Three Lower Counties (Delaware), the other depicting the long West Line between Pennsylvania and Maryland, each showing a strip of land three miles wide on either side of the surveyed line including settlements, rivers, mountains, trails and other details of the terrain.

Mason and Dixon could not, at the time, have foreseen the prodigious significance their survey and map would take on in the subsequent history of America. Fully half a century later, Congress, in its bitter debates of 1819-20 over the institution of slavery in the newly-opened western territories, seized upon the West Line of the Pennsylvania-Maryland border, which never extended further west than 233 miles, as an expedient line of demarcation between lands where man could or could not hold another man in slavery. The Mason and Dixon Line thus crystallized into an imaginary, but iron clad, frontier reaching across an entire continent, symbolically dividing it and its people by political orientation and social customs into North and South. The name of an obscure surveyor was, in the process, tranformed into "Dixie", the popular name for a region, a cultural milieu and a state of mind.

Two different Philadelphia engravers were employed to engrave the finished map on large copper plates, and on August 16 1768, 200 copies of the two-section map were printed at the order of the Boundary Commission. A few copies of this beautiful map were carefully mounted on linen and joined together to depict the entire length of the boundary, from the Atlantic shoreline to the 233 mile marker in the western Appalachians. Lot 21, estimated at $8,000 to $12,000, was one of these mounted copies. In spirited bidding, it sold for $35,200 (£19,556).

The next lot was a linen-mounted copy of the Mason-Dixon map of special significance: an officially certified and validated copy, with a lengthy legal certification in a decorative 18th century hand, and bearing the prominent signatures and wax seals of most of the members of the Pennsylvania-Maryland Boundary Commission, including those of Benjamin Chew and the Governor of Maryland, Horatio Sharpe. A private collector, Benjamin Coates, was the successful bidder at $39,600 (£22,000).

An even more remarkable document from the Chew Family Papers followed: Charles Mason's original drawing for the map of the West Line delicately rendered in pen and ink, with an attractive cartouche of trees around its hand-lettered title and, at its lower corner, the neat signatures of both Mason and Dixon. This was the drawing from which the engraving had originally been prepared. The drawing for the eastern portion of the map, it was learned, had been given away by one of Chew's descendants as early as 1864, and had passed, in time, to the Princeton University Library. The drawing for the West Line, a strip of linen-backed paper about six inches wide and over six feet long, was framed and prominently displayed throughout the pre-sale exhibition, and had attracted considerable attention from the press, potential buyers and the general public. A palpable air of electricity gripped the crowded saleroom when the lot, estimated at $40,000 to $60,000 was announced. In a few moments of relentless bidding between Benjamin Coates and Malcolm Forbes, jun., a noted collector of American autographs and manuscripts, the map was sold to Forbes for the astonishing sum of $396,000 (£220,000): the highest price paid at auction for any Americana manuscript and the highest ever achieved by a map.

The final lot of the sale was arguably the most important single piece of paper ever printed in America: the broadside of the Declaration of Independence, set in type by a Philadelphia printer, John Dunlap, probably only hours after the famous document had been approved and signed by John Hancock and other delegates of July 4th 1776. The size of Dunlap's edition is not known, but the fragile broadside survives today in only 21 copies, many of those damaged or

IN CONGRESS, JULY 4, 1776.

A DECLARATION

BY THE REPRESENTATIVES OF THE

UNITED STATES OF AMERICA,

IN GENERAL CONGRESS ASSEMBLED.

WHEN in the Course of human Events, it becomes neceffary for one People to diffolve the Political Bands which have connected them with another, and to affume among the Powers of the Earth, the feparate and equal Station to which the Laws of Nature and of Nature's God entitle them, a decent Refpect to the Opinions of Mankind requires that they fhould declare the caufes which impel them to tle Separation.

We hold thefe Truths to be felf-evident, that all Men are created equal, that they are endowed by their Creator with certain unalienable Rights, that among thefe are Life, Liberty, and the Purfuit of Happinefs—-That to fecure thefe Rights, Governments are inftituted among Men, deriving their juft Powers from the Confent of the Governed, that whenever any Form of Government becomes deftructive of thefe Ends, it is the Right of the People to alter or to abolifh it, and to inftitute new Government, laying its Foundation on fuch Principles, and organizing its Powers in fuch Form, as to them fhall feem moft likely to effect their Safety and Happinefs. Prudence, indeed, will dictate that Governments long eftablifhed fhould not be changed for light and tranfient Caufes; and accordingly all Experience hath fhewn, that Mankind are more difpofed to fuffer, while Evils are fufferable, than to right themfelves by abolifhing the Forms to which they are accuftomed. But when a long Train of Abufes and Ufurpations, purfuing invariably the fame Object, evinces a Defign to reduce them under abfolute Defpotifm, it is their Right, it is their Duty, to throw off fuch Government, and to provide new Guards for their future Security. Such has been the patient Sufferance of thefe Colonies; and fuch is now the Neceffity which conftrains them to alter their former Syftems of Government. The Hiftory of the prefent King of Great-Britain is a Hiftory of repeated Injuries and Ufurpations, all having in direct Object the Eftablifhment of an abfolute Tyranny over thefe States. To prove this, let Facts be fubmitted to a candid World.

He has refufed his Affent to Laws, the moft wholefome and neceffary for the public Good.

He has forbidden his Governors to pafs Laws of immediate and preffing Importance, unlefs fufpended in their Operation till his Affent fhould be obtained; and when fo fufpended, he has utterly neglected to attend to them.

He has refufed to pafs other Laws for the Accommodation of large Diftricts of People, unlefs thofe People would relinquifh the Right of Reprefentation in the Legiflature, a Right ineftimable to them, and formidable to Tyrants only.

He has called together Legiflative Bodies at Places unufual, uncomfortable, and diftant from the Depofitory of their public Records, for the fole Purpofe of fatiguing them into Compliance with his Meafures.

He has diffolved Reprefentative Houfes repeatedly, for oppofing with manly Firmnefs his Invafions on the Rights of the People.

He has refufed for a long Time, after fuch Diffolutions, to caufe others to be elected; whereby the Legiflative Powers, incapable of Annihilation, have returned to the People at large for their exercife; the State remaining in the mean time expofed to all the Dangers of Invafion from without, and Convulfions within.

He has endeavoured to prevent the Population of thefe States; for that Purpofe obftructing the Laws for Naturalization of Foreigners; refufing to pafs others

THE CHEW FAMILY PAPERS: *The Declaration of Independence* (detail)
United States of America. In Congress, July 4, 1776. A Declaration by the Representatives of the United States of America, in General Congress assembled
Signed by Order and in Behalf of the Congress, John Hancock, President. Attest, Charles Thompson, Secretary
Philadelphia: printed by John Dunlap
1776
Folio broadside, overall size 42.1 x 39.5 cm, originally folded twice horizontally and twice vertically
Sold 1.4.82 in New York for $313,500 (£174,167)

imperfect. The Chew copy was not only in the finest possible condition, without signs of wear or handling, but was of special interest for its distinguished colonial provenance. It was difficult to predict what it might be sold for: in 1969, when only 15 copies had been recorded, a sixteenth had come to light and had sold at auction in Philadelphia for an astounding $404,000 (£168,330) to a determined Texas collector. This price remained a world auction record for a printed item until Christie's sale of The Gutenberg Bible in 1978 for $2,200,000 (£1,176,000). The Chew broadside was discovered in the family papers in about 1970 and, after the sale at Christie's in London in July 1975 of another copy for $92,000 (£40,000), it became the subject of considerable speculation prior to the auction. In a stiff contest between the New York dealers, Hans P. Kraus and John Fleming, the broadside was sold for $313,500 (£174,167) to Fleming. A few days later it was announced that it had been presented by the Robert Wood Johnson Charitable Trust to one of New York's most distinguished public institutions, The Pierpont Morgan Library. The sale of the Declaration was a fitting cadenza to a highly exciting and beautifully orchestrated sale.

Manuscripts by Bach and Debussy

STEPHEN C. MASSEY

The nucleus of Christie's auction devoted to music, on May 21, the second of its kind in New York, was the consignment of 13 items belonging to The Curtis Institute of Music in Philadelphia. Four other consignors contributed significant pieces to make up a sale of only 17 lots, which sold for a total of $751,355 (£417,419). In October 1978 Christie's New York sold The Curtis Institute's superb Richard Wagner collection and secured a world record auction price of $242,000 (£121,000) for the manuscripts of Tannhauser, so this spring sale, which again attracted many of the world's leading collectors and dealers, had the atmosphere of a reunion, (highlighted by recorded music!) before the spirited bidding began.

There would appear to be a definite trend among American teaching institutions to offer for sale by auction major works of art, literature and music. The Curtis Institute's course of action was a factor in the decision taken by Boston's New England Conservatory to include in the sale the most important and extensive autograph manuscript of Claude Achille Debussy's only opera, *Pelléas et Mélisande*, written between 1893 and 1901 and comprising 124 pages of music, many with corrections and markings in coloured inks and pencil. A fierce contest for this manuscript between John Fleming of New York, acting on behalf of the Pierpont Morgan Library, and Pierre Beres for the Bibliothèque Nationale in Paris, produced the unexpected price of $385,000 (£213,880): a new record auction price. It should be borne in mind by those who express concern that this manuscript did not return to France, that it has been in the U.S.A. at least since 1910, and that it has been added to the Pierpont Morgan Library's extensive Debussy collection, now the most important in the world.

The Curtis Institute's complete autograph manuscript of Johann Sebastian Bach's delightful Cantata BWV 180 ("Schmucke dich, o liebe Seele"), which had previously belonged to an illustrious series of musicians, including Felix Mendelssohn-Bartholdy, was purchased for $198,000 (£110,000), a record price for a Bach manuscript, by the German dealer Hans Schneider, bidding on behalf of the Gemeinutzige Stiftung "Internationale Bachakademie" in Stuttgart, a new centre for Bach studies. It is their first major manuscript by the German master.

The earliest known manuscript in the sale was also owned by The Curtis Institute. Known as "The Ileborgh Tablature", it was written on seven vellum leaves in 1448 by a Franciscan monk, Brother Adam Ileborgh at Stendal in the March of Brandenburg. It comprises eight compositions for the organ and is one of the earliest known pieces of keyboard music.

Hans Kraus of New York was the purchaser at $35,200 (£19,550).

CLAUDE ACHILLE
DEBUSSY: *Autograph
manuscript of the short
Score of Pelléas et
Mélisande*
Signed with his
monogram in 5 places
Paris, September
1893-September 1901
Sold 21.5.82 in
New York for
$385,000 (£213,888)
Record auction price
for a musical
manuscript

JOHANN SEBASTIAN BACH:
Autograph manuscript, "Schmücke dich, o liebe Seele"
Cantata BWV 180, full score for chorus and orchestra
Leipzig, probably just before
22 October 1724
Sold 21.5.82 in New York for
$198,000 (£110,000)

ITALIAN CARRARA MARBLE CENTRE
TABLE: The central scene of
Romulus and Remus with the
She-Wolf surrounded by twelve
views of the Antiquities and
sights of Rome
19th century
121 cm diam; 83 cm high
Sold 2.11.81 at Leonardslee,
Sussex, for £19,250 ($34,650)

Sales on the Premises

Christie's King Street

7/8.10.81	Birr Castle, Co. Offaly, Ireland	IR£335,493	(£291,879)
15.10.81	Stoneleigh Abbey, Kenilworth, Warwickshire	£249,356	($466,295)
21.10.81	Avebury Manor, Marlborough, Wiltshire	£122,762	($229,564)
2.11.81	Leonardslee, Lower Beeding, Horsham, Sussex	£197,835	($369,951)
5.4.82	The Nash, Kempsey, Worcestershire	£177,409	($319,336)
26/27.4.82	Merdon Manor, Hursley, Hampshire	£324,130	($583,434)
9/10.6.82	Adare Manor, Co. Limerick, Ireland	IR£945,000	(£812,700)

Christie's South Kensington

17/18.9.81	The Bath Club, 41 Brook Street, London	£194,775	($370,072)
24.5.82	Sunrising House, Edgehill, Nr. Banbury	£69,400	($124,920)
7.6.82	Comilla House, Amesbury, Wiltshire	£54,362	($97,851)
22.6.82	Sefton Court, 51 Ullett Road, Liverpool	£137,920	($248,256)

Christie's and Edmiston's, Glasgow

7.9.81	Denork, Fife,	£105,607	($197,485)
16.11.81	Morland, Ayrshire,	£44,112	($82,489)
17.5.82	Auchineden, Blanefield, Stirlingshire	£58,210	($104,778)
24.5.82	24 Rothesay Terrace, Edinburgh	£54,710	($98,478)

Christie's Park Avenue, U.S.A.

13.7.82	Duck Creek, Old Lyme, Connecticut,	$365,299	(£200,713)
10/11.8.82	Iroquois Mansion, Cooperstown, New York	$865,018	(£508,834)

FRANCESCO GUARDI:
Church in the Venetian Lagoon with Gondolas and Shipping
45.7 x 35.5 cm
Sold 7.10.81 at Birr Castle, County Offaly, for IR£52,500
(£45,052)

Suite of Chinese painted paper panels
The panels and papier-mâché borders were supplied in 1764 by Bromwich and Leigh as part of the extensive redecoration at Stoneleigh, mainly on the bedroom floor, carried out for Edward, 5th Lord Leigh, following his coming of age in 1763
Sold 15.10.81 at Stoneleigh Abbey, Warwickshire, for £17,600 ($32,912)

George III marquetry
bureau de dame
Attributed to
Pierre Langlois
89.5 cm wide;
51.4 cm deep;
97.8 cm high
Sold at Adare Manor,
Co. Limerick for
IR£70,250 (£60,863)

Massive pair of Sèvres-pattern green-ground
ormolu-mounted vases and covers, on ormolu-
mounted ebonized fluted classical column bases
125.7 cm high overall. Bases 76.2 cm high
Sold 22.6.82 for £9,800 ($17,052)

One of a pair of George II giltwood console tables
170.2 cm wide
Sold 22.6.82 for £20,000 ($34,800)
Both sold at Sefton Court, 50 Ullett Road, Liverpool

The Adare Manor Sale

DESMOND FITZ-GERALD, Knight of Glin

"He that hath Pity on the Poor, lendeth to the Lord." "If it be Possible, as much as lieth in you, live Peaceable with all men." These were but two of the Biblical texts painted on tin scrolls that hung in the great vaulted kitchen in the basement of Adare. They were Lot 933, almost at the end of the sale, and were included with all the varied contents of one of the basement rooms, and I had missed them! Thanks to kind Liz Vincent, the dealer from near Devizes, they now hang self-righteously in the kitchen at Glin with the remains of Caroline, Countess of Dunraven's copper *batterie de cuisine*. Adare is not far away from Glin and my grandmother Rachel Wyndham-Quin was married from Adare in 1897, so the Manor and its collection has always been an absorbing interest to me. Since childhood I remember our visits there, and on arrival recall the flash and ripple of the sunlight on the Tudor revival leaded panes of the many and varied mullioned windows. I remember also the strange grotesque gargoyles and elaborate coats of arms incorporated into the stonework, the carved and crested zigzagged chimney stacks on the acres of roof, best seen from the mysterious fly-haunted empty rooms at the top of the Wyndham tower. Inside the house it was always the long gallery that I used to escape to, while the grown-ups gossiped below over tea in the drawing-room. Canvas after canvas of strange faces – stern and ruffled Elizabethans, sultry doe-eyed Restoration beauties, stiff Anglo-Irish squires – hung on every available space not taken up with Flemish carved woodwork or embrasured window. It now all seems like a dream.

The intense excitement of a great sale does much to stifle all ones' inevitable nostalgia. A successful house sale is one of the most electric experiences both for the auctioneers and the buyers that I can think of, and the sale of Adare Manor held on the 9th and 10th June, after months of planning, was no exception.

Most of the contents of the Manor were formed in the early Victorian period by Windham, 2nd Earl of Dunraven and his heiress wife Caroline Wyndham from Dunraven in South Wales to furnish their new house which they slowly built between 1828 and 1862. When he wrote to her on a buying trip in London in 1840 that "Nothing looks so well in old places as old portraits and old glass. We have plenty of each", he was not exaggerating and the fruits of their combined efforts realized excellent prices during the sale. Their full-length double portrait by Thomas Phillips in the robes they wore for Queen Victoria's coronation was bought by the National Museum of Wales for IR£4,320 (£3,745). An Elizabethan portrait of a lady by Marcus Gheeraerts the Younger fetched IR£14,040 (£12,074). An example of the Dunraven's continental picture buying were the set of four out of the 12 Allegories of the Months signed and dated by Pieter Syners in 1727, IR£21,600 (£18,576). Also bought on the continent especially for the long gallery were the four magnificent North German walnut armoires. They reached a collective total of IR£16,848 (£14,489).

186

A view of the Great Hall, Adare Manor, Co. Limerick

Anything associated with A.W.N. Pugin who was but one of the galaxy of architects that contributed to the design of Adare Manor caused a great deal of interest. For instance a pair of brass and steel andirons with the Wyndham and Quin arms fetched IR£3,132 (£2,715) and even the functional Pugin oak wash stands and writing tables reached as much as IR£562 (£483) and IR£1,620 (£1,393) respectively.

Some of the collection sold came from the old house at Adare that stood on the site of the present one. Other pieces filtered in from Clearwell Court and Dunraven Castle, the English and Welsh houses once owned by the family. A number of grand tour pictures collected in Italy in the 1770s by the first Earl of Dunraven did extremely well. The most spectacular was the Vanvitelli Roman Views which peaked at IR£70,200 (£60,865) and two Italian views attributed to Joli and Canaletto of Rome and Venice made IR£21,600 (£18,576) and IR£22,680 (£19,504) each. Of the Irish pictures always in the family the National Gallery of Ireland bought the charming primitive bay racehorse with jockey on the Curragh by the Irish D. Quigley for IR£7,560 (£6,501), and again in the sporting line Caroline Dunraven's father's lifesize hound attributed to John Boultbee went for IR£16,200 (£13,932). A group of furniture originally from Clearwell and Dunraven included some lacquer: a pair of Regency side cabinets, £20,520 (£17,790), a pair of coffers on stands, IR£10,800 (£9,288) and the Palladian style giltwood mirrors with the Wyndham crest made IR£17,064 (£14,675). The remaining highest prices for furniture were all pieces associated with the Quin side of the family, most notably the George III marquety *bureau de dame* attributed to Pierre Langlois, IR£70,200 (£60,865), a George III marquetry writing table in similar French taste IR£15,120 (£13,003), and a pair of Florentine scagliola table tops by Don Petro Belloni IR£17,280 (£14,860).

The second day's sale saw the dispersal of the silver, porcelain, and glass, arms and armour, and the remaining furniture. The library of books were sold concurrently in the long gallery, and the total of the second day's sale was IR£61,902 (53,235), bringing up the final grand total to IR£945,000 (£812,700).

It still surprises me how quickly all is dispersed and when I looked again at another of the neatly lettered texts on the tin scrolls in my kitchen the message seemed curiously apt: "Gather up the Fragments That Nothing be Lost".

FURNITURE AND
WORKS OF ART

One of a pair of Queen Anne gilt-gesso mirrors
198 x 86 cm
Sold 19.11.81 in London for £52,800 ($100,848)

One from a set of four early George III mahogany side chairs
Sold 19.11.81 in London for £24,200 ($46,222)

One from a set of ten George I walnut dining-chairs
Sold 19.11.81 in London for £66,000 ($126,060)
Formerly in the collection of the Dukes of Leeds at
Hornby Castle

One of a pair of
George I gilt-metal
and verre églomisé-
mounted walnut side
chairs
Sold 30.1.81 in
New York for $39,600
(£21,063)
Originally made for
Nicholas, 4th Earl of
Scarsdale of Sutton
Scarsdale, *c*.1724

Early George III painted and gilded side table
*c.*1770
Stamped G IV R 55
90 cm wide
Probably designed by Sir William Chambers for King George III at Buckingham House and bearing the inventory mark of King George IV
Sold 17.10.81 in New York for $52,800 (£28,852)
From the collection of Henry Ford II

Regency rosewood and amboyna ormolu-mounted sofa table
Early 19th century
114.5 cm wide
Sold 17.10.81 in New York for $63,800 (£34,863)

One of a pair of George III marquetry commodes
131 cm (and 129 cm) wide; 55.5 cm deep; 90 cm high
Sold 19.11.81 in London for £88,000 ($168,080)
Formerly in the collection of Henry Hirsch and previously sold in these Rooms 10 June 1931

Pair of George III rosewood and marquetry commodes
Attributed to John Linnell
108 cm wide; 87 cm high; 48 cm deep
Sold 15.4.82 in London for £135,000 ($240,300)
The design for these commodes is based on a drawing by John Linnell of *c*.1765 in the Victoria and Albert Museum

Yew-wood gateleg dining-table
17th century
183 x 156 cm; 71 cm high
Sold 19.11.81 in London for £23,100 ($44,121)
Record auction price for a gateleg table

Charles II oak bookcase
249 cm high; 50 cm deep;
149 cm wide
Sold 19.11.81 in London for
£50,600 ($96,646)
Record auction price for any
piece of oak furniture
This bookcase was made for
Charles Sergison (1654-1732),
Pepys's successor as Clerk of the
Acts of the Navy Board, and is
modelled on Pepys's own
bookcases, now in the Pepys
Library at Magdalene College,
Cambridge

Pair of Anglo-Indian ivory open armchairs
Late 18th century, Vizagapatam
The seats 52 cm wide; the back 89.5 cm high
Sold 15.4.82 in London for £25,920 ($46,137)
From the collection of Lord Astor of Hever

Victorian ivory-inlaid ebony cabinet in the Italian Renaissance style
206 cm wide;
287 cm high
Sold 15.10.81 in London for £15,400 ($28,798)
Designed by Alfred Lorimer and made by Jackson and Graham, probably for the Earl of Bective, at a cost of £4,000 in 1867
Exhibited in Paris that year and again in London in 1871 and Vienna in 1873
Sold at Christie's 4 December 1885 for 500gns, and subsequently owned by the poet Siegfried Sassoon by whose descendants it was sold again

Louis XV ormolu and
Ming celadon
porcelain vase
75.5 cm high;
the base 43 cm wide
Sold 3.12.81 in
London for £77,000
($150,920)
A drawing now in the
Metropolitan
Museum shows a
nearly identical vase
which probably
belonged to the Duke
and Duchess of
Sachsen-Teschen,
Marie-Antoinette's
sister and brother-in-
law who were
Governors of the Low
Countries from
1780-92

Far right

Louis XIV ebony and boulle clock and bracket
From a design by A.-C. Boulle published *c.*1724
152 cm high overall; clock 54.5 cm wide
Sold 3.12.81 in London for £16,500 ($32,340)
From the Stoneleigh Abbey collection

Right

Louis XIV ormolu-mounted boulle cartel clock and barometer
109 cm high; 25.5 cm wide
Sold 1.7.82 in London for £28,080 ($48,297)
From the collection of Colonel S.L. Green

Pair of Louis XVI ormolu and porphyry
gueridons
45 cm diam; 79 cm high
Sold 3.12.81 in London for £30,800 ($60,368)

Opposite

Suite of Louis XV giltwood seat furniture,
comprising a canapé and six fauteuils
Mid-18th century
Each stamped I Pothier
Canapé 192.5 cm wide
Sold 12.11.81 in New York for
$192,500 (£100,260)
From the collection of Henry Ford II

Louis XIV ormolu-mounted kingwood and parquetry commode
Early 18th century
143 cm wide
Sold 12.11.81 in New York for $126,500 (£65,885)

Louis XV/XVI kingwood and marquetry commode
Mid-18th century
Stamped P.A. Foullet
143.5 cm wide
Sold 12.11.81 in New York for $126,500 (£65,885)
From the collection of Henry Ford II

Louis XV black and gold lacquer bureau en pente known as the Vallière Bureau
By Jacques Dubois
21 cm wide; 104 cm high; 52 cm deep
Sold 3.12.81 in London for £143,000 ($280,280)
This desk, together with a lacquer screen, was given to the Marquis de Vallière (1717-76) by
Charles III of Spain in recognition of his services to the Spanish army as artillery and engineering
adviser. He was famous as an artilleryman and is known as the inventor of the gun which bears his name

Transitional tulipwood bureau à cylindre
By J.-F. Oeben
141 cm wide; 87.5 cm deep; 123 cm high
Sold 22.4.82 in London for £69,120 ($123,033)
Formerly in the collection of the Baroness Burton and previously sold at Christie's 24 November 1950

Louis XV ormolu-mounted kingwood bureau plat
Attributed to Charles Cressent
163 cm wide; 81 cm high; 83 cm deep
Sold 1.7.82 in London for £102,600 ($174,420)
From the collection of the Earl of Normanton

The *bureau plât* or large flat-topped writing table is one of the most characteristic forms of 18th century French furniture. It emerged in the 1720s as a distinct type, clothed in rococo form, losing in the process the central four legs and stacked drawers at either side familiar in the *bureau Mazarin*, its lineal predecessor. Among the Parisian *ébénistes* who first mastered this new form – and indeed the new rococo idiom – Charles Cressent was probably the most distinguished. As a sculptor as well as *ébéniste* he managed to create in his furniture a homogeneity and unity between gilt bronze and wood, exemplified in the Normanton *bureau plât*, which has rarely been equalled. This particular piece has an interesting saleroom history prior to its sale in King Street in July. It was bought by the 2nd Earl in 1851 for 55 guineas at his brother-in-law, the 12th Earl of Pembroke's, sale at Christie's. Both men were contemporaries and rivals of the Prince Regent; Lord Pembroke, who died in Paris, may well have purchased the table there

Louis XVI amaranth bureau plat
By J.-F. Leleu
183 cm wide; 98 cm deep; 80 cm high
Sold 3.12.81 in London for £330,000 ($646,800)
From the collection of the Marquis of Lansdowne, removed from Meikleour, Perthshire

A similarly interesting Anglo-French history surrounds the spectacularly grand *bureau plât* made by Jean-François Leleu in the early 1770s and sold at King Street last December. It came from the celebrated collection of French furniture and *objets d'art* formed by Margaret, Baroness Nairne and Keith, and her husband the Comte de Flahaut, Talleyrand's natural son, for their Paris house, the Hôtel de Massa. Leleu trained in the workshop of J.-F. Oeben in company with J.-H. Riesener and both later employed some of the same techniques learnt from their master. While Cressent's bureau captures the incipient delicacy of the early rococo, Leleu's bureau majestically and lavishly embodies the stern masculinity of early neoclassicism: advanced in the use of strongly delineated architectural forms, at the same time it looks back in some respects – as so much of the finest Louis XVI furniture – to the grandeur of the golden age of Louis XIV

Louis XIV boulle bureau Mazarin
148.5 cm wide; 77.5 cm deep; 85 cm high
Sold 3.12.81 in London for £33,000 ($64,680)

German amaranth and marquetry commode
Stamped three times P.S. Claise
Mid-18th century
135 cm wide; 53 cm deep; 89 cm high
Sold 3.12.81 in London for £20,900 ($40,964)
From the collection of Eva, Countess of Rosebery, D.B.E.

Two from a set of four Italian polychrome painted chairs
Late 18th century
Sold 1.7.82 in London for £7,992 ($13,586)

South German
pewter-inlaid walnut
bombé bureau
Mid-18th century
80 cm wide;
97 cm high;
57 cm deep
Sold 10.12.81 in
London for £33,000
($63,360)
From the collection of
the Marquis of
Lansdowne, removed
from Meikleour,
Perthshire

The Goddard and Townsend Cabinet Makers

RALPH CARPENTER

Newport, Rhode Island, was one of the five largest port cities of Colonial America and a major centre of domestic furniture production in the 18th century. The wealthy merchants of Providence and Newport, enriched by a prosperous sea trade, commissioned furniture from the prominent Goddard and Townsend families of cabinet makers.

John Brown of Providence, owner at one time of 25 ships, bought much of his furniture from John Goddard, including the blocked and shell-carved kneehole desk illustrated here. The Goddards and Townsends embellished their furniture with distinctive designs of Baroque influence. Another example of John Goddard's style of carving is shown on the knees of the table on page 217. But it was their blocked drawers with three large shells, two convex and one concave, that has established their reputation as some of the most innovative and successful furniture designers in 18th century America. There are relatively few extant examples of block and shell carving. As of today, we know of 10 desks and bookcases, three slant-lid desks, and 50 chests of drawers.

Among this select group, the John Brown kneehole desk combines an important provenance, rare figured mahogany, a top drawer fitted with unique compartments and a writing surface, a commendable small size, and fine proportions. This desk, like all Goddard-Townsend pieces, excels in the selection of both secondary and primary woods, in the meticulous dovetailing, and in the structural designs used to give strength to the frame.

Goddard and Townsend furniture first received recognition when H.F. du Pont paid $29,000 at public auction for a tea table in 1930. Prices advanced steadily but rather slowly until the early 1970s. In October 1978, a blocked and shell-carved kneehole desk, similar to the one illustrated here, sold for $140,000 (£252,000) at Christie's New York, establishing a new record for American furniture.

Since then, demand has grown, until today Goddard-Townsend furniture prices continue to set auction records and exceed prices paid for furniture from other American cabinet making centres.

214

John Brown Chippendale figured mahogany block-front and shell-carved kneehole desk
Goddard or Townsend Shop, Newport, Rhode Island
1760-80
80.3 cm high; 90.8 cm wide; 51.4 cm deep
Sold 12.6.82 in New York for $385,000 (£215,085)
From the collection of Charles A. Kilvert

Federal inlaid and carved satin-wood tambour lady's writing desk
Attributed to the shop of John and Thomas Seymour, Boston, Massachusetts
1794-1800
125.7 cm high; 100 cm wide; 51.8 cm deep
Sold 23.1.82 in New York for $121,000 (£63,684)

Chippendale mahogany circular card table
Probably by John Goddard, Newport, Rhode Island
1760-80
64.8 cm high; 89.2 cm wide; 89.2 cm deep (top open)
Sold 12.6.82 in New York for $286,000 (£159,776)

Louis XIV Beauvais
tapestry
From the Italian grotesque
by Philippe Béhagle after
the designs of Jean Bérain
2 m.89 cm x 2m.1 cm
Sold 1.7.82 in London for
£24,840 ($42,228)

Late Renaissance tapestry fragment
Brussels, c.1520
Sold 12.11.81 in New York for $44,000 (£22,916)
From the Collection of the Metropolitan Museum of Art, New York

European Sculpture and Works of Art

CHARLES AVERY

This season saw a continuation of the success story of Renaissance and Baroque bronze statuettes within the sculpture market: exceptional examples fetched phenomenal prices which confirmed an accelerating upward trend.

In the first of the three major annual sales of sculpture on 8 December a unique and unpublished model of a prancing stallion incisively modelled in the circle of Mantegna sold unexpectedly well for £18,700 ($36,652). An exceptionally fine grotesque Paduan oil lamp, combining forms as diverse as a pelican, elephantine and leonine faces and a negroid head, made £12,100 ($23,716). Bronzes from the Venetian school did particularly well: a gilt salt cellar of a kneeling man supporting a scallop shell, a model long associated with Girolamo Campagna, was fought over by several collectors, reaching £7,150 ($14,010), as was a finely cast and chased statuette of a man representing *Autumn*, attributed to Campagna's contemporary Tiziano Aspetti, which went for £4,950 ($9,700). Other Venetian bronze figures from andirons, all, however, of exceptional quality, made satisfactory prices: a pair of *Hercules* and *Venus* by Roccatagliata £4,950 ($9,700) and a group of *Venus and Cupid*, attributed to Danese Cattaneo, the same price.

The highlight of the year was the collection of Mediaeval and Renaissance sculpture from Hever Castle, which predictably excited great interest internationally, partly owing to its sheer variety and quality and partly, no doubt, because it was virtually unknown, even to specialists. Lord Astor's bronze statuettes, a small but distinguished collection, excited keen competition. The finest 15th century bronze was a reduction of one of the Graeco-Roman horses of San Marco, while among the 16th century ones the rarest was a bust by the little-known French sculptor Ponce Jacquio of Mary Stuart, Queen of Scotland and France, one of the only three casts known. However the highest price of £18,360 ($32,680) was paid for a ravishingly beautiful statuette of *Fortuna* balancing on a globe, after Giambologna. An exquisite small Fanelli bronze of *Cupid on a Dolphin* went as high as £5,400 ($9,612).

The other component of Lord Astor's collection, more in keeping with the character of Hever Castle, was a group of late medieval sculpture in various sorts of stone and wood. A very refined early 15th century Burgundian marble statuette of a *Kneeling Donor* fetched the highest price, at £59,400 ($105,730), while two pretty 16th century French stone carvings of *St Barbara* and the *Virgin and Child* also made substantial figures at £10,800 ($19,220) and £11,880 ($21,146) respectively. Among the other works of art from Hever, the most surprising price was the £10,800 ($19,220) paid for a tiny German *Memento Mori Skull*, which opened to reveal microscopic carvings, a coat of arms and the date 1515.

North Italian
Renaissance bronze
statuette of a kneeling
youth holding a shell
Early 16th century
From the circle of
Antonio Lombardi
25.5 cm high
Sold 21.4.82 in
London for £81,000
($144,180)

Venetian bronze
model of one of the
Horses of San Marco
Late 15th century
24 x 25 cm
Sold 21.4.82 in
London for £15,120
($26,913)

In the rest of the sale the highest price was £81,000 ($144,180) paid for a unique and most attractive 16th century North Italian bronze figure of a *Kneeling Boy*, tentatively attributed to Antonio Lombardi. The next highest price was £16,200 ($28,836), paid for a bronze group of *Charity* by Giuseppe Mazzuoli, while the continuing popularity of Florentine late Baroque bronzes was attested by the sum of £10,250 ($18,245) paid for a Soldani cast of Giambologna's marble group of *Florence triumphant over Pisa*.

Paduan bronze oil lamp of a Pelican pecking its breast
Mid-16th century
10.5 cm high
Sold 8.12.81 in London for £12,100 ($23,716)

A gruesome but cunningly carved boxwood statuette of *Death* was the most spectacular German sculpture at £10,800 ($19,220), while an appealing French marble statuette of *La Fillette à l'Oiseau et la Pomme* signed by J.-B. Pigalle and dated 1784, an autograph second version of a statuette in the Louvre, was bought by a private collector for £24,800 ($42,720).

The summer sale on 23 June was notable for the £64,800 ($113,400) achieved by a splendid bronze statuette of *Mercury Playing a Flute* attributed after considerable research to the important Parisian court-sculptor Barthélémy Prieur (*c*.1540-1611). The rare subject, Mercury lulling the giant Argus to sleep before killing him, corresponds with the description of a bronze in the inventory of the collection of Andre le Nôtre which appears among a number of other statuettes now firmly connected with Prieur. Close stylistic analogies with bronzes by him now in the Louvre corroborate the present attribution.

Sculpture

Far left

Florentine bronze
statuette of Fortune
After Giambologna
Late 16th century
55 cm high
Sold 21.4.82 in
London for £18,360
($33,680)

Left

French bronze
statuette of Mercury
playing a flute
Late 16th century
Attributed to
Barthélémy Prieur
47 cm high
Sold 23.6.82 in
London for £64,800
($110,160)

French bronze bust of
Mary, Queen of Scots
Late 16th century
Attributed to
Ponce Jacquio
27 cm high
Sold 21.4.82 in
London for £14,040
($24,991)

The Fruit Stall
From a set of 18th century Neapolitan crib figures
Sold 21.4.82 in London for £4,536 ($8,074)

CLOCKS AND WATCHES

JOSEPH KNIBB, LONDON: Charles II walnut and olivewood
longcase clock
c.1682-5
213 cm high
Sold 7.10.81 in London for £15,150 ($28,331)
From the collection of the late Dr G.C. Thornley

The Mostyn Tompion:
Links with the Court Team of Craftsmen

RICHARD GARNIER

In the field of clocks it is a pleasant change to encounter such a thorough record through nearly 200 years as is furnished for the Mostyn Tompion by its winding book. Equally exciting are the clues, considering the consistency of the decoration of Tompion's royal productions, that this clock gives towards the identification of his collaborators and their sources of ornament. Clocks, frequently allowed beauty, have chiefly been considered ingenious mechanical devices; at first scantily recorded, they have more recently been studied principally from the standpoint of horology.

Undoubtedly Tompion's masterpiece, the Mostyn clock is arguably the finest spring clock ever made. Year-going, spring as opposed to weight drive, with hour strike and quarter-repeat, it represents a considerable technical advance not only over the few year-going longcases then made (commonly mere timepieces) but also over the two or three earlier German spring clocks of year duration by Johan Sayller in Ulm and Hans Buschmann in Augsburg. They had found it necessary to simplify the problem with a remontoire by which the subsidiary spring driving the hands is rewound daily by the mainspring. Tompion's mainsprings engage through their fusees directly with the trains, and furthermore the striking train has to sound out the hours when the quarter-repeat is operated. The efficacy of his solution is today demonstrated by the fact that one of the springs is still strong enough even though it is riveted back together having at some stage fractured.

Made for William III *c.* 1695-1700, the clock passed at his death as a perquisite to Henry Sydney, Earl of Romney. When the Sydney family died out in the mid-18th century, the clock passed from the last and childless Sydney daughter, Elizabeth, Lady Sherard, to her adopted daughter, Lady Yonge, whose own daughter married a Lloyd. Lady Lloyd's great nephew married the Mostyn heiress and the Lloyds then changed their name to Mostyn, being created Barons Mostyn in 1831.

On receiving the clock, Lady Lloyd recorded first winding it on 16 June 1793, and so began a process that was to evolve into the winding book in which all windings, repairs and exhibitions of the clock have been noted to this day. Previously the clock had been deemed by Romney's great nephew Philip, 4th Earl of Leicester, in his will as an heirloom and it is also described in various inventories at Penshurst.

In contrast to such subsequent documentation, the royal archives are curiously reticent concerning patronage of Tompion. It is to Lady Lloyd that we owe the tradition that the clock originally cost £1,500 and to Hooke's diaries much of our information about Tompion's initial work for Charles II.

Thomas Tompion
London: William III's
celebrated year-going
Spring clock
Of small size, hour
striking and with pull
quarter-repeat
*c.*1695-1700
71.1 cm high
Sold prior to the
14.7.82 sale by private
treaty to the
British Museum for
£500,000 net
($865,000)
Record price for any
clock
From the collection of
The Lord Mostyn,
M.C.

Having been thus brought to royal notice, Tompion was to find an even more enthusiastic patron in William III and perhaps his finest and most ambitious achievements were made for William and Mary. The Mostyn clock is of a magnificent appearance, contrasting with the sobriety of Tompion's normal case design. Such a studied sense of design is continued in his other clocks and barometers made for the joint monarchs and they are all prime examples of the particular Baroque style of Daniel Marot favoured by their court. Without a surviving design for the clock it is not possible to be definite about the role of Marot, but his engravings, published in 1702 and reissued in 1712 (some of which were reproduced in the sale catalogue) include numerous similarities of decorative detail to Tompion's royal commissions. These probably indicate an overseeing role – he was William III's *dessinateur en chef* and had been summoned to England in 1694 by the Queen to design her apartments at Hampton Court.

Figure 1 and 2 of a pattern book published *c.* 1690 by Jean Berain

The front plate of the Mostyn Tompion

The superb engraving on the front plate of the clock is superior to any clock engraving of the period, even within Tompion's *oeuvre*. Like the engraving on the de Grey ewers and basin (*see* illustrations opposite) it has been confidently placed within the corpus of the hitherto unidentified engraver recognized by the late Charles Oman and dubbed by him "The Master of George Virtue" but shortly to be published on the basis of Arthur Grimwade's research as Blaise Gentot, the engraver of the signed table-top from Chatsworth. Additionally it is now put forward that the eagle pinioning a serpent (though with wings further upswept) and also the lion heads towards the base of this frontplate are repeated in two of the plates engraved by Virtue's other master, Vander Gucht, for Tijou's *New Book of Drawings* of 1693. The motif on the regulation arm, seemingly engraved by another hand from Gentot's, is composed of elements from Fig. 1 and 2 of a pattern book published *c.* 1690 by Jean Berain, the master of Marot.

That the clock was made by Tompion for William III has never been in doubt but it is very rewarding to be able now to suggest some of those who contributed to its creation, seemingly the best of their respective callings and members of the circle patronized by the court. The price of £500,000 ($925,000) net to the owner, after tax, settled with the British Museum just before the auction sale confirms the clock's importance, and allows it to be studied by all.

Charles II early
table clock
Signed by Ahasuerus
Fromanteel Londini
Fecit
*c.*1660-5
53.5 cm high
Sold 14.7.82 in
London for £54,000
($93,960)

Thomas Tompion,
No.376
Ebonized striking
bracket clock with
quarter-repeat
34 cm high
Sold 14.7.82 in
London for £23,760
($41,342)

Marine Chronometer No. 176 by John Arnold

DAVID HARRIES, F.R.G.S., F.B.H.I.

The owners of a marine chronometer – John Arnold No. 176 – which for many years had stood on a hall table in their house in a small village in the south of England, found it almost unbelievable when told by Christie's that it had a unique history and formed a very important part of our maritime heritage.

It had been in their possession for a long time, having been left to them by a branch of their family, but they knew nothing at all of its early history and were completely unaware that it had been issued by the Board of Longitude to Captain William Bligh, R.N. in 1806. Since that date it had not been heard of again, in spite of the fact that Bligh was written to in January 1812 with the request that he advise the Board of its whereabouts. Our own further research into its provenance was to bring to light the fact that it was very closely connected with the early maritime history of both Canada and Australia.

In the closing years of the 18th century and the early years of the 19th, the use of chronometers by the Admiralty was restricted to those ships of the Royal Navy engaged primarily on the great voyages of exploration that now form part of our political history. Almost without exception they were ordered by the Board of Longitude, often for particular ships and specific voyages, and the number they purchased was very limited. They came from the workshops of the very few 18th century chronometer makers then in business, many of whom, like John Harrison, Thomas Mudge, Larcum Kendall, John Arnold and Thomas Earnshaw, hold an important place in horological history.

Research, carried out on behalf of the owners in the Board of Longitude Papers at Royal Greenwich Observatory and the records of both the Ministry of Defence and the National Maritime Museum at Greenwich, were to show that Arnold No. 176 was probably the most historically important marine chronometer still in private hands to be offered for sale this century. Very few chronometers were purchased by the Board of Longitude, and the handful still extant are mainly in the public collections of the British Museum and the National Maritime Museum.

Documentary evidence relating to the history of No. 176 was obtained from original documents, such as the appropriate Minutes of the Board of Longitude and John Arnold's invoice to them dated 21 December 1791, the latter showing that the chronometer was delivered to the Astronomer Royal at Greenwich Observatory on 21 June 1791. It was ordered specifically for Captain George Vancouver R.N., after whom the city of Vancouver, British Columbia is named, who, by this date, had already sailed in *H.M.S. Discovery* on his voyage of exploration to the coast of North West America, the Pacific Ocean and thence round the world.

Historically important, documented, 50-hour 'Expedition' marine chronometer, completed 1791 for the Board of
Longitude, with Arnold spring detent, compensated balance undersprung
11.0 cm diam. of dial
Sold 25.11.81 in London for £39,600 ($76,032). Now in The Vancouver Maritime Museum

It was dispatched to him in the store-ship *Daedalus* and reached him via Rio de Janeiro and the Falkland Islands. Vancouver arrived back in the River Thames on 24 September 1795 and No. 176 was then returned to the custody of the Board.

After examination and repair by the son of the maker, John Roger Arnold, it was next issued in 1801 to Captain Matthew Flinders, R.N. for his "Voyage to Terra Australis" but his Journal shows that by February 1802 it had become so defective that he found it necessary to return it, along with another John Arnold chronometer (his No. 82), to the Astronomer Royal. This Flinders arranged to do while at Port Jackson, and both chronometers came back to England in the whaler *Speedy*. After repair by John Roger Arnold it was issued to Bligh in 1806, by the express instructions of the Board of Longitude, shortly before he took up his appointment as Governor of New South Wales.

There was no subsequent trace of No. 176 until it was found, quite unexpectedly, in July 1981. While it was with Christie's and prior to its sale, it was completely taken apart. During this process positive dating evidence for the year 1791 was discovered marked inside the great wheel of the fusee and this, together with the research work carried out on No. 176, has added considerably to the history of John Arnold.

The chronometer was sold on 25 November 1981 to Vancouver Maritime Museum for £39,600 ($76,030), a world record for an Arnold marine chronometer. It is the only fully authenticated maritime artefact of Vancouver owned by Canada. We hope that John Arnold No. 82, which also forms an important part of the maritime heritage both of the United Kingdom and of Australia, may one day be re-discovered.

Far right

Early German
chamber clock
16th century,
probably lower Rhine
57 cm high
Sold 25.11.81 in
London for £27,500
($52,800)
From the Textor
Collection, F.D.R.

Right

Gold and enamel
watch and châtelaine
Inscribed on the
cuvette Breguet A
Paris
Early 19th century
4.4 cm diam.; 14.5 cm
total length
Sold 18.11.81 in
Geneva for
Sw.fr.60,500 (£18,006)

Gold and enamel Peto cross detent
pocket chronometer
Signed Ilbery, London No.5994
6.3 cm diam.
Sold 28.4.82 in London for £16,200
($28,988)

French diamond-set gold verge watch, key
and chain
Signed L'Epine A Paris
Late 18th century
4.8 cm diam.
Sold 18.11.81 in Geneva for Sw.fr.104,500
(£31,101)

Gold and enamel duplex watch
Signed Vancher Fleurier
5.8 cm diam.
Sold 7.10.81 in London for £7,150
($13,371)

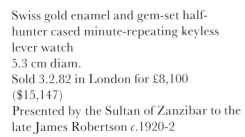

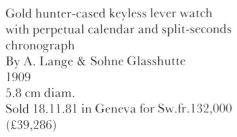

Gold hunter-cased keyless lever watch
with perpetual calendar and split-seconds
chronograph
By A. Lange & Sohne Glasshutte
1909
5.8 cm diam.
Sold 18.11.81 in Geneva for Sw.fr.132,000
(£39,286)

Swiss gold enamel and gem-set half-
hunter cased minute-repeating keyless
lever watch
5.3 cm diam.
Sold 3.2.82 in London for £8,100
($15,147)
Presented by the Sultan of Zanzibar to the
late James Robertson c.1920-2

Early Huaud gold and
enamel watch
Movement signed
David Rousseau à Geneve
c.1675-80
3 cm diam.
Sold 28.4.82 in London for
£16,200 ($29,988)

The Falmouth
Stradivari: Italian
violin
By Antonio Stradivari
Cremona 1692
Length of back
36.3 cm
Sold 2.6.82 in London
for £102,600
($184,600)
This violin was once
owned by the Earl of
Falmouth, a notable
collector, who sold it
in 1853 for £110

Italian violoncello
By Nicolo Gagliano
Naples, 1782
Sold 2.6.82 in London for £21,600 ($38,880)

Far left

Italian viola
By Joannes Florenus
Guidantus
Bologna, 1737
Length of back
41.4 cm
Sold 2.6.82 in London
for £21,600 ($38,880)

Left

Italian violin
By J.B. Guadagnini
Turin
Length of back 35.3 cm
Sold 2.4.82 in London
for £23,760 ($42,530)

JEWELLERY

Fancy yellow diamond bracelet
Sold 16.10.81 in New York for $154,000 (£82,795)

The Emperor Maximilian Diamond

MARY M. MURPHY, F.G.A.

Combining exceptional size, extraordinary luminosity, a royal provenance and a fascinating legend, the Emperor Maximilian Diamond epitomizes the allure of precious gems. The sale of this legendary diamond by Christie's New York attracted worldwide attention, transforming the auction of magnificent jewels into an historic event.

The diamond was named after Emperor Maximilian of Mexico who acquired it in 1860. At 41.94 ct, the gem is one of the largest diamonds ever mined in Brazil, where diamond mining began in 1720, nearly 150 years earlier than the discovery of diamonds in South Africa.

Maximilian (1832-1867) was the second son of Archduke Francis Charles of Austria and the younger brother of Emperor Francis Joseph. At an early age he developed a keen interest in the sciences, particularly botany. After serving as commander in the Austrian Navy and as Viceroy of the Lombardo-Venetian Kingdom, he retired to private life, residing mainly at Trieste with his young bride, Princess Charlotte (Carlotta), daughter of Leopold I of Belgium.

It was in 1859 that Maximilian was first approached by Mexican exiles proposing that he assume the throne of Mexico, then in a state of anarchy. Although he refused this initial proposal, Maximilian nevertheless had a burning desire to visit the New World. In 1860 he journeyed to the tropical forests of Brazil on a botanical expedition. While in Brazil, he acquired two exceptionally large diamonds which were to be named after him, the Emperor Maximilian and the Maximilian II.

The first was a 41.94 ct diamond with a strong blue fluorescence under ultraviolet light. The diamond absorbs the ultraviolet light, invisible to the human eye, and re-emits it as light of a blue colour, which, due to its longer wavelength, can be seen by the eye as a soft glow. Although fluorescence is not an uncommon characteristic of diamonds, few stones exhibit the phenomenon as strongly as the Emperor Maximilian. Indeed, the fluorescence of this stone is so strong that even the relatively weak concentration of ultraviolet rays in natural daylight is enough to activate the phenomenon. So the Emperor Maximilian diamond glows with a soft blue luminosity, adding considerable beauty to the brilliant gem.

The second diamond, the Maximilian II, was of a greenish-yellow tint and weighed 33 ct. After his return from Brazil, Maximilian presented this stone to his wife, who wore it mounted as a pendant. He kept the larger diamond for himself.

In 1863, under pressure from Napoleon III and from his wife, Maximilian consented to accept the Mexican crown. He and Carlotta journeyed to Mexico in 1864 to reside in a beautiful Spanish colonial castle in Chapultepec, where they lived in a most lavish style. Indeed, during his first six months in Mexico, Maximilian's wine bill alone was over $100,000. However, from the very outset, his reign was highly troubled. By 1866, the necessity for his abdication was obvious to everyone outside Mexico, including Napoleon himself. Nevertheless, Maximilian refused to desert his followers. Fearing for her husband, Carlotta returned to Europe in order to plead for aid. In May 1867, Maximilian was court-martialed and sentenced to death.

Maximilian was executed by firing squad on June 19 1867, along with his two highest ranking generals. This dramatic moment was depicted by Edouard Manet in his work *The Execution of Maximilian*. Manet painted four versions of this scene, all of them in 1867, and three of them of immense size. The one regarded as the "tableau definitif" hangs in

244

The Emperor Maximilian
Cushion-shaped diamond weighing 41.94 carats, of Brazilian origin
Mounted as a ring by Cartier
With a gemological certificate stating that the diamond is VS, and "I" colour with a very strong blue
fluorescence, due to which the stone appears different in varying lighting conditions
Sold 20.4.82 in New York for $726,000 (£403,333)

the Städtische Kunsthalle in Mannheim (*see* page 246); the version in the National Gallery, London, was damaged – it is not clear how or when – but Degas bought the picture and actually stitched three pieces of it together. This version was bought by the National Gallery, London, in the Degas sale in 1918.

Legend says that Maximilian was wearing the Emperor Maximilian Diamond in a small bag tied around his neck when he faced the firing squad. Following the execution, his remains were returned to Vienna and the Emperor Maximilian Diamond returned to his widow.

Carlotta had showed signs of mental illness during her final months in Mexico. Following the tragic death of her husband, she completely succumbed to insanity. She lived into the 20th century, dying in January 1927 at the age of 86.

The Emperor Maximilian Diamond was reportedly sold to help pay Carlotta's medical expenses. The sale may have occurred in 1919, the year two other important Habsburg diamonds, the 137.27 ct Florentine diamond (dating back to 1477) and the 44.62 ct Frankfurt Solitaire were reputedly sold in South America.

In 1919 the Emperor Maximilian diamond was acquired by an American jeweller, Ferdinand Hotz. The diamond was displayed at the 1934 Chicago World's Fair as the highlight of a $5,000,000 exhibition which reproduced a diamond mine with "native labourers."

EDOUARD MANET: *The Execution of Maximilian*
One of four versions all painted in 1867
Reproduced by kind permission of the Städtische Kunsthalle, Mannheim

Mr Hotz refused to sell the diamond, and it remained in his possession until his death in 1946. It was subsequently acquired by a titled private owner in whose collection it remained until it was consigned to Christie's by the trustees of her estate.

The Emperor Maximilian Diamond was offered as the last of 288 lots in a sale which also included magnificent jewels from the estate of Marjorie Merriweather Post. There was a standing-room-only crowd for the auction which was filmed by six television networks. Tension, combined with celebration, mounted as the bidding for the Emperor Maximilian, having opened at $200,000, quickly surpassed the high estimate of $300,000. At $500,000 six determined buyers were still competing. The hammer finally went down after $726,000 (£427,050) was bid by London jeweller Lawrence Graff. He called the Emperor Maximilian "the most beautiful, luminous diamond I have ever seen."

Sapphire and diamond
bracelet
Cushion-cut sapphire
weighing approx.
58.33 carats
Signed by Cartier
Sold 16.10.81 in
New York for $968,000
(£520,430)

Opposite

Sapphire and diamond
pendant necklace
The pendant is
detachable and can be
worn as a clip brooch
Sold 13.5.82 in Geneva
for Sw.fr.242,000
(£67,978)

Sapphire ring set with a
cut-cornered rectangular
sapphire weighing 28.08
carats
Sold 13.5.82 in Geneva
for Sw.fr.154,000
(£43,258)

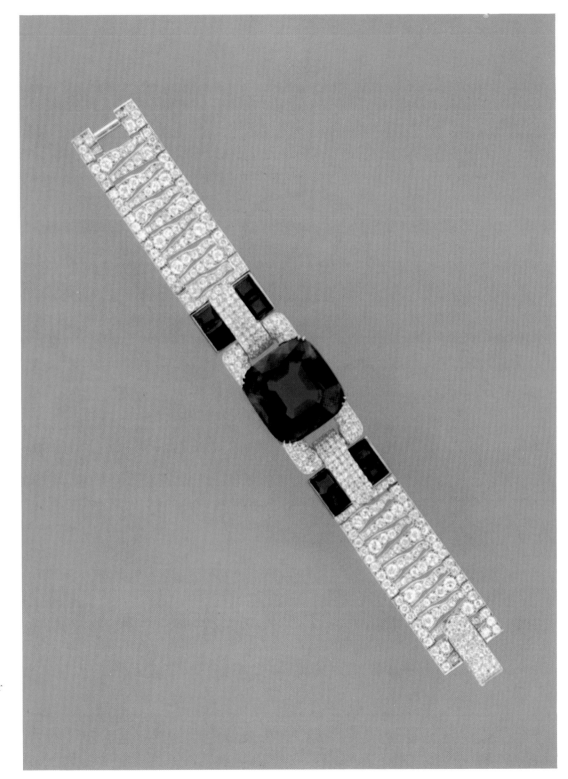

Diamond and ruby
pendant necklace
Sold for £8,640
($15,466)

Cabochon ruby and
brilliant and baguette-
cut diamond double
clip brooch
Sold for £1,620
($2,900)

Art Deco ruby and
diamond ring
Sold for £20,520
($36,731)

Emerald-cut diamond
single-stone ring,
diamond weighing
approximately
10.50 carats
Sold for £15,120
($27,065)

Art Deco cabochon
ruby, brilliant and
baguette-cut diamond
triple section flexible
bracelet
Sold for £3,780
($6,766)

All sold 31.3.82 in
London

Ruby and diamond necklace
Signed by Van Cleef & Arpels
Sold 20.4.82 in New York for $616,000 (£342,222)

Antique ruby and diamond necklace
Sold for £22,000
($42,020)

One of a pair of ruby and diamond collet and ribbon loop clip brooches
Sold for £23,100
($44,121)

Victorian diamond, synthetic and natural sapphire and ruby butterfly brooch
Sold for £1,870
($3,571)

Pair of diamond, ruby and emerald circular cluster earrings
Sold for £2,860
($5,462)

Victorian ruby and diamond bee brooch
Sold for £2,640
($5,042)

Jade and diamond flexible bracelet
Sold for £6,600
($12,606)

All sold 16.12.81 in London

Ruby and diamond necklace
Signed by Bulgari
Sold 19.11.81 in Geneva for Sw.fr.1,210,000 (£370,030)

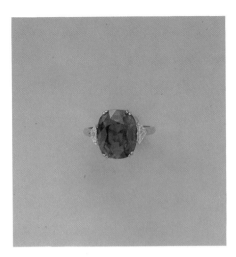

Sapphire and diamond ring, the cushion-shaped sapphire weighing 8.38 carats
With an expertise by Gübelin stating that the sapphire is from Kashmir
Sold 19.11.81 in Geneva for Sw.fr.264,000 (£80,733)

Pair of sapphire and diamond ear-pendants weighing 16.48 carats
Sold 13.5.82 in Geneva for Sw.fr.187,000 (£52,528)

Above centre

Cabochon sapphire and diamond brooch
Sold 13.5.82 in Geneva for Sw.fr.308,000 (£86,517)

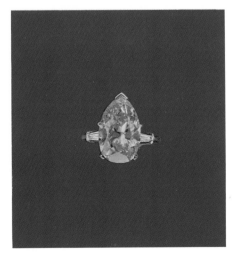

Ruby and diamond ring, the pear-shaped ruby weighing 3.99 carats and the pear-shaped diamond weighing 2.42 carats
With a certificate for the diamond by the Gemological Institute of America: colour D, clarity VS[1]
Sold 19.11.81 in Geneva for Sw.fr.132,000 (£40,366)

Fancy pink diamond ring weighing approximately 7.13 carats
With gemological certificate number 1913183 stating that the diamond is of natural colour
Sold 20.4.82 in New York for $572,000 (£317,777)

Below

The Marjorie Merriweather Post diamond
Antique cushion-cut diamond weighing
31.20 carats
Mounted as a ring by Tiffany & Co.
With gemological certificate number 1305147
stating that the diamond is colour D
and VS[1]
Sold 20.4.82 in New York for $594,000
(£330,000)

Antique diamond cluster brooch
Set with a circular-cut diamond weighing
12.74 carats
Sold 13.5.82 in Geneva for Sw.fr.275,000
(£77,247)

Below

Pair of diamond ear-pendants, each set with
an oval-cut diamond weighing 21.97 carats
and 19.28 carats respectively
Signed by Bulgari
Sold 19.11.81 in Geneva for Sw.fr.825,000
(£252,293)

Above centre

Diamond ring set with a cushion-shaped
diamond weighing 15.00 carats
With an expertise by Gübelin: colour E,
clarity internally flawless
Sold 19.11.81 in Geneva for Sw.fr.825,000
(£252,293)

Yellow diamond ring: fancy yellow diamond
weighing 5.70 carats
With a certificate by the Gemological
Institute of America stating that the colour is
natural
Sold 13.5.82 in Geneva for Sw.fr.82,500
(£23,174)

Emerald-cut diamond ring weighing
12.62 carats
With an expertise by Gübelin: colour
River E, clarity VS[1]
Sold 13.5.82 in Geneva for Sw.fr.319,000
(£89,607)

Emerald bead two-row necklace
Sold for Sw.fr.110,000 (£30,899)

Pair of diamond ear-pendants
weighing 19.08 carats
Sold for Sw.fr.187,000 (£52,528)

Both sold 13.5.82 in Geneva

Emerald and diamond bracelet
Signed by Bulgari
Sold 19.11.81 in Geneva for
Sw.fr.495,000 (£151,376)

Antique emerald intaglio and gold ring
Italian, 18th century
Photo enlarged
Sold 13.5.82 in Geneva for
Sw.fr.28,600 (£8,034)

Antique emerald and diamond pendant
mounted with a cut-cornered
rectangular emerald weighing
12.62 carats
Sold 13.5.82 in Geneva for
Sw.fr.41,800 (£11,742)

Pearl and diamond brooch
pendant
The pearl was formerly tested
by Gübelin
Sold 13.5.82 in Geneva for
Sw.fr.93,500 (£26,264)

Pair of pearl and diamond
ear-pendants
Signed by Chaumet
With an expertise by Gübelin
stating that the pearls are
natural
Sold 13.5.82 in Geneva for
Sw.fr.71,500 (£20,084)

Black pearl and diamond
clip brooch
Mounted by Cartier
With a certificate by the
Gemological Institute of
America stating that the pearl
is natural
Sold 13.5.82 in Geneva for
Sw.fr.30,800 (£8,652)

Opposite

Diamond necklace
Mounted by Cartier
Sold 19.11.81 in Geneva for
Sw.fr.572,000 (£174,923)

Pair of diamond ear-pendants
By Cartier
Sold 19.11.81 in Geneva for
Sw.fr.121,000 (£37,003)

Jewellery

Jade and diamond
necklace and a pair of
ear-clips *en suite*
Sold for Sw.fr.198,000
(£55,617)

Pair of jade and
diamond ear-pendants
Sold for Sw.fr.82,500
(£23,174)

Pair of jade cuff-links
Sold for Sw.fr.30,800
(£8,651)

All sold 13.5.82
in Geneva

Antique pink topaz and
diamond brooch
Sold for £6,264 ($11,275)

Antique emerald and
diamond ring
Sold for £9,180 ($16,524)

Cushion-shaped
alexandrite single-stone
ring, alexandrite
weighing approximately
10.70 carats
Sold for £10,800
($19,440)

Art Deco diamond,
emerald and sapphire
flexible bracelet.
Sold for £12,960
($23,328)

Jade and diamond ring
Sold for £3,456 ($6,220)

Art Deco diamond,
sapphire, emerald,
demantoid garnet,
amethyst and coral
rectangular panel brooch
Sold for £6,480 ($11,664)

All sold 16.6.82
in London

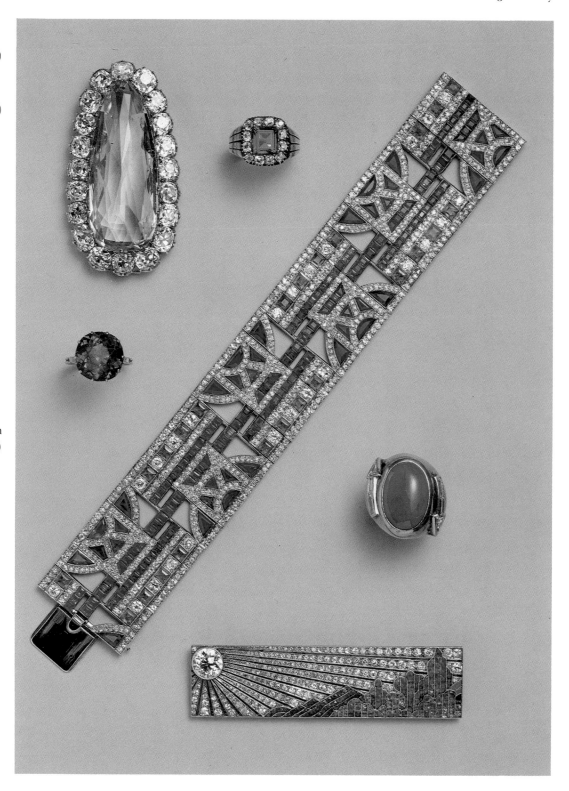

Gold-mounted
necklace set with
garnets and foiled
crystals
c.1800
42 cm long
Sold 8.6.82 in London
for £3,240 ($5,864)

Silver-mounted
jewelled dress
ornament
c.1760
9 cm long
Sold 8.6.82 in London
for £2,268 ($4,105)

ART NOUVEAU
AND ART DECO

Art Nouveau gold, sapphire, diamond and enamel
pendant necklace
Signed by Gautrait
Sold 19.11.81 in Geneva for Sw.fr.28,600 (£8,511)

Laburnum leaded glass and
bronze table lamp
By Tiffany Studios
71 cm high; 56 cm diam.
of shade
Sold 3.10.81 in New York
for $52,800 (£28,540)

Far right

"Iris et Libellule": marqueterie-de-verre, applied and engraved glass vase
Engraved Gallé
39 cm high
Sold 16.11.81 in Geneva for
Sw.fr.253,000 (£76,435)

Right

Applied, engraved, intercalaire, overlay and marqueterie-de-verre glass vase
Engraved and gilt Gallé and with a paper label "Collection Roger Marx" on the base
43.2 cm high
Sold 16.11.81 in Geneva for
Sw.fr.506,000 (£152,870)
Record auction price for a Gallé vase

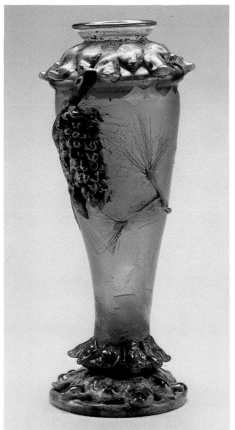

Far right

Etched, applied, martelé and engraved coquillage coupe
Engraved Gallé
11.7 cm high
Sold 16.11.81 in Geneva for
Sw.fr.176,000 (£53,172)

Right

Triple-overlay, applied and engraved glass vase
Engraved Gallé
19 cm high
Sold 16.11.81 in Geneva for
Sw.fr.264,000 (£79,758)

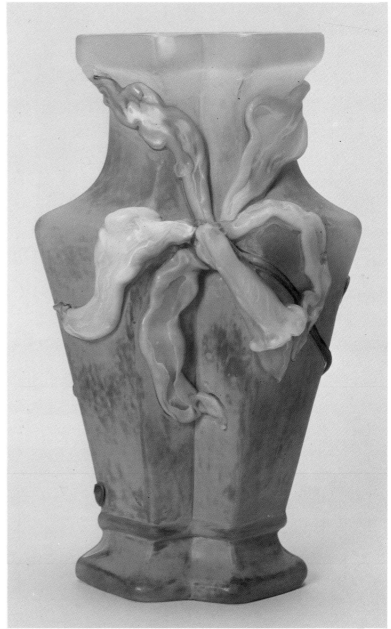

Bronze mounted, double overlay and martelé glass
table lamp
By Daum and L. Majorelle
69.5 cm high
Sold 10.5.82 in Geneva for Sw.fr.143,000 (£40,625)

Orchid applied and carved glass vase
By Emile Gallé
c.1900
23 cm high
Sold 20.11.81 in New York for $132,000 (£71,351)

VITTORIO ZECCHIN: *Le Tre Grazie*
Signed with monogram lower left
Tempera and gold paint on unprimed fabric
108 x 108 cm
Sold 23.9.81 in London for £33,000 ($61,380)

Mahogany and glass vitrine
By L. Majorelle
244 cm high; 147 cm wide; 42 cm deep
Sold 3.10.81 in New York for $28,600 (£15,459)

"Harlequin": silvered, enamelled, and cold-painted bronze, ivory and glass table lamp
Cast and carved from a model by
Marcel Bouraine
Signed Bouraine and inscribed Etling Paris
55.3 cm high
Wired for electricity
Sold 5.12.81 in New York for $20,900 (£10,829)
Record auction price for a work by the artist

Selection of
Lucie Rie
pottery
Sold 16.3.82 in
London for a
total of £9,800
($17,836)

Group of Hans Coper
stoneware vases
Sold 23.9.81 in
London for a total of
£14,850 ($27,621)

White marble figure of a jester
By Sarah Bernhardt, signed 1877
42.6 cm high, including separate shaped marble base
Sold 2.10.81 in New York for $19,800 (£10,102)

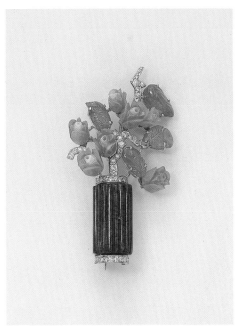

Above

Art Deco ruby, diamond, lapis-lazuli
and coral vase of flowers brooch
Signed by Van Cleef & Arpels
Sold 19.11.81 in Geneva for Sw.fr.11,000
(£3,273)

Above right

Art Deco diamond and glass brooch
mounted with a Samurai swordsman
Sold 19.11.81 in Geneva for Sw.fr.19,800
(£5,892)

Right

Art Deco lapis-lazuli, onyx and diamond
card case
Signed by Janesich
Sold 19.11.81 in Geneva for Sw.fr.16,500
(£4,910)

Art Deco rock crystal, rose quartz, diamond, enamel and mother-of-pearl mystery clock
Signed by Cartier
*c.*1925
41.9 x 29.8 cm
Sold 20.4.82 in New York for $198,000 (£110,000)

Art Deco mother-of-pearl, enamel
and gem-set case
9 x 5 cm
Sold 19.11.81 in Geneva for
Sw.fr.37,400 (£11,130)

Art Deco desk clock
Signed by Cartier
Made in 1929
8.4 x 8.4 cm
Sold 19.11.81 in Geneva for
Sw.fr.121,000 (£36,011)

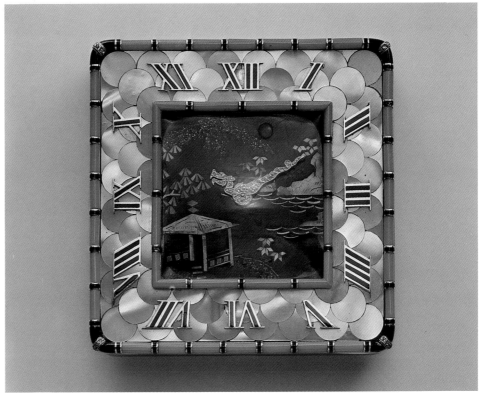

Aristee: tapestry from an original design of 1932 by René Perrot
Executed at Aubusson 1946
200 x 300 cm
Sold 16.3.82 in London for £5,400 ($9,828)

SILVER

Dutch Sabbath and festival hanging lamp
By Pieter Bartolomeus von Linden
Amsterdam, 1762
90 cm high
Sold 12.5.82 in Geneva for Sw.fr.132,000 (£37,078)

James I silver-gilt standing cup
and cover
Maker's mark probably WI, with the
animal's head between the initials
1604
47.6 cm high
Sold 2.12.81 in London for £31,900
($62,843) by order of the Trustees of
The Pierpont Morgan Library
The inscription records that the cup
was made from the matrix of the Great
Seal of Ireland, for Adam Loftus, Lord
Chancellor of Ireland of the day.
Originally the cup was surmounted by
a "steeple" which has been lost

Pair of William III silver-gilt ewers and a basin
By Benjamin Pyne
1699
61.6 cm diam. of basin
Sold 24.3.82 in London for £226,800 ($410,508)
All three pieces are engraved with the arms of Anthony Grey, 11th Earl of Kent (d.1702). Attributed to the Huguenot engraver Blaise Gentôt (*see* Richard Garnier, *The Mostyn Tompion*, p.228) the engraving on the basin is among the most accomplished and imposing of the period to have survived. The sophisticated craftsmanship and the finely balanced sense of proportion that characterize the ewers show how unjustified is the view that native English goldsmiths of the late 17th century were invariably less capable than their immigrant Huguenot contemporaries

George I two-handled
cup and cover
By Paul de Lamerie
1720
31.3 cm high
Sold 7.7.82 in London
for £27,000 ($73,980)

George II shaped oval
cake-basket
By Paul de Lamerie
1743
35.5 cm long
Sold 24.3.82 in
London for £32,400
($58,676)

Queen Anne toilet-service
By Colin McKenzie
Edinburgh, 1703
Sold 24.3.82 in London for £172,800 ($312,768)
This is the only known complete Scottish toilet-service of the period. It is engraved with the cypher of the Hon. Marian Stewart, daughter of Alexander, 5th Lord Blantyre, who married James Stirling of Keir in 1704. The toilet-service was possibly a wedding or betrothal gift, and remained in the Stirling family until it came to Christie's for sale

Regency two-handled tray
By Paul Storr
1812
The engraved royal arms are attributed to Walter Jackson
71.8 cm long
Sold 11.2.82 in New York for $56,100 (£31,166)

George IV silver-gilt charger
By James Fray
Dublin, 1828
68.6 cm diam.
Sold 14.6.82 in New York for $121,000 (£67,977)
From the collection of C. Ruxton Love
The applied arms are those of Thomas Manners-Sutton, first Baron Manners (1756-1842), who was Lord Chancellor of Ireland until 1827

The Ascot Jubilee cup 1887
By C.F. Hancock
1867
Sold 21.10.81 in London for
£23,100 ($42,735)
The cup was modelled by the
sculptor H.H. Armstead,
R.A., and illustrates scenes
from Tennyson's *Idylls of the
King*. When presented in
1887 it was valued at £1,000

Victorian parcel-gilt table garniture
By Elkington and Co.
Birmingham, 1879
Design attributed to Léonard Morel-Ladeuil
Length of centrepiece: 89 cm
Sold 21.10.81 in London for £44,000 ($81,400)

The De Witt Clinton
Plateau
By John W. Forbes
New York, *c.*1825
Length of plateau
161.3 cm
Sold 12.6.82 in
New York for
$264,000 (£148,314)
Presented to Governor
De Witt Clinton by
the citizens of the
State of New York
upon the completion
of the Erie Canal in
1825. Only three other
American plateaux of
this period are known,
including one of
identical design in the
collection of the White
House. The dessert-
stand in the centre is
by Benjamin Smith II,
London, 1823

Pair of standing cups
By John Edwards
Boston, 1694-1729
19.4 cm high
Sold 12.6.82 in
New York for $55,000
(£30,898)
Engraved with the
Dummer crest within
cartouche above an
engraved inscription
reading "Dedicated by
Wm. Dummer Esqr.
to the Church of
Newbury Falls, for the
Communion-Table,
1729."

The Fitzwilliam Ewer and Basin

TIMOTHY SCHRODER

The silver-gilt ewer and basin sent for sale by the Countess Fitzwilliam epitomizes the somewhat ambiguous character of late Renaissance display plate. Ostensibly intended for use, it is so designed as to render the functional object secondary to the work of art. This was due partly to changing social custom that was gradually making the ewer and basin a redundant piece of equipment, but also to a prevalent attitude towards works of art that failed to draw the modern distinction between "fine" and "applied" art.

During the 16th century the ewer and basin was essential to civilized dining. Prior to the general acceptance of the fork, it was used to wash the hands between courses and was a standard item on any substantial inventory of plate. The Royal Jewel House inventory of 1574, for example, lists only two forks of gold and 13 of silver. On the other hand, it lists no fewer than 30 ewers with basins and many more unpaired ones. Similarly, the inventory of Hardwick Hall, compiled in 1601, lists no forks at all, but 12 ewers with basins, and again further individual ones. As late as 1617 Fynes Moryson, writing in his *Itinerary*, advises the cosmopolitan traveller that it would be prudent, upon returning to England, to "lay aside the spoone and forke of Italy, the affected gestures of France, and all strange apparell."

The decline of the functional role of the ewer and basin, together with its substantial intrinsic value as bullion, ensured the disappearance of all but a few examples of this category of plate. But by the same token, it also enabled the goldsmith to treat it entirely as an object of display, without need to compromise his design through considerations of practicality. In this respect the Fitzwilliam ewer and basin represents a transitional stage. Clearly it cannot ever have been intended for use: the basin is too shallow, while certain flaws in the ewer would have made it unacceptable to a patron who intended it as anything other than a work of art. But the ornament on the basin is still arranged around the centre, as if to be seen from above. By the second decade of the 17th century basins were beginning to be designed to be viewed standing, with the decoration organized in the vertical plane. The Paulus van Vianen "Diana and Acteon" basin of 1614 in the Rijksmuseum and the Lomellini basins divided between the Victoria and Albert, the Ashmolean and the Birmingham City Museums are all of this type.

The internationalism of goldsmiths' work during the late 16th and early 17th centuries frequently makes specific attributions in the absence of hallmarks very difficult. The attribution to Northern Italy in this case is tentative, but is based on the form of the ewer and on certain decorative details on the basin. Together they are decorated with eight episodes from the story of Susanna and the Elders (Book of Daniel, chapter 13), popularly regarded as a parable of grace. The source of the design has yet to be identified, but is most likely of Flemish origin and was presumably in circulation in printed form. The design of the ewer, on the other hand, is quite closely related to drawings by the Florentine artist Antonio Salviati. Moreover, certain drawings of basins by the same artist also treat the border in exactly the same way as the Fitzwilliam basin. Again, the sculptural quality of the handle and the grotesque cast masks beneath the lip and the lower junction of the handle are directly suggestive of Italian workmanship.

Italian silver-gilt ewer and basin
Early 17th century
Unmarked
Height of ewer 39.4 cm; diam. of basin 58.9 cm
Sold 7.7.82 in London for £118,800 ($201,960)

German Renaissance parcel-gilt mounted glass goblet
The mounts by Friedrich Hillebrand, Nuremberg, late 16th century; the associated glass engraved by Georg Schwanhardt the Elder
*c.*1630
Sold 8.11.81 in Geneva for Sw.fr.110,000 (£32,738)

German parcel-gilt
centrepiece of Diana as
Huntress
By Abraham Drentwett II
Augsburg, *c.*1680
30 cm high
Sold 18.11.81 in Geneva for
Sw.fr.242,000 (£72,023)

One of a pair of covered soup-tureens and stands
Tureens by Berthold Christian Schlepper,
St. Petersburg, 1774; stands by Antoine Boullier,
Paris, 1780
Length of stands 49 cm
Sold 12.5.82 in Geneva for Sw.fr.115,500 (£32,443)

Opposite

Pair of George III ormolu candlesticks
*c.*1800-10
36 cm high
Sold 15.4.82 in London for £14,580 ($25,952)
The distinctive heraldic motifs used on the bases of these
candlesticks and beneath the sockets make it almost
certain that they once formed part of the collection built
up by William Beckford (1760-1844) at Fonthill Abbey
in Wiltshire. Throughout his life Beckford was obsessed
by his ancestry, and much of the furniture and plate at
Fonthill incorporated the charges from his coat-of-arms
in their decoration.

The C. Ruxton Love Collection of Silver-Gilt

ANTHONY PHILLIPS

The 13 magnificent lots of European silver-gilt from the collection of the late C. Ruxton Love were perhaps the finest group of such pieces to come on the market since the sale at Christie's in London, June 1971, of the collection of the late Anna Thomson Dodge. Indeed two lots were directly comparable with those in the Dodge sale: a pair of wine-coasters and a pair of superb wine-coolers originally from the Demidoff service made by the Paris maker Odiot in the early 19th century. The price differential between the two sales was staggering. In 1971 four wine-coasters fetched just under $4,000 (£1,660) while in 1982 an identical pair made $13,200 (£7,760). Again, in 1971 the wine-coolers made $18,150 (£11,210) while in 1982 the matching pair made $330,000 (£185,390). These extraordinary increases in auction values in just over a decade obviously reflect not only inflation, but also the auction cliché that in today's market collectors will pay almost anything for the best in any given field. French Empire silver varies greatly in quality, but the finest works of Odiot and Biennais rival in elegance and grandeur the best silver of any period, anywhere. Such elegance and grandeur is typified not only by the two pieces mentioned, but also by a pair of smaller coolers and a pair of circular tureens of the same service sold in the Love collections. According to the original account dated December 5 1817, from Odiot (who generously allowed us to reproduce it and several of the designs in the catalogue) the service consisted, apart from the knives, forks, and spoons, of almost 60 pieces of "hollow ware". From the variety of design and the fact that while most of the pieces are hallmarked for the period 1809-19, some date from 1798-1809, it seems that Demidoff went to Odiot and made a selection from existing stock, rather than ordering a new service from scratch.

The "Mr de Demidoff" of the account has traditionally been identified as Count Nikolai Demidoff. He was born near St Petersburg in 1772. He entered the Imperial Guard at a young age and by 1792 he was promoted to Lieutenant-Colonel. Two years later he was made a Gentleman of the Bedchamber, having married into the illustrious Stroganoff family. He retired from the army, travelled widely, and very successfully developed mines and ironworks on his lands in Russia. He rejoined the army in 1812 and fought at the battle of Borodino. After 1815 he lived for several years in Paris where his house became the centre for the most distinguished artists and literary figures. He was also known for his philanthropy, distributing every month some 2,000 francs to the poor of the city. He moved to Florence where he died in 1828, leaving his immense wealth to his sons Paul and Anatole.

One of a pair of
French silver-gilt
wine-coolers
By Jean-Baptiste-
Claude Odiot
Paris, 1809-19
36.9 cm high
Sold 14.6.82 in
New York for
$330,000 (£185,393)
From the collection of
C. Ruxton Love

The Demidoff service was re-sold as the property of "an anonymous English Gentleman of Title" in the sale of "Magnificent creations in gold plate made by Claude Odiot for Count Nikolai Demidoff" at the American Art Association Anderson Galleries, New York, December 15 1928.

Apart from the Demidoff pieces, the silver-gilt sold in New York in June this year included an important octagonal tray with the arms of Napoleon as King of Italy, and a fine pair of double salt-cellars also by Odiot. The work of Odiot's rival Biennais was exemplified by a small but beautifully designed coffee-pot, that had been sold in London in1973 for $2,250 (£937), and in June of this year made $33,880 (£19,030).

The Love collection sold included three non-French items: a rare, early 17th century, Augsburg nautilus cup; an extraordinary Irish charger made by James Fray in Dublin, 1828, for the retiring Lord Chancellor of Ireland, Thomas, Lord Manners on his retirement from office; and a remarkable "Egyptian style" tea-urn by Digby Scott and Benjamin Smith II, London, 1806, which has the most unusual feature of handles that fold down to form the shoulder decoration.

The variety and quality of the 13 lots offered, which fetched a total of $1,451,630 (£815,520) are alone enough to justify Ruxton Love's standing as one of the great post-war collectors of European silver.

One of a pair of
French silver-gilt
soup-tureens
By Jean-Baptiste-
Claude Odiot
Paris, 1809-19
28 cm diam.
Sold 14.6.82 in
New York for
$429,000 (£241,011)
From the collection of
C. Ruxton Love

One of a pair of
French silver-gilt
wine-coolers
By Jean-Baptiste-
Claude Odiot
Paris, 1798-1809; also
with Paris marks for
1809-19
21.3 cm high
Sold 14.6.82 in
New York for
$126,500 (£72,061)
From the collection of
C. Ruxton Love

OBJECTS OF ART
AND VERTU

Rectangular jewelled and enamelled two-colour gold
Imperial presentation frame with an oval painted
miniature-portrait of Tsar Nicholas II
By Fabergé
Workmaster Henrik Wigström
St Petersburg, 1899-1908
10.5 cm high
Sold 17.11.81 in Geneva for Sw.fr.88,000 (£26,190)

Silver-gilt Peter the Great presentation kovsh, the centre with a chased portrait medallion of the Tsar
*c.*1703
Unmarked
42 cm long
Sold 11.5.82 in Geneva for Sw.fr.71,500 (£20,312)

Parcel-gilt bratina, the gilt rim engraved Cyrillic *Bratina of Maksim Yakovlev, son of Stroganov*
*c.*1635
Unmarked
23 cm diam.
Sold 11.5.82 in Geneva for Sw.fr.104,500 (£29,687)

Rectangular gold-mounted porcelain
snuff-box, the cover painted with the
coat of arms of Count Grigory
Orlov, the interior with his portrait
signed by Andrei Chernov
Impressed double-headed
eagle mark
Imperial Porcelain Factory
St Petersburg, c.1768
9 cm long
Sold 17.11.81 in Geneva for
Sw.fr.154,000 (£45,833)

Hardstone group of a horse drawn sleigh and coachman
By Fabergé
Workmaster Henrik Wigström
St Petersburg, 1908-17
Base 27.5 cm long
Sold 17.11.81 in Geneva for Sw.fr.125,000 (£37,202)

Gold-mounted hardstone spray of wild cherries
By Fabergé
13.3 cm high
Sold 17.11.81 in Geneva for Sw.fr.121,000 (£36,011)

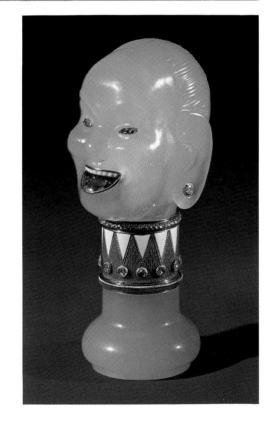

Above

Agate carving of a vulture
Workmaster Henrik Wigström
St Petersburg, 1908-17
4.8 cm high
Sold for Sw.fr.49,500 (£14,732)

Above right

Grey and violet jasper carving of a seated mandrill,
the eyes set with rose-cut diamonds
By Fabergé
4.8 cm high
Sold for Sw.fr.52,800 (£15,714)

Right

Jewelled gold-mounted and enamelled pale-green
jade hand-seal
By Fabergé
St Petersburg, 1899-1908
9 cm high
Sold for Sw.fr.66,000 (£19,642)

All sold 17.11.81 in Geneva

Gold-mounted, enamelled and hardstone miniature Easter eggs
By Fabergé
Sold 17.11.81 in Geneva on behalf of a European Princely House for Sw.fr.102,300 (£30,446)
From a collection of objects of vertu and jewellery owned by the Grand Duchess Maria Alexandrovna, wife of Alfred, Duke of Edinburgh

Right Enamelled silver-gilt frame
By Fabergé
Workmaster Victor Aarne
St Petersburg, 1899-1908
10.3 cm high
Sold 11.5.82 in Geneva for Sw.fr.28,600 (£8,125)

Below Enamelled two-colour gold and silver-gilt desk
clock enamelled in the Rothschild racing colours
By Fabergé
Workmaster Henrik Wigström
St Petersburg, 1908-17
8.5 cm high
Sold 11.5.82 in Geneva for Sw.fr.55,000 (£15,625)

Below right Enamelled gold box, the cover painted
en camaïeu sepia with a view of the fortress of St Peter
and St Paul in St Petersburg
By Fabergé
Workmaster Henrik Wigström
1899-1908
5.8 cm long
Sold 11.5.82 in Geneva for Sw.fr.55,000 (£15,625)

Enamelled silver-gilt
mounted white quartz
clock shaped as a
classical temple
By Fabergé
Workmaster Julius
Rappoport
St Petersburg,
1899-1908
28 cm high
Sold 11.5.82 in
Geneva for
Sw.fr.121,000
(£34,375)

Icon of the Deesis,
depicting the Saviour
enthroned flanked by
the Virgin and St
John the Baptist
Cretan School,
16th century
On gold ground
43 cm high
Sold 21.4.82 in
London for £8,640
($15,380)

JOHN SMART:
Nelly Garnett
Signed with initials
and dated 1770
3.8 cm high
Sold for £1,600
($2,847)

Far left

GEORGE ENGLEHEART:
Mrs John Holford
4.8 cm high
Sold for £2,700
($4,800)

Left

GEORGE ENGLEHEART:
Mrs Stubbs
5 cm high
Sold for £2,808
($4,773)

Centre

JOHN PLOTT: *A Lady*
3.8 cm high
Sold for £972 ($1,730)

Far left

SAMUEL SHELLEY:
Captain Harvey
6.3 cm high
Sold for £3,240
($5,767)

Left

RICHARD COSWAY:
Henrietta,
Viscountess Belgrave
6 cm high
Sold for £3,780
($6,728)

All sold 15.6.82
in London

PIERRE ADOLPHE HALL:
*Miniature of a lady, perhaps a
daughter of the artist*
8 cm high
Sold 23.3.82 in London for
£12,420 ($22,356)

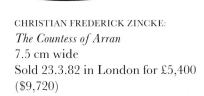

CHRISTIAN FREDERICK ZINCKE:
The Countess of Arran
7.5 cm wide
Sold 23.3.82 in London for £5,400
($9,720)

SAMUEL COOPER: *Elizabeth Claypole
(née Cromwell)*
Signed with initials and dated 1654
6.6 cm high
Sold 23.3.82 in London for £11,880
($21,384)

Perhaps by CORNELIUS JOHNSON
after Van Dyck: *Miniature of
Queen Henrietta Maria*
Oil on copper
9.3 cm high
Sold 15.6.82 in London for £3,456 ($6,152)

THOMAS FORSTER:
*Elizabeth Keyt,
Viscountess Tracy*
Signed and
dated 1703
10.5 cm high
Sold 15.6.82 in
London for £4,320
($7,690)

ROWLAND LOCKEY:
*Gentleman of the
Barker family of
Suffolk*
5 cm high
Sold 15.6.82 in
London for £7,020
($12,495)

Far right

PIERRE LOUIS BOUVIER:
*Le Comte de Beaujolais,
as a child*
In the cover of a rectangular
gold-lined tortoiseshell box,
maker's mark PAM
Paris, June 1798 to
August 1809
Sold 15.6.82 in London
for £2,160 ($3,845)

Right

JEAN THEODORE PERRACHE,
after SIR JOSHUA REYNOLDS:
*Mrs Abington as Roxalana
in The Sultan*
Signed on reverse and
dated 1785
7 cm high
Sold 23.3.82 in London for
£1,500 ($2,700)

Far right

EMANUEL PETER, after
MICHAEL MORITZ DAFFINGER:
*Maria Sidonia,
Princess Lobkowicz*
Signed
9.8 cm high
Sold 23.3.82 in London for
£4,860 ($8,748)

Right

GEORGE ENGLEHEART:
An Infantry Officer
7.5 cm high
Sold 23.3.82 in London for
£4,860 ($8,748)

311

RICHARD CROSSE:
*Miniature of the artist's
father, John Crosse*
In a Chinese
Chippendale giltwood
frame
14.7 cm high
Sold 15.6.82 in
London for £9,180
($16,340)

Ornate Chinese silver
shrine containing an
ivory figure of the
infant Christ
Mid-late Quing
Dynasty
Bed 6.2 cm high;
35.5 cm wide;
23.5 cm deep
Sold 24.11.81 in
London for £17,600
($33,440)
The shrine is believed
to have been taken by
Brigadier General
Draper at the Seige of
Manila in 1762

Elizabethan gold and foiled crystal signet-ring with two silver-mounted ivory desk-seals
Each seal 9 cm long
Sold 7.7.82 in London for £22,680 ($39,463)
The arms on the above are those of Sir Thomas Smijth (1513-77), diplomat, statesman and author, who was twice appointed Secretary of State and who served as Ambassador to France during the reign of Queen Elizabeth. It is very rare to find a group of personal seals of this date. The set is now in the British Museum

Documented set of five Italian vari-coloured agate cameos
By Giuseppe Girometti
Featuring the five famous artists of the golden age of Leo X: inscribed Raffaele Da Urbino,
Michel Angelo Bonaroti, Tiziano Vecellio, Antonio Da Coreggio and Leonardo Da Vinci. Each sitter
profiled against a different coloured ground and each signed
*c.*1830
With plain silver-gilt mounts each 4.2 cm high
Sold 8.6.82 in London for £3,780 ($6,804)
From the collection of Lord Astor of Hever

Frederick the Great Snuff-box

DR GEZA VON HABSBURG

The few examples of Frederick the Great's snuff-box collection to come on the market in recent times – not more than six in the last 30 years – all reflect his taste for luxury in art. Of the boxes listed after his death (specialists have reconstructed a collection of some 300) only a very small number were not embellished with precious stones. The present table snuff-box (now in a private collection in Los Angeles) is one of the most lavish of the group which comprises but a tenth of the original number today. Obviously such a collection must have represented a considerable drain on Prussia's finances – costing up to 12,000 *Thalers* a piece. One of the boxes was, however, to save the King's life when a Russian bullet ricocheted off it during the Battle of Kunersdorf, which led the monarch to comment: "(and, to say that) I am constantly reproached for spending too much on my box collection."

The *friederizianische* snuff-boxes can be divided into five groups:

1) Rectangular enamelled gold boxes with diamond-set thumbpiece, painted by Daniel Chodowiecki or in his style
2) Rectangular gold boxes encrusted with hardstones and with diamond-set thumbpiece, some of which bear the mark of Daniel Baudesson
3) Cartouche-shaped gold boxes with a portrait of the King, surrounded by diamonds, of a French mid-18th century type
4) Cartouche-shaped gold boxes painted with *grisaille* subjects on pink or turquoise ground with diamond borders connected with the models produced by Jean-Guillaume George Krüger
5) Large cartouche-shaped hardstone boxes, mostly in chrysophrase, figured agate or jasper, in chased gold mounts encrusted with diamonds, for which a number of drawings by Krüger exist

The present box, its gold body covered with mother-of-pearl panels applied with hardstone flowers and profusely encrusted with diamonds and rubies, belongs to this last group.

316

Frederick the Great cartouche-shaped, jewelled, mother-of-pearl, hardstone and vari-coloured
gold snuff box
Berlin, 1760-5
10.4 cm wide
Sold 11.5.82 in Geneva for Sw.fr.1,540,000 (£435,028)
Record auction price for any gold snuff-box
Sold on behalf of a German Royal Family

The Rothschild Gold Boxes

ARTHUR GRIMWADE

In March 1904 at King Street the first four days' sale occurred of the huge collection of gold snuffboxes and bibelots formed by Charles Hawkins of Portland Place, then recently dead, which was to continue to be dispersed for several years. Scholarship had scarcely begun on the subject and little more than a period dating could be attempted in the catalogues of the day. But taste and enthusiasm for these most jewel-like of functional objects was as acute then as now, even if little informed, and the finest of them commanded figures equal to those obtained for old masters. The Hawkins sales were probably the first opportunity many had to appreciate the great range of technique and superb craftsmanship embodied in these golden handfuls, which must now be scattered world-wide in many collections.

It was therefore particularly interesting to be confronted in the sale on June 30th this year with a group of such creatures which had been mainly inherited from the Collection of Baron Carl von Rothschild of Frankfurt. At his death in 1886 the collection had been divided among his five daughters, a factual illustration of the dissemination of taste within this famous family. Modern research has done much in such catalogues as those of the Waddesdon Manor Collection, the Wallace Collection and others to increase our knowledge of particular makers and origins of such *tours de force* as the solid gold varicoloured box chased with the Palace of Schönbrunn by Johann Paul Kolbe of Vienna, *c.* 1760, which fetched £118,800 ($206,712), or the rarity of the inset hardstone rustic scenes on the box by Heinrich Taddel of Dresden, by whom only four other such boxes are yet recorded which achieved £140,400 ($244,296).

So many facets are present in gold box design that all tastes can be suited whether it be for the charming enamelled domestic scenes after Boucher on the box by Louis-Phillipe Demay, Paris 1759, which sold for £86,400 ($150,336); the restrained elegance of the lapis lazuli panels in narrow gold borders by Jean Ducrollay, Paris 1758, which sold for £48,600 ($84,564); or the diamond-rayed, cloud-enthroned Apollo with his attendant pink putti by Jean François Breton, Paris 1753, which made £56,160 ($97,718). Classical severity was saluted in the grisaille panels of maidens and putti on the raspberry red enamel ground of the octagonal box by Louis Roucel, 1765, which achieved £41,040 ($71,409) or chinoiserie by the inlaid hardstone smoking Chinaman on a mother-of-pearl ground in a box of likely German origin which sold for £25,920 ($45,100). Perhaps for many the most appealing box in its simplicity was the Dresden rock-crystal example carved with Dido and Aeneas by Johann Georg Klett which made £34,560 ($60,134), and the most surprising the unmarked example, inlaid with subtly tinted enamel butterflies in what the guide book to Baron Carl's Collection by Ferdinand Luthmer had dubbed "very curious technique" which sold for £8,100 ($14,094). A short sale, certainly, but one to linger long in the memory.

Louis XV shaped
octagonal gold and lapis
lazuli snuff-box
By Jean Ducrollay
Paris, 1758-9 and
1759-60
8 cm long
Sold 30.6.82 in London
for £48,600 ($84,564)

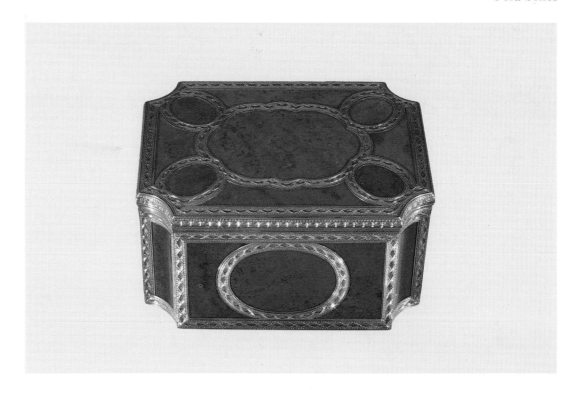

Louis XV rectangular
jewelled, gold and enamel
snuff-box
By Jean François
Breton
Paris, 1753-4
With charge and
décharge of Julien
Berthe, the flange
engraved No.27
8 cm long; 6 cm wide
Sold 30.6.82 in London
for £56,160 ($97,718)
Both from the collection
of Lord Rothschild
G.B.E., G.M., F.R.S.

Dresden oval jewelled, gold
and hardstone snuff-box
By Heinrich Taddel
*c.*1760
Unmarked
9.6 cm long; 7 cm wide
Sold 30.6.82 in London for
£140,000 ($244,296)

Austrian oval vari-coloured
gold snuff-box
Signed by Johann Paul
Kolbe, maker's
initials ISP and IS
*c.*1760
8.6 cm long; 6 cm wide
Sold 30.6.82 in London for
£118,800 ($206,712)
The cover is chased and
engraved with a view of the
Palace of Schönbrunn
Both from the collection of
Lord Rothschild,
G.B.E., G.M., F.R.S.

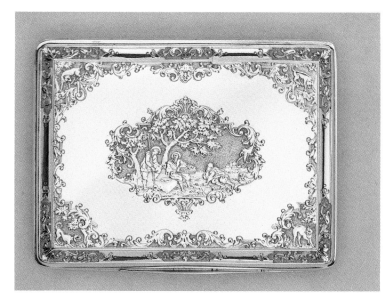

Above left

French Regence oblong gold snuff-box
Paris 1717-22
8.2 cm long
Sold 7.7.82 in London for £16,200 ($28,188)
Traditionally supposed to have been presented to
Archbishop Wake by Queen Caroline on her
Coronation, 11th October, 1727
From the collection of Sir Anthony Rumbold,
Bt. K.C.M.G., K.C.V.O., C.B.

Above

Swiss enamelled gold musical automaton snuff-box
Attributed to J.F.V. Dupont père
Inscribed No.5078 on the flange, the movement signed
PM for Piguet et Meylan
In original fitted red leather case, with original key
8.5 cm wide
Sold 17.11.81 in Geneva for Sw.fr.286,000 (£85,119)

Left

Frederick the Great diamond-set chased gold snuff box
carved with scenes from the Seven Years' War
Signed Sahler (under the thumbpiece)
Berlin, *c.*1760
9.1 cm long
Sold 11.5.82 in Geneva for Sw.fr.220,000 (£62,146)

Swiss vari-coloured gold musical box with nautical automata, *c.* 1790 bearing Paris prestige marks for 1783-1789
8 cm long
Sold 14.6.82 in New York for $71,500 (£42,058)

Australia
Half-sovereign
1861
£1,150 ($2,139)

Germany
Brunswick-
Wolfenbüttel
Ducat 1733
£630 ($1.171)

Augustus
(27 BC-AD 14)
Denarius
£320 ($569)

Trajan
(AD 98-117)
Denarius
£140 ($249)

Hadrian
(AD 117-138)
Denarius
£230 ($409)

Valentinian I
(AD 364-375)
Solidus
£460 ($814)

Russia
10-Roubles
1778
£390 ($725)

Macedon Philip II
(359-336 BC)
Tetradrachm
£320 ($553)

Germany, Frankfurt
"Sturm Doppel
Dukat"
1710
£2,200 ($4,092)

Italy, Carmagnola
Ludovico II
(1475-1504)
Cavalotto
£280 ($495)

Middlesex
Swainson's Token
c.1800
£300 ($519)

Nero (AD 54-68)
Sestertius
£600 ($1,062)

Hadrian (AD 117-138)
Sestertius
£700 ($1,239)

Segovia, Ferdinand
and Isabella
4-Excellentes
Sw.fr.15,000 (£4,545)

Segovia, Charles II
8-Escudos
1687
Sw.fr.17,000 (£5,151)

Lima, Philip V
Cob 8-Escudos
1743
Sw.fr.4,000 (£1,230)

Catalonia, Ferdinand VII
8-Escudos
1814
Sw.fr.13,000 (£4,000)

Madrid, Provincial Government
100-Pesetas
1870
Sw.fr.380,000 (£115,000)
Record auction price for a European gold coin

Madrid, Amadeo I
100-Pesetas
1871
Sw.fr.170,000 (£52,000)

The Kurt Hommé Collection of Spanish and Spanish American gold coins

Raymond Sancroft Baker

The above six coins are from the Kurt Hommé Collection of Spanish and Spanish American gold coins that were sold in Geneva on November 25 and 26 1981. The collection was formed in the early 1960s at a time when the dedicated collector could quite easily put together an extensive series of coins, including then unrecognized rarities, by buying from dealers' stocks and the auction rooms in Europe and America. The importance of the collection to the specialists in the series is demonstrated not least by the fact that authors such as Lopez-Chaves recorded and in many cases illustrated coins from this collection in their works of reference.

The sale attracted collectors and dealers from all over Europe as well as North and South America. The highlight of the auction was the 100 Pesetas of the Provincial Government struck in 1870. Very few of these coins exist, and this one exceeded the estimate when it sold for Sw.fr. 380,000 (£115,000), a record price for a European gold coin. This was our first coin sale in Geneva and proved a useful addition to the already successful series of sales held in Switzerland.

324

From left to right

Charles II
Five-guineas
1668
£4,400 ($7,612)

William and Mary
Five-guineas
1691
£3,300 ($5,709)

William III
Five-guineas
1701
£2,600 ($4,498)

Anne
Five-guineas
1714
£2,900 ($5,017)

George I
Five-guineas
1716
£5,200 ($8,996)

George II
Five-guineas
1729
£2,700 ($4,671)

Anne
Two-guineas
1711
£3,600 ($6,228)

William and Mary
Two-guineas
1693
£3,200 ($5,536)

USA, 10-Dollars,
1795
$7,700 (£3,989)

USA, 5-Dollars,
1804
$6,270 (£3,248)

USA, 5-Dollars,
1805
$5,500 (£2,849)

USA, 5-Dollars,
1807
$2,860 (£1,481)

USA, 10-Dollars,
1801
$9,900 (£5,129)

USA, 5-Dollars,
1810
$2,750 (£1,424)

USA, 5-Dollars,
1853
$2,310 (£1,196)

USA, Proof
3-Dollars, 1858
$28,600 (£14,818)

USA, Proof
3-Dollars, 1874
$24,200 (£12,538)

USA, Matte Proof
10-Dollars, 1915
$13,200 (£6,839)

The J. Hambleton Ober Collection of United States gold coins

The J. Hambleton Ober Collection of gold coins was sold in New York on 9 December for a total of $702,000 (£369,473). The collection consisted entirely of United States gold coins, the earliest being a 10-Dollars, 1795, and the most recent, a 2½-Dollars, dated 1929. The strength of the collection lay in the series of proof 3-Dollars (1854-89), the most expensive of which, dated 1858, fetched $28,600 (£15,000). There were also some very fine Eagles and Half-Eagles ($10 and $5) from the first few years of the 19th century; these proved extremely popular, as common coins in mint condition, because of their rarity, are still in great demand. Another factor that ensured good prices was that the collection was formed over 30 years ago.

Far right

Germany, Saxony,
Military Order of
Saint Henry
Embroidered Star and
gold enamel Badge
£5,000 ($9,300)

Right

Austria, Order of the
Golden Fleece
Neck Badge in gold
and enamel
£6,200 ($11,532)

The Most Illustrious
Order of the House
of Chakri
(Maha Chakrakri)
Collar, two Badges
and Star
Awarded to Grand
Duke Michael
Alexandrovitch of
Russia, brother of
Tsar Nicholas II,
in 1897
£4,600 ($7,958)

Deruta blue-ground coppa-amatoria
Attributed to Franceses Urbini
c. 1525-30
25 cm diam.
Sold 5.4.82 in London for £15,200 ($27,512)

CERAMICS AND GLASS

Yellow-ground bouquetière
Veuve Perrin
*c.*1760
24.5 cm high
Sold 9.5.82 in Geneva for Sw.fr.30,800 (£8,750)
Formerly in the Papillon, Gaymard, Lacroix and Maurin collections

Pair of Louis XV
bouquetières and
covers
Fauchier Neveu
*c.*1760
29.5 cm high
Sold 9.5.82 in Geneva
for Sw.fr.26,400
(£7,500)

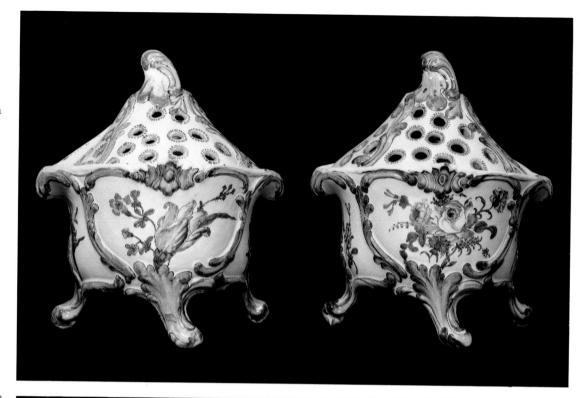

Pair of ice-buckets and
covers
Veuve Perrin
*c.*1770
31 cm high
Sold 9.5.82 in Geneva
for Sw.fr.49,500
(£14,062)

Monsieur Boucher's Basket

HUGO MORLEY-FLETCHER

Although he confined his talents to painting and drawing, François Boucher exercised a profound influence on the products of the Sèvres factory. Many of its wares and figures are redolent of his art. It is known that he possessed examples of the factory's products because several were included in the sale of his effects after his death in 1771 and because the Sèvres archives record one piece that was presented to him by the factory. An entry in the ledger for December 1757 reads: "A Monsieur Boucher: 1 pannier f. vert et or, 2ème grandeur ... 240£" This basket was not included in Boucher's sale (it has been suggested that his widow decided to keep it), and no other similar piece would appear to have been produced.

Although apparently very simple, this basket must have been technically quite difficult to produce: the ribbons at the base of the handle posed particularly tough problems in their construction. The apple green colour of the ground had only just been introduced, and thus the production of the perfect colour was by no means a certainty. In any event, it was successfully fired and decorated and, having disappeared at Boucher's death, was lost to students of Sèvres except for a brief appearance in Sir Charles Mills' Collection during the last century, until it resurfaced recently in France and was sent from there for sale in London. Fierce competition from the United States and the Antipodes finally saw it bought by a New York dealer for £30,240 ($51,408).

In December we offered another great Sèvres rarity, not however recorded in the archives: a gold mounted knife with rose-Pompadour handle. The mounts bear the décharge of Eloy Brichard who, besides being the Fermier Général of Paris silver, was titular holder of the "privilège" under which the Sèvres factory operated. This too set sail for America for £2,420 ($4,743).

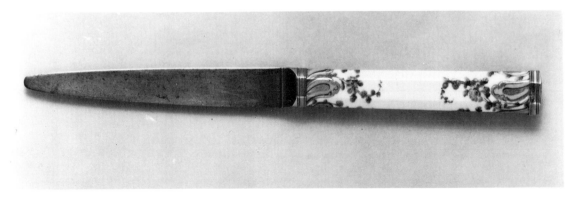

Louis XV gold-mounted Sèvres porcelain knife handle 1756-62
Sold 30.11.81 in London for £2,420 ($4,743)

Vincennes green-
ground basket
Blue interlaced L
marks enclosing the
date letter D for 1756
and incised marks PZ
22 cm high
Sold 28.6.82 in
London for £30,240
($51,408)

Vezzi flattened
oviform teapot and
recessed cover
grey Ven.a. and
incised C mark
*c.*1725
15 cm wide
Sold 5.10.81 in
London for £18,700
($34,595)

The Wares of the Vezzi Factory

HUGO MORLEY-FLETCHER

The products of the Vezzi factory, which was operated in Venice from 1720 to 1727 by Giovanni Vezzi and his family, are rare and mostly recorded. It was therefore remarkable that in a few months we were able to offer three hitherto unknown examples of the factory's output.

The first to appear was a teapot, similar to the example in the Correr Museum, Venice, but with differences in the construction of the cover and spout. This bore the typical Ven$^{\underline{a}}$ mark of the factory and sold for £18,700 ($34,595). Six weeks later, in Geneva, a greater rarity appeared. Unmarked save for the diagonally placed incised letters to be found on most Vezzi wares, this was the first polychrome plate from the factory to come to light. Fortunately for the member of our staff to whom it was shown, the decoration of archers shooting geese also occurs on a teapot we sold in June 1968, from the Cartwright Collection, and identification was swiftly made. Despite spirited efforts from Milan the plate found its home in Geneva for Sw.Fr.99,000 (£29,910). The last piece to appear was an octagonal teabowl, moulded with stiff leaves and without its saucer. This fetched £4,860 ($8,650), a modest sum when compared with the two other pieces, but a high price for a small and incomplete specimen.

Unrecorded Venice (Vezzi) polychrome circular plate
Centre painted by *Duramano*, reverse incised with A and N
*c.*1725
24.5 cm high
Sold 16.11.81 in Geneva for Sw.fr.99,000 ($£29,910)
Record auction price for a piece from this factory

Capodimonte
(Carlo III) group
Modelled by
Guiseppe Grucci
*c.*1745
21.5 cm high
Sold 28.6.82 in
London for £41,040
($69,768)
Record auction price
for a piece from this
factory

Naples (Ferdinand IV) topographical plates and dishes from the so-called Fiordalisi service produced in the 1790s
Sold individually 30.11.81 in London for a total of £16,445 ($32,232)
From the collection of Eva, Countess of Rosebery, D.B.E.

Pair of Zürich (soft paste) Italian comedy figures
Bases incised K3/1 and K3/3
c.1770
16.2 cm and
15 cm high
Sold 16.11.81 in Geneva for
Sw.fr.66,000 (£19,940)

Tureen from a Frankenthal armorial royal presentation dinner-service
Sold 28.6.82 in London for £41,040 ($69,768)
From the collection of Monsieur Michael von Jenner

Meissen chinoiserie
tea-service
Painted by
J.G. Herold and
P.E. Schindler
1724-5
Sold individually
5.10.81 in London for
a total of £73,590
($136,141)

Pair of Meissen lobed squat saké-bottles and
stepped covers with Augsburg Hausmalerei
decoration
*c.*1725
25.5 cm high
Sold 28.6.82 in London for £15,120 ($25,704)

Meissen lobed square saké-bottle and cover
painted in bright colours and *Böttger-lustre*
By Johann Ehrenfried Stadler
*c.*1730
22.5 cm high
Sold 28.6.82 in London for £4,320 ($7,344)

Vienna du Paquier famille rose globular two-handled pot and cover
1720-5
22.5 cm high; 20 cm diam.
Sold 5.10.81 in London for £17,600 ($32,560)

Above

Staffordshire slipware dish
By William Simpson
*c.*1700
34 cm diam.
Sold 14.12.81 in London for £3,520 ($6,688)

Above right

Liverpool Delft blue and white shell-moulded
sauceboat
*c.*1760
Sold 19.4.82 in London for £345 ($610)
From the collection of the late
Mrs J.C. Paterson

Right

Bristol Delft blue and white inscribed and dated
oviform jug
1730
23.5 cm high
Sold 14.12.81 in London for £1,430 ($2,717)

Wedgwood and Bentley compressed urn-shaped porphyry vase and cover
Impressed Wedgwood & Bentley Etruria mark within a circle
*c.*1775
Sold 21.4.82 in New York for $14,300 (£7,729)

Liverpool large oblong
octagonal dish
Richard Chaffer's
Factory; *c*.1765
41.5 cm long
Sold for £418 ($806)

Derby powder-blue
ground oviform vase
c.1765; 12.5 cm high
Sold for £1,210 ($2,335)

Liverpool swelling flared
vase; Seth Pennington's
Factory; *c*.1780
15 cm high
Sold £264 ($509)

Bow foliate stand for a
finger-bowl
c.1750; 14.5 cm diam.
Sold for £792 ($1,528)

Liverpool miniature
pear-shaped bottle
William Reid's Factory
c.1758; 6 cm high
Sold for £792 ($1,528)

Lowestoft pear-shaped
bottle; *c*.1765
22.5 cm high
Sold for £418 ($806)

Liverpool miniature
pear-shaped bottle
William Reid's Factory
c.1758; 6.5 cm high
Sold for £792 ($1,528)

Worcester baluster
cream-jug; *c*.1754
10.5 cm high
Sold for £792 ($1,528)

All sold 12.10.81
in London
From the collection of
Gilbert Bradley, Esq.

Chelsea figure of Pu-Tai Ho-Shang
1746-9
8 cm high
Sold 14.12.81 in London for £1,650
($3,135)

Chelsea fluted leaf-shaped cream-jug
Red anchor mark
c.1753
11 cm wide
Sold 2.11.81 in London for £2,860
($5,291)

Worcester herring-bone moulded coffee-pot and domed cover
c.1760
25 cm high
Sold 2.11.81 in London for £3,520
($6,512)

Lowestoft blue and white dated birth-tablet
7 cm diam.
Sold 14.12.81 in London for £1,210 ($2,299)

Pair of Bow groups of
Venus and Mars with
Cupid
c.1762
24 cm high
Sold 19.4.82 in
London for £1,058
($1,873)

Worcester teabowl
and saucer
c.1753
Sold for £864 ($1,581)

Worcester flared
beaker-vase
Painted by
James Rogers
c.1758
13.5 cm high
Sold for £950 ($1,738)

Worcester teabowl
and saucer
c.1754
Sold for £378 ($692)

All sold 17.5.82
in London
From the collection of
R.H. Newsholme

Venetian diamond-engraved armorial dish
Engraved with the Arms of the Medici Pope Pius IV
Third quarter of the 16th century
27 cm diam.
Sold 26.5.82 in London for £35,640 ($64,865)
From the collection of the late Count Antoine Seilern

Clichy turquoise-overlay close
concentric mushroom weight
8.5 cm diam.
£2,592 ($4,406)

Baccarat marguerite weight
7.5 cm diam.
£2,052 ($3,488)

St Louis close concentric
millefiori weight
9 cm diam.
£1,620 ($2,754)

Baccarat blue carpet-ground
dated scattered millefiori
weight
8 cm diam.
£2,160 ($3,672)

Baccarat yellow clematis-spray
weight
7.5 cm diam.
£1,620 ($2,754)

All sold 25.6.82
in London

Selection of glass
paperweights
Sold 27.10.81 in New York
for a total of $145,376
(£79,439)
From the Cheney Wells
Collection

Pair of white-enamelled Electioneering decanters
Each of mallet shape inscribed "Sir Jno Anstruther
For Ever" and "Lady Anstruther For Ever"
1765-8
Decorated by a member of the Beilby family
Decanters 22 cm high
Sold 6.10.81 in London for £6,050 ($11,192)

Newcastle Dutch-engraved
armorial goblet for the Dutch
East India Company
c.1750
19 cm high
Sold 26.5.82 in London for £5,940
($10,810)

French "Gorge de Pigeon" opaline
ormolu-mounted clock
c.1830
33 cm high
Sold 6.10.81 in London for £15,950
($29,507)

Façon-de-Venise diamond-
engraved tazza
Spain or Venice
Last quarter of the 16th century
16.5 cm high; 15 cm diam.
Sold 26.5.82 in London for £5,184
($9,435)

ORIENTAL CERAMICS AND WORKS OF ART

Imperial white jade vase and cover
Base incised on each side with a four-character Qianlong mark and
of the period, reading Qianlong pang gui
39 cm high overall
Sold 24.2.82 in New York for $77,000 (£41,621)

Archaic bronze
pear-shaped vessel
and cover, *zhi*
Late Shang/early
Western Zhou
Dynasty
17.5 cm high
Sold for £30,240
($53,827)

Archaic bronze vessel
and cover, *fang yu*
Early Western Zhou
Dynasty
17 cm high
Sold for £10,800
($19,224)

Both sold 17.6.82
in London
From the estate
of the late
Count Antoine
Seilern

Green-glazed buff pottery tripod cylindrical jar and shallow domed cover, the interior under a yellow glaze with areas of orange-red pigment remaining Tang Dynasty
23 cm high
Sold 17.6.82 in London for £70,200 ($124,956)
From the estate of the late Count Antoine Seilern

Sancai buff pottery broad oviform jar
Tang Dynasty
26.5 cm diam.; 26 cm high
Sold 17.6.82 in London for £21,600 ($38,448)
From the estate of the late Count Antoine Seilern

Henan broad oviform
wine jar, *meiping*
Song Dynasty
40 cm high
Sold 17.6.82 in
London for £48,600
($85,440)
From the estate
of the late
Count Antoine
Seilern

Early Ming blue and white vase, *meiping*
Yongle period
36.4 cm high
Sold 14.6.82 in London for
£302,400 ($541,296)
From the collection of the
late Mr and Mrs R.H.R. Palmer

Opposite top

Early Ming blue and white
dice bowl
Xuande six-character mark in
underglaze blue below the lip and
of the period
28 cm diam.
Sold 23.6.82 in New York for
$82,500 (£47,965)

Opposite below

Brilliant small junyao tripod
narcissus bowl
Song Dynasty
19 cm diam.
Sold 23.6.82 in New York for
$66,000 (£38,372)

Early Ming blue and white leys jar, *zhadou*
Encircled Xuande six-character mark in the stepped recessed base and of the period
16.6 cm diam.; 14.5 cm high
Sold 14.6.82 in London for £64,800 ($115,992)
From the collection of the late Mr and Mrs R.H.R. Palmer

Early Ming blue and
white tankard
Unenclosed Xuande
six-character mark at
the shoulder opposite
the handle and of the
period
13.3 cm high
Sold 14.6.82 in
London for £86,400
($154,656)
From the
collection of
the late Mr
and Mrs
R.H.R. Palmer

Ming blue and white palace bowl
Encircled Chenghua six-character mark and of the period
15.5 cm diam.
Sold 14.6.82 in London for £183,600 ($328,644)
From the collection of the late Mr and Mrs R.H.R. Palmer

Ming blue and white dish
Unenclosed Chenghua six-character mark in a line below the rim and of the period
29.9 cm diam.
Sold 14.6.82 in London for £345,600 ($618,624)
From the collection of the late Mr and Mrs R.H.R. Palmer

Ming green dragon saucer-dish
Encircled Hongzhi six-character mark and of the period
18 cm diam.
Sold 14.6.82 in London for £19,440 ($34,797)

Extensive famille rose
"tobacco-leaf" dinner-
service
Sold 29.3.82 in
London for £56,160
($101,088)

元人松溪垂釣

MING HUA HUI JIN: *Imperial album of ten Song and Yuan Dynasty paintings*
In brown dragon brocade covers
12th/13th century
Sold 24.6.82 in New York for $330,000 (£191,860)
Record auction price for an album of Chinese paintings

SHEN ZHOU
(1427-1509):
*Flowers of the Four
Seasons*
Handscroll, ink and
colour on paper
Signed
25.7 x 49.1 cm
Sold 24.6.82 in
New York for $60,500
(£35,174)

Shanghai, the Bund
American and British
trading vessels in the
foreground
Period Chinese frame
19th century
Sold 23.6.82 in
New York for $66,000
(£38,372)

Group of 18th century famille rose porcelain which sold for a total of £10,190 ($19,564)
It includes a tureen, cover and stand with the arms of Frederick the Great of Prussia which sold for
£2,600 ($4,992)
All sold 16.11.81 in London

Kakiemon shallow
bowl
c.1700
13.3. cm diam.
Sold for £270 ($483)

Pair of Kakiemon
deep bowls
Late 17th century
Both approximately
19 cm diam.
Sold for £7,560
($13,532)

Early Kakiemon dish
Late 17th century
21.3 cm diam.
Sold for £864
($15,465)

Kakiemon kikugata
bowl
c.1700
13.1 cm diam.
Sold for £702 ($2,565)

Kakiemon decagonal
dish
c.1700
22.6 cm wide
Sold for £1,404
($2,513)

All sold 6.4.82
in London

Rounded rectangular
document box
(ryoshibako) and
matching writing box
(suzuribako)
19th century
28.8 x 25.2 cm
Sold 27.10.81 in
London for £6,050
($11,011)

Five-case red
ground inro
19th century
Sold for £4,620
($8,454)

Four-case silver-
ground inro
Signed Kajikawa Saku
Probably early 19th
century
Sold for £7,920
($14,493)

Four-case inro
Signed Jokasai Saku
Late 18th/early
19th century
Sold for £2,860
($5,233)

Four-case sleeve inro
19th century
Sold for £3,520
($6,442)

All sold 28.10.81 in
London

The Yaddo Namban Retable

WILLIAM TILLEY

The Japanese lacquer travelling shrine, containing a European painting of the Holy Trinity, was made for the Christian market and dates from the Momoyama period (1573-1614).

Such is the rarity of these portable Namban shrines that only 11 examples are known, and their very existence went unrecognized until one in Utrecht was published by Martha Boyer in 1959 (Japanese Export Lacquers, Copenhagen 1959, p.XXVII 23).

The successful evangelism of the Jesuits led by Saint Francis Xavier, who landed at Kagoshima in 1549, meant that the religious artefacts they brought with them were soon exhausted. The Japanese, accustomed to focusing their faith on representations of the Buddhist pantheon, constantly requested the missionaries to provide a Christian equivalent in the form of pictures of the Saviour, the Virgin Mary and the various Saints. The Jesuits sent to the Curia in Rome for supplies to meet this demand, but since several years could pass before they were received, local artisans were increasingly used as the "Christian Century" progressed. By 1580 there were an estimated 150,000 Japanese Christians, mostly in and around Nagasaki where the Portuguese ships usually anchored.

Although a large amount of Christian art was produced at this time, much of it was to be destroyed in the fierce repression of Christianity during the first decades of the 17th century, culminating in the massacre of some 37,000 Christians at Shimabara and the end of overt Christianity in Japan.

Japanese lacquer travelling shrine for the Christian market
Momoyama period
29 cm wide; 40.5 cm high
Sold 24.6.82 in New York for $198,000 (£115,116)

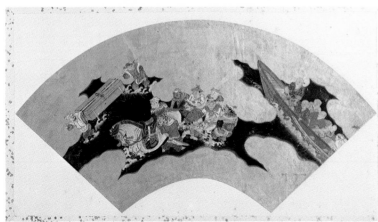

Album containing fifty fan-
shaped paintings
Attributed to Kano
Naganobu (Kyuhaku)
Early Edo period
Album leaf 30.5 x 54 cm
Sold 27.7.82 in London for
£4,860 ($8,748)

Six-leaf screen
Momoyama/early
Edo period
Fitted wood box
Each leaf
approximately
119 x 53 cm
Sold 9.3.82 in London
for £9,180 ($16,891)

Bronze figure of a standing windswept immortal
Signed in a rectangular reserve Miyao zo
Late 19th century
Fitted rectangular wood stand
49 cm high
Sold 6.7.82 in London for £9,180 ($16,065)

Black lacquered wood Church-style chest
Momoyama period
Chest 61.5 x 52 x 42.5 cm
Sold 8.12.81 in London for £4,950 ($9,702)

Rectangular tansu
19th century
146.8 cm high
Sold 8.12.81 in London for £8,800 ($17,248)

Armour made for a member of
the Matsudaira family
Helmet 16th century;
remainder 18th century
Sold 22.6.82 in London for
£6,480 ($11,664)

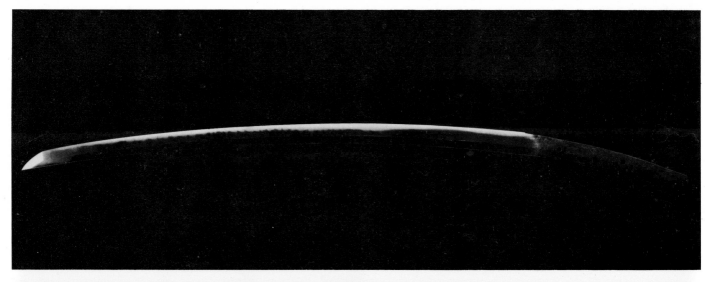

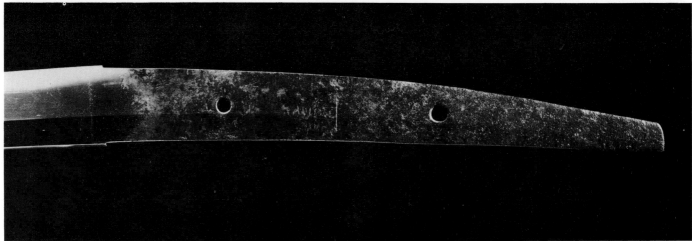

Ichimonji tachi blade known as the Imaaranami
Attributed to Norifusa of Bizen and Bitchu, an Ashikaga heirloom
Mid-13th century
Sold 22.6.82 in London for £32,400 ($55,080)
This splendid sword is typical of the broader, heavier blades demanded by the warriors of Kamakura, so different from the slender graceful blades of the preceding Heian period. Japan was now under threat of invasion by the Great Khan Kublai, grandson of Genghis, and his "Golden Horde" of Mongols from Northern Asia; this was the type of weapon used by the Japanese (whose martial traditions called for single combat between knightly warriors) against the invading, and well-armed, mass formations of Mongols, Chinese and Koreans. Such blades, and the providential typhoons known to history as "kamikaze", saved Japan and served to confirm its inhabitants' belief in their divine origins

HIROSHIGE: *Oban tate-e Triptych, a snow scene at the Kiso Gorge*
Sold 27.7.82 in London for £4,536 ($8,164)

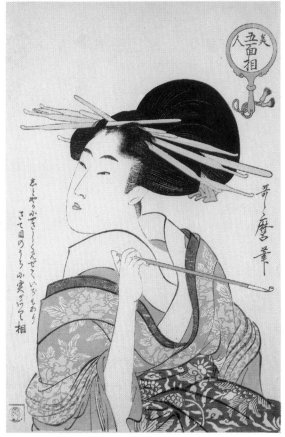

UTAMARO: *Oban tate-e: an okubi-e portrait of a courtesan smoking her pipe*
From the series Bijin gomen so
Sold 28.9.81 in New York for $18,700 (£10,500)

Extremely rare "vase" carpet
Persia
17th century
538 x 202 cm
Sold 22.4.82 in London for £97,200 ($173,015)

Velvet panel
(Later applied metal thread edging)
Possibly Shah Jahan
Late 17th century
103 x 103 cm
Sold 22.4.82 in London for £7,560 ($13,456)

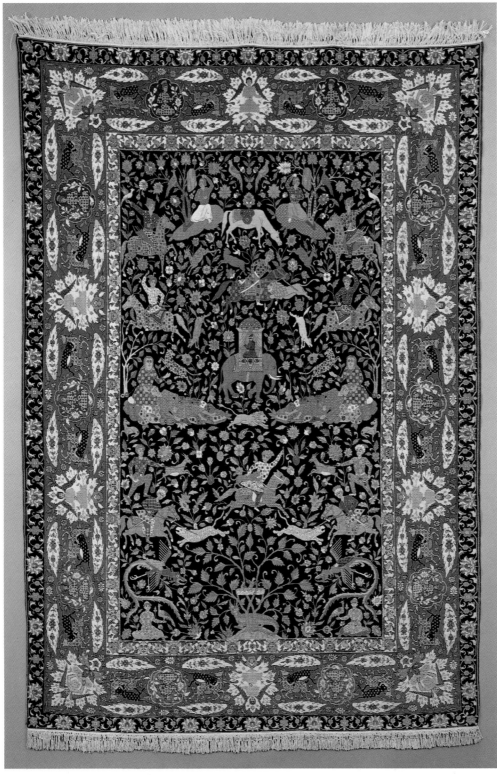

Antique silk Hereke-rug
211 x 147 cm
Sold 15.10.81 in London for
£15,400 ($28,644)

Antique silk Tabriz
carpet
376 x 279 cm
Sold 4.2.82 in London
for £37,800 ($71,064)

Antique Senna rug
193 x 137 cm
Sold 4.2.82 in London for
£16,200 ($30,456)

Antique qashqai millefleurs prayer rug
213 x 137 cm
Sold 22.4.82 in London for
£18,360 ($32,680)

Far right

Pair of wooden figures of Kali
Cera 15th/16th century
114 cm high
Sold 29.10.81 in London for
£5,500 ($10,065)

Right

Hoyasola grey stone stele
12th century
86 cm high
Sold 1.4.82 in London for
£8,100 ($14,418)

Far right

Tibetan gilt-bronze figure
of Tara
19th century
39 cm high
Sold 29.10.81 in London for
£1,320 ($2,416)

Right

Nepalese gilt-bronze figure
of Padmapani
Inscribed and dated (1596)
Circular base
16th century
22 cm high
Sold 1.4.82 in London for
£2,160 ($3,845)

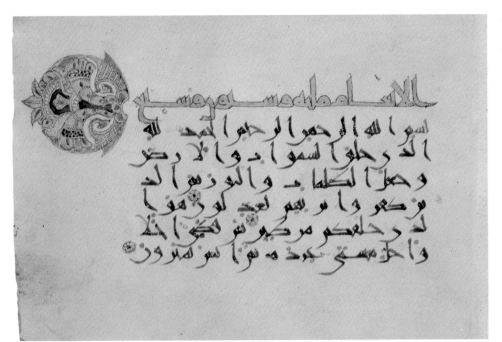

Qur'an Section: Juz'7
Probably Kairouan
9th or early 10th century
Sold 1.4.82 in London for £70,200
($124,956)

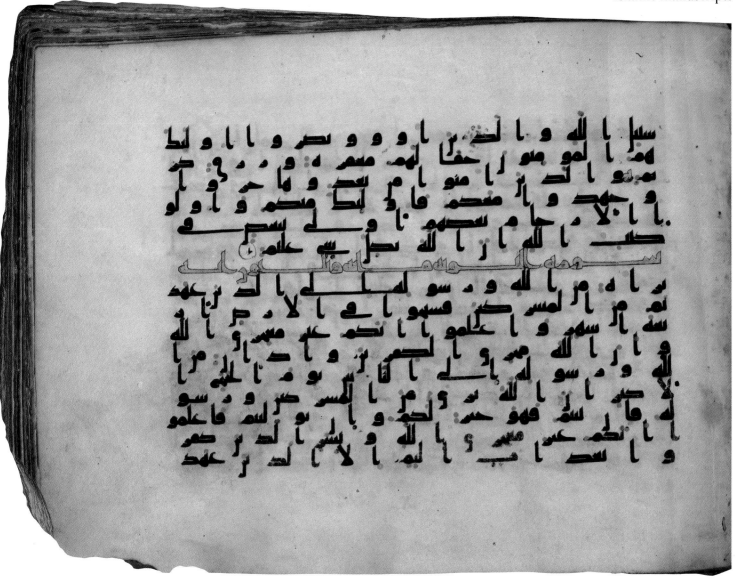

Qur'an Juz'I
Probably Abbasid
9th century
Folio 18.5 x 15.5 cm
Sold 1.4.82 in London for £38,880 ($69,206)

Portrait of a Persian Dignitary
Golconda
*c.*1640-60
32.4 x 20.2 cm
Sold 1.4.82 in London for
£9,180 ($16,340)

Illustration to the Baburnama
Outline by Kanhe, painted by Ikhlas
Mughal, *c.*1589
22.5 x 13.5 cm
Sold 1.4.82 in London for
£11,880 ($21,146)

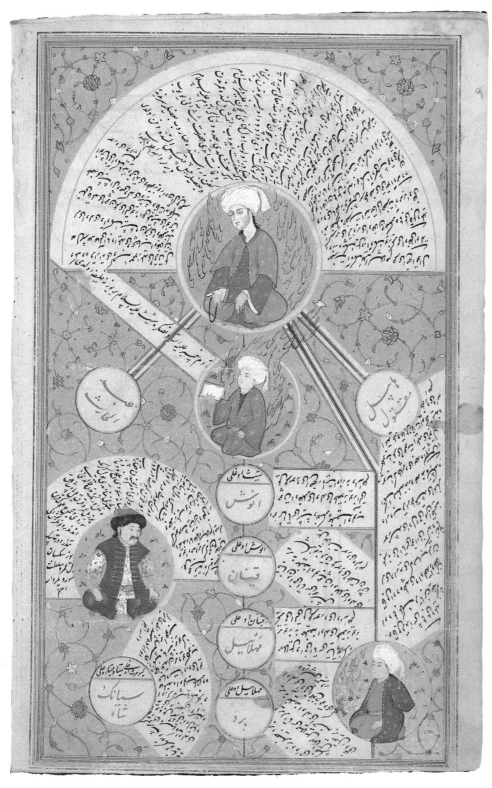

Zubdei Tarih (Cream of
Genealogies)
Ottoman, *c.*1550-1600
Folio 24.5 x 17 cm
Sold 1.4.82 in London for
£8,640 ($15,379)

ANTIQUITIES AND ETHNOGRAPHICA

Romano-Egyptian portrait of a man painted in
encaustic on panel
Second half of 2nd century AD
37.2 cm high
Sold 2.7.82 in London for £18,360 ($32,130)

Attic black-figure neck
amphora, near the
Antimenes Painter
c.520 BC
41 cm high, intact
Sold 10.12.81 in London for
£15,400 ($29,568)

Opposite

Caeretan black-figure
hydria, Herakles in
combat with the Hydra
Second half of 6th century
44.5 cm high; 41 cm wide
at handles
Sold 2.7.82 in London for
£162,000 ($283,500)
From the collection of the
late Count Antoine Seilern

Sarmatian gold
bracelet
*c.*2nd century BC
4.6 cm high;
6.4 cm diam.
Sold 2.7.82 in London
for £32,400 ($56,700)

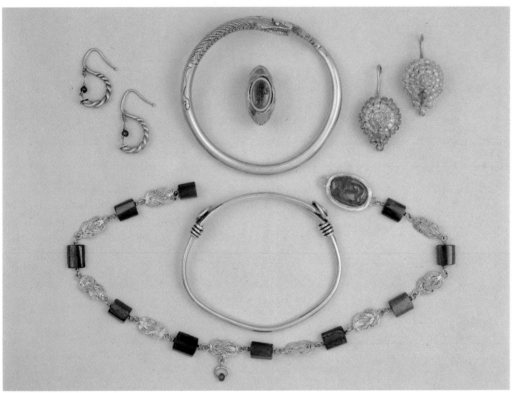

Selection of Greek and Roman jewellery
Sold 2.7.82 in London for a total of £13,727 ($24,022)

Male
6th century BC
15.1 cm high
Sold 10.12.81 in London for
£11,000 ($21,120)

Iberian bronze figure of a horse
c.6th century BC
10 cm high
Sold for £7,150 ($13,728)

Iberian bronze figure of a horse
and warrior
c.3rd century BC
7.8 cm high
Sold for £5,500 ($10,560)

Both sold 10.12.81 in London

Tahiti wood stool, iri or nohora
Late 18th/early 19th century
99 cm wide
Sold 7.7.82 in London for £25,920 ($45,100)

This magnificent stool, similar in form to the headrests so typical of the Society Islands, is the largest of the only four that appear to be recorded and to have survived the intervening 200 years of continuous European contact with Tahiti. One is in the George Ortiz collection. A smaller stool (56.5 cm wide), collected by Sparrman on Cook's Second Voyage, is in the Statens Etnografiska Museum, Stockholm. The fourth is in the collection of a descendant of Tobias Furneaux, Commander of the Adventure, who brought Omai to England from Huahine in 1774, and may be the one that is held by Omai in the portrait attributed to Nathaniel Dance.

William Ellis gives the best account of these stools: "In general they sat cross-legged on mats spread on the floor, but occasionally used a stool which they called iri or nohora. This resembled the pillow in shape, and, though much larger, was made out of a single piece of wood ... The rank of the host was often indicated by the size of this seat, which was used on public occasions, or for the accommodation of a distinguished guest ..."

Far right

Haida or Tsimshian wood
raven rattle
Early 19th century
32 cm long
Sold 7.7.82 in London for
£8,640 ($15,033)
From the collection of the
late James Hooper

Right

Early wood claw-and-ball
club
Iroquois or Algonquin
First half of the
17th century
43 cm long
Sold 7.7.82 in London for
£18,360 ($31,946)

Hawaiian Wooden Figure

HERMIONE WATERFIELD

This aggressive little figure is from the temple Hale-o-Keawe at Honaunau in Kealakekua Bay, in the Kona district of western Hawaii Island. On 15 July 1825 Lord Byron and other members of the ship's company of H.M.S. Blonde visited the temple. (They had previously visited Oahu to deposit for burial the bodies of King Liholiho (Kamehameha II) and Queen Kamamulu who had died of measles in London.) In the temple they found the preserved bones of chiefs of the Island, "curious carved wooden idols," "tapa," calabashes etc. They were allowed to remove artefacts and "the Blonde soon received on board almost all that remained of the ancient deities of the Islands." The old priest in charge of the temple did not allow them to touch the bones. From there they sailed back to England via New Zealand.

An old and worn label on the foot of the figure reads "This idol was taken out of the only remaining Morai Sandwich Islands 1825." This is similar to the entry of another Hawaiian statue which Andrew Bloxam, the naturalist on the Blonde, presented to the Ashmolean Museum, Oxford, and which is now in the Pitt Rivers Museum there. It would therefore seem very possible that Bloxam may have collected the Kona figure, but unfortunately when Richard Cuming acquired it on 30 December 1848 for his museum in Southwark, London, no one recorded from whom it was purchased. A suggestion has been made that it is a statue Bloxam is known to have given Lord Byron, but as there is no evidence to substantiate the fact, we can only be certain that it must have come from Hawaii on H.M.S. Blonde.

Hawaii wood figure,
'aumakua ki'i
41 cm high
Sold 7.7.82 in London
for £18,360 ($31,946)
From the collection of
the late James Hooper

Fang wood female figure, bieri
Equatorial Guinea (Rio Muni)
40.5 cm high
Sold 31.3.82 in London for £32,400 ($58,320)
Collected by a civil engineer attached to the
Spanish Delegation to Rio Muni until 1933

ARMS AND ARMOUR AND MODERN SPORTING GUNS

One of a pair of silver-mounted flintlock holster pistols
By Bate
London, 1769
40.6 cm
Sold 9.6.82 in London for £5,940 ($10,751)

The Brunswick Armour

CLAUDE BLAIR,
Keeper of Metalwork at the Victoria and Albert Museum

In 1928 a sensation was produced among students of English armour by the discovery, in an obscure German castle, of an armour given by Henry Frederick, Prince of Wales (1594-1612), Charles I's elder brother, to his cousin Prince Friedrich Ulrich of Brunswick-Wolfenbuettel (1591-1634). This had been known from documents relating to its manufacture in the royal armour-workshops at Greenwich, but was thought to have long since disappeared. Its reappearance, however, was only to be a temporary one. In 1951, when the Tower of London Armouries held an important loan exhibition of *Armour Made in the Royal Workshops at Greenwich*, it was the only one of the two major surviving products of the workshops not included, since, according to the exhibition catalogue, it was unobtainable because it was "in Russian hands". Events were to prove this last statement to be untrue: 30 years later the armour emerged from obscurity even more sensationally to be sold at Christie's on 18 November 1981 for £418,000 ($802,560), the highest price ever paid for any armour at public auction.

The armour as it now exists comprises a complete suit for a man, and a defence (*shaffron*) for the front of his horse's head decorated *en suite*. The closed helmet with which the suit is equipped is fitted with a visor designed for the type of tournament known as the tilt, which derives its name from the barrier separating the two contestants. The armour also has attachments for various tilt reinforcing-pieces that no longer survive. It may also have had other pieces for converting it for use in other forms of tournament and in the field, like a similar armour, now at Windsor Castle, made for Prince Henry himself. Apart from the loss of these pieces and of the gauntlets – which appear to be the similarly-decorated pair in the Metropolitan Museum, New York – the armour is in astonishing condition. One of its most remarkable features is the retention of nearly all its original leather and textile fittings.

The decoration consists of recessed bands running across the main surfaces, and recessed borders, all of which contain etched strapwork, foliage and other motifs. The bands are alternately broad and narrow. The broad ones are simple parallel-sides strips, the narrow ones are represented as if tied at intervals into double knots with Tudor roses set between them. These bands and borders, as also the buckles and hinges on the armour, retain their original fire-gilding in brilliant condition, while the plain surfaces between retain most of their fire-bluing. This last now varies in colour from its pristine lustrous peacock blue to russet brown.

On the shaffron for the horse, (*see* illustration page 407), is a gilded escutcheon etched with a crested shield of the arms of Brunswick-Wolfenbuettel. The tinctures are coloured with what in Germany is called *Kaltemail* (cold enamel), something that survives on no other English armour. A preliminary analysis of a small sample at the Victoria and Albert Museum indicates that this is merely a kind of wax-based paint.

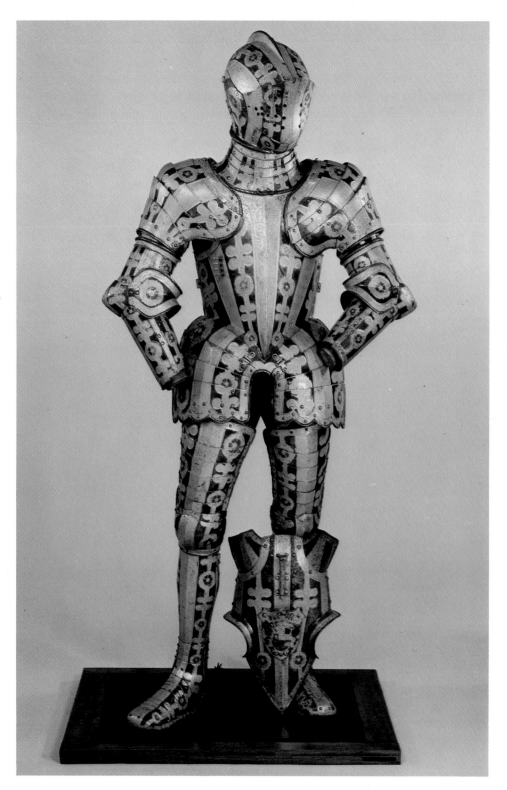

Greenwich armour ordered by
Henry, Prince of Wales for the
Duke of Brunswick, and made
under the Mastership of William
Pickering between 1610 and 1613
Sold 18.11.81 in London for
£418,000 ($802,560)
A record auction price for a suit of
armour and for any item in the
field of arms and armour

In construction and decoration the suit relates closely to a well-known group of rich armours made for various Elizabethan courtiers and illustrated in the so-called *Almain Armourer's Album*, a book of designs in the Victoria and Albert Museum associated with Jacob Halder, a German (*Almain*) who was Master Workman at Greenwich from 1576 to 1608. Since its purchase by the Museum in 1894, the *Album* has been justifiably regarded as the key to the study of the Greenwich workshops, though, in fact, not one of the armours depicted in it can be directly documented as one of their products. As will be shown later, the Brunswick armour *is* so documented, and therefore provides the only absolutely firm evidence for the origins of the armours in the *Album* that it so closely resembles.

The Greenwich workshops were established in the royal palace there by Henry VIII in 1515, and initially staffed with Germans. Apart from a brief sojourn in Southwark they remained at Greenwich until they closed down during the Civil Wars. During most of this time the workshops' main function was to provide armour for the monarch's own person and, to quote a commission set up to investigate the armouries in 1630, "such noble men as bring warrant under the King's hand." It was an expensive privilege to be allowed to purchase an armour from them, and they seem to have worked exclusively for the aristocracy, except perhaps at the very end. In consequence, the standard of workmanship remained very high, though from the last quarter of the 16th century it was allied to extremely conservative design and decoration.

The Brunswick armour is the last major decorated suit known to have been made in the workshops. There can be little doubt that it was ordered in 1610, when Prince Friedrich Ulrich visited England. His cousin, Prince Henry, was given special responsibility for his entertainment, and would no doubt have taken him to the Greenwich workshops, then under the Mastership of Halder's successor, William Pickering (1608-18). The earliest firmly-dated reference to it, however, is in a warrant of 1 May 1612 (Public Record Office E351/2793), authorizing Prince Henry's Treasurer to pay £100 "towards the guilding and compleat garnishing of an Armor for the Duke of Brunswick" to John Pickering, William's son, who worked at Greenwich but was also Henry's personal armourer. An undated, but probably slightly earlier, payment of £80 "to Pickering the Armourer for guilding one Armour for the Duke of Brunswick and for other woorkes" is recorded in the Prince's privy-purse accounts covering the last two years of his life (P.R.O. E351/2794). Half of this £80 must have been for the "other woorkes", since the warrant authorizing final payment of £200 for the armour states that this was the balance owing on a total cost of £340. The warrant (P.R.O., S.P.39/111/4), issued in the King's name on 11 July 1614, 20 months after Henry's death, refers merely to "one rich Armour with all peeces complete fayrely guilt and graven" which "was made in the office of our Armery of Greenwich by William Pickering our Master Workeman...by the Commaundement of our Late deere sonne Prince Henry." That this was the Brunswick armour is in no doubt, however, because the warrant is the only document connected with the completion of the Prince's affairs that can possibly relate to the two payments previously mentioned.

August, Duke of Brunswick (1579-1666)

Despite the date on the authorizing warrant, Pickering was not actually paid his £200 until March 1615 (F. Devon, *Issues of the Exchequer*, 1836, p.173). The armour itself, however, had long since gone to its owner. This is shown by a warrant issued in February 1613 for the payment of £40 travelling and other expenses to "John Douglas, Gentleman, appointed to go to the Prince of Brunswick with armour and other thinges prepared by the late Prince to be sent unto him" (Devon, p.159). The "other thinges" were perhaps a "new Tylting sadle of cullered velutt richly embrodered with other furniture for the same" also made for the Prince of Brunswick at a cost of £198.16s.3d., and "a rich petticoate wrought with three borders all over vpon white sattin grounde with gould silver & silke", costing £116.1s.0d., made for his sister, both of which are mentioned in Prince Henry's wardrobe account for 1611-12 (P.R.O., A.O.1/2346/40).

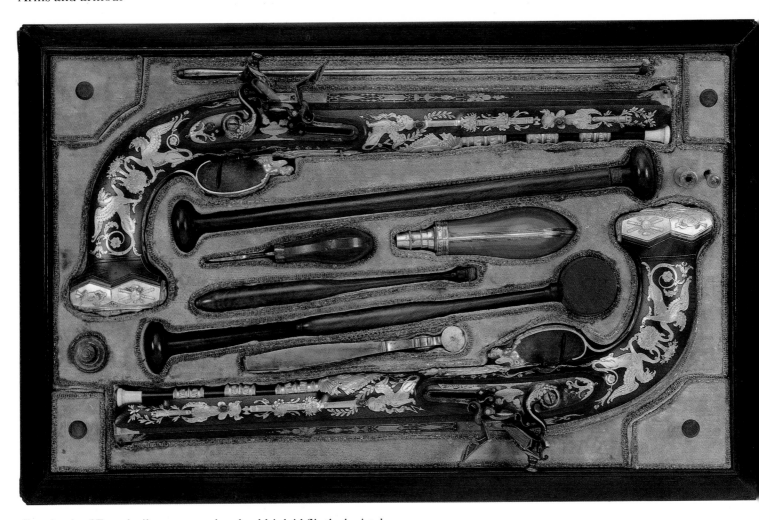

Cased pair of French silver-mounted and gold-inlaid flintlock pistols
By Boutet
Versailles, No.13
40.6 cm
Sold 18.11.81 in London for £66,000 ($126,720)
From the collection of Mrs N. Chamberlayne-Macdonald
Presented in 1796 by Murat, later King of Naples, to the Hereditary Prince of the Two Sicilies

Irish stirrup-hilted cavalry officer's
presentation sword
Signed Jno. Read, Maker,
College Green, Dublin, c.1799
Blade 69.1 cm
Sold 7.4.82 in London for
£5,940 ($10,514)
Now in The Armouries,
H.M. Tower of London

Swedish cruciform-hilted sword of
honour
Signed Liljedahl
Stockholm, c.1840
Blade 83.8 cm
Sold 7.4.82 in London for
£3,240 ($5,735)
Now in The Armouries,
H.M. Tower of London

French silver-gilt hilted presentation
sword
Inscribed "Récompense Nationale" and
signed "Manuf^{re} Imp^{le} à Versailles,
Boutet et Fils"
Paris silver hallmarks for 1789-1809,
maker's mark NB, a pistol between
Blade 79.3 cm
Sold 7.4.82 in London for £4,536
($8,029)

These swords were removed from Loughton, County Offaly, the seat of the first and second Barons Bloomfield. They
are believed to have belonged to Benjamin, first Baron Bloomfield (1768-1846), who was a close friend of the
Prince Regent (later King George IV)

The Colt/Christie's Auction

PETER HAWKINS

The arms sale held in association with Colt Industries on October 7 1981 at our Park Avenue premises was an historic occasion in many ways. It was our first gun sale in New York, the first by any company in the city for many years, probably the most distinguished public auction of American firearms ever held, and without doubt the most highly acclaimed and widely publicized.

Since the idea was first suggested some two years in advance, the combined efforts of Colt's, firearms historian Larry Wilson, and Christie's own experts had created widespread interest (and a measure of controversy) in the gun-collecting world. The sale brought together an unprecedented array of collectors' pieces, among them many guns previously owned by famous people – Ernest Hemingway, Charles Lindbergh, Mrs Teddy Roosevelt and Kit Carson.

Anwar Sadat was assassinated in Egypt on Tuesday, October 6, but the next day in gun-conscious New York our saleroom was filled to overflowing. As well as establishing a record for catalogue sales (6,000 copies were printed, of which only 100 remained unsold on the day of sale), over 20 new auction records were set, including:

$104,500 (£55,882) for a modern sporting gun (*see* page 417)
$82,500 (£44,117) for a Colt firearm (illustrated overleaf)
$55,000 (£29,411) for a Kentucky rifle
$55,000 (£29,411) for a shoulder-stocked Colt revolver (illustrated overleaf)
$49,500 (£26,470) for a Winchester firearm (*see* page 420) and
$33,000 (£17,647) for a Colt Paterson revolver (illustrated opposite)

To these records must be added the auction's most significant achievement: its contribution towards the growing public awareness of firearms as works of art. The skill of some of the world's greatest engravers, both past and present, featured prominently in the 116 lots. In the words of the reporter of the *New York Times*: "Guns for once brought pleasure and commerce to New York City last week...the care with which they were handled demonstrated their meaning and value...the auction at Christie's was not so much a display of arms but art."

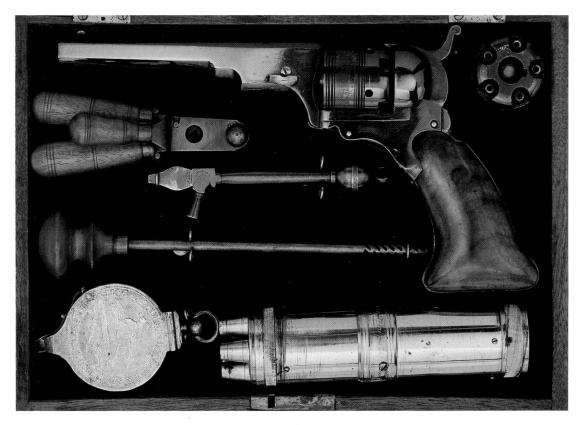

Cased No.3 Belt Model Colt Paterson Revolver, No.684
Barrel 11.6 cm
Sold 7.10.81 in New York for $33,000 (£17,647)
From the Collection of Colt Industries, Colt Firearms Division

Cased Colt Model 1851 Navy
with attachable canteen shoulder
stock, No.91997
Decorated by the Gustave Young
shop in an unusual arabesque
variant pattern
*c.*1859
Barrel 19 cm
Sold 7.10.81 in New York for
$55,000 (£29,411)

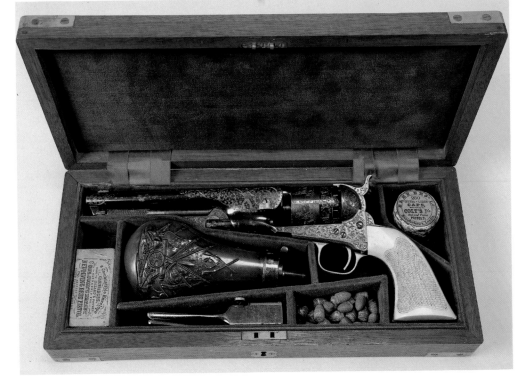

The Cox Navy: cased Colt model
1861 Navy revolver, No.23371IP,
presented to New York banking
executive William H. Cox
Engraving attributed to
Gustave Young
Barrel 19 cm
Sold 7.10.81 in New York for
$82,500 (£44,117)
Now in the Colt Industries
Collection
Both from the collection of
Mr Jerry D. Berger of
Kansas City

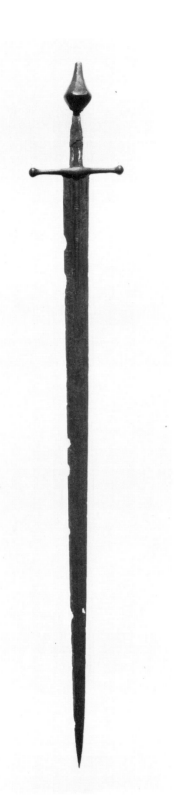

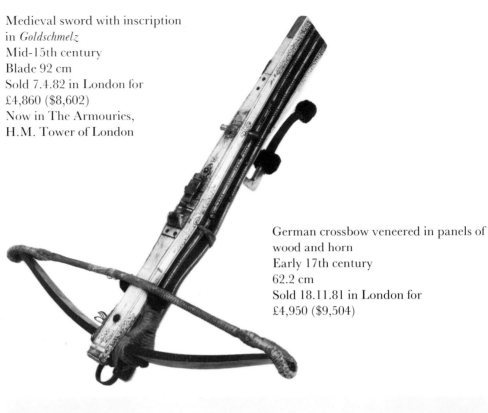

Medieval sword with inscription
in *Goldschmelz*
Mid-15th century
Blade 92 cm
Sold 7.4.82 in London for
£4,860 ($8,602)
Now in The Armouries,
H.M. Tower of London

German crossbow veneered in panels of
wood and horn
Early 17th century
62.2 cm
Sold 18.11.81 in London for
£4,950 ($9,504)

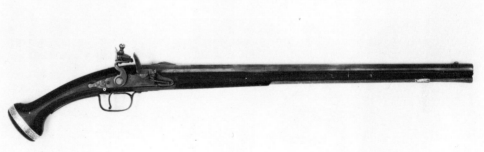

Dutch long flintlock holster pistol with
ebony stock
By Jan Aerts
Maestrecht, mid-17th century
72.9 cm
Sold 7.4.82 in London for £7,560
($13,381)

Portions of a half-armour for the field, probably made in the Greenwich workshops for William Herbert, 1st Earl of Pembroke *c*.1540-50
Sold 18.11.81 in London for £18,700 ($35,904)
Now in The Armouries, H.M. Tower of London
From the armoury of the Earls of Pembroke and Montgomery, Wilton House
Previously sold in 1921

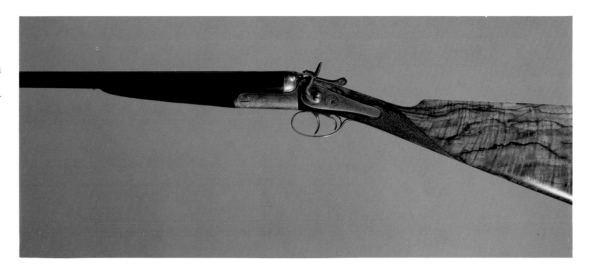

Pair of hammer
ejector 12-bore
D.B. guns
By J. Purdey, London
Built in 1897 and still
in original nitro proof
Sold 17.3.82 in
London for £9,504
($17,582)

Modern Sporting Guns and Vintage Firearms

CHRISTOPHER BRUNKER

Why some antique firearms are included in this section is a paradox that may warrant explanation. Briefly, it stems from the Firearms Act, 1968. This exempts any "antique firearm" kept as "a curiosity or ornament" from the controls imposed on all other firearms. The exemption makes good sense, but difficulties have arisen in its application because the Act defines "firearm", but not "antique".

The police have to administer the law, whether it is clear or not. Where the police believe there is doubt, they may feel obliged to draft rules of interpretation. These do not have the force of law, but they do make clear how the police will apply the law, subject to the Courts. A Metropolitan Police ruling on "antique firearm" is currently used in many police areas: principally, it excludes from consideration as "antique" all cartridge breech-loaders, irrespective of age. This definition by type is simple and practicable from a police viewpoint, but essentially unsatisfactory in seeking to amend, rather than interpret, a statute. If the exemption referred to "obsolete" firearms, a definition by type alone might well be appropriate, but as the word is "antique", one cannot reasonably dismiss the relevance of age. Case law supports this view, but prosecutions are still brought under the "type" definition, and more positive guidance is required. In the meantime, it is safer to conform to local police practice.

In the absence of a statutory definition, only the Courts can say what constitutes "antique" in law, but those best qualified to say what "antique" means in fact are the specialist collectors, dealers, auctioneers and others familiar with firearms and antiques. It is time we pooled and clarified this expertise, for the benefit of all.

415

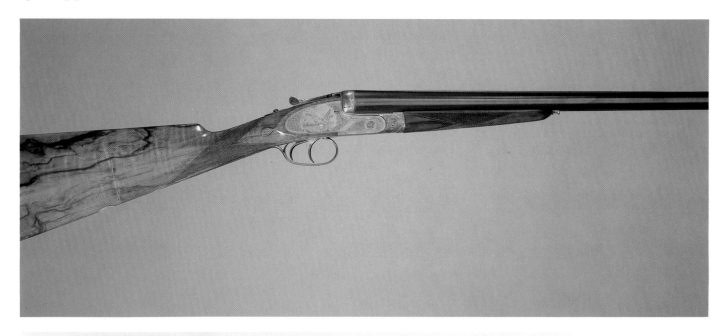

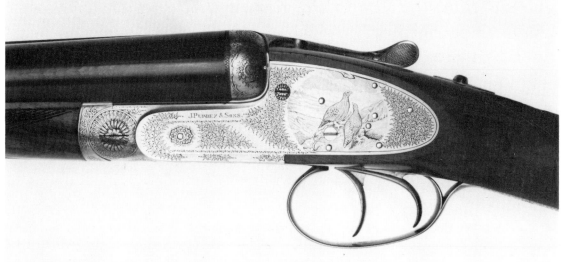

Pair of "London best" sidelock ejector 12-bore (2¾ in) D.B. guns with game engraving
By J. Purdey, London
Built in 1980
The engraving, though apparently unsigned, is by Stephen Kelly and includes pairs of mallard, pheasant, grey partridge and red grouse in characteristic settings
Sold 16.6.82 in London for £18,900 ($34,398)

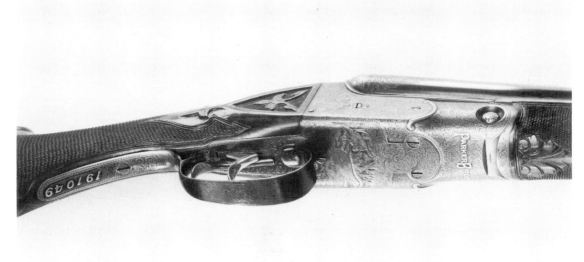

Parker "A-1 Special" 28-bore (2¾ in) D.B. boxlock ejector gun with gold-inlaid name and
serial number
By Parker Bros, Meriden, Connecticut
Built *c.*1920
L.L. Baer, *The Parker Gun*, estimates that of approximately 320 Parker "A-1 Specials" built, only about
eight were 28-bores. He also refers to the rarity of gold-inlays
Sold 7.10.81 in New York for $104,500 (£56,440)
Record auction price for a modern sporting gun

Sporting guns

Pair of single-trigger
sidelock ejector 12-bore
D.B. guns
By Boss, London
Built in 1898 (barrels of
one gun sleeved by Boss
in 1981)
Sold 17.3.82 for £8,640
($15,984)

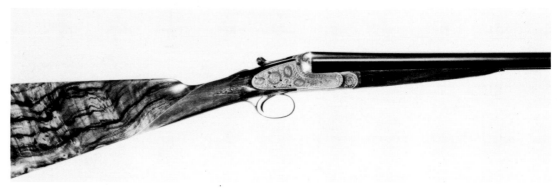

Pair of "Utility XXV"
boxlock ejector 12-bore
D.B. guns
By E.J. Churchill,
London
Built in 1931
Sold 30.9.81 for £3,300
($6,237)

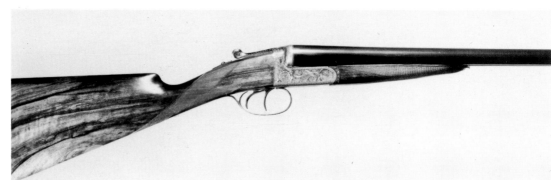

Sidelock ejector 16-bore
D.B. gun with single-
trigger
By F. Beesley, London
Built in 1911, when it
cost 63 guineas
Sold 16.6.82 for £3,672
($6,609)

Ornate under-and-over
16-bore (2¾ in) D.B.
boxlock ejector gun with
dummy sideplates
By Simson, Suhl
Built c.1964
Sold 7.12.81 for £3,190
($5,901)

All sold in London

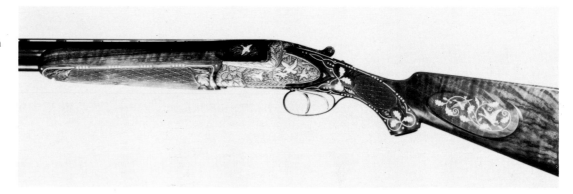

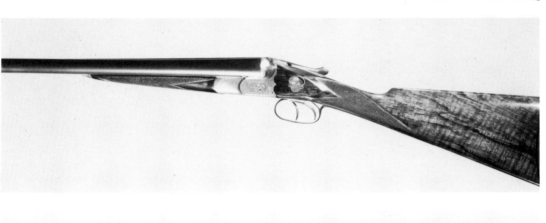
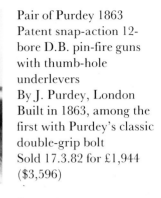

Pair of Purdey 1863
Patent snap-action 12-
bore D.B. pin-fire guns
with thumb-hole
underlevers
By J. Purdey, London
Built in 1863, among the
first with Purdey's classic
double-grip bolt
Sold 17.3.82 for £1,944
($3,596)

Pape 1867 Patent snap-
action 12-bore D.B.
hammer gun with
thumb-underlever
By W.R. Pape,
Newcastle-upon-Tyne
Built c.1870
Sold 17.3.82 for £756
($1,398)

Pair of "Royal" boxlock
non-ejector 12-bore D.B.
guns
By W.W. Greener,
Birmingham
Built c.1886/7
A variant of Greener's
"Facile Princeps"
hammerless action
Sold 7.12.81 for £1,650
($3,052)

Pair of Lancaster 1879
Patent ejector 12-bore
D.B. backlock guns
By F.T. Baker,
London
Built c.1890
Sold 16.6.82 for £1,728
($3,110)

All sold in London

"Royal" sidelock ejector .300 (H&H Magnum Belted Rimless) D.B. rifle, with telescope
By Holland & Holland, London
Built in 1965
Sold 30.9.81 in London for £9,350 ($17,297)

Winchester Model 1873 "1 of 1000" rifle in .44-40 calibre with factory-engraved frame
By Winchester Repeating Arms Co, New Haven, Connecticut
Built in 1875
Only about forty Model 1873 "1 of 1000" rifles are known and very few of these have frame engraving
Sold 7.10.81 in New York for $49,500 (£26,735)
Record auction price for a Winchester firearm

Lancaster 1881 Patent four-barrelled .455 oval-bore pistol
By C. Lancaster, London
Built c.1884
Sold 16.6.82 in London for £756 ($1,360)

SALES IN ITALY, THE NETHERLANDS, CHRISTIE'S EAST, NEW YORK AND AT CHRISTIE'S & EDMISTON'S, GLASGOW

Neapolitan bureau bookcase
18th century
242 x 105 cm
Sold 28.4.82 in Rome for L.28,000,000 (£11,965)

FRANCESCO HAYEZ: *Fleeing before the Storm*
155 x 115 cm
Sold 18.5.82 in Rome for L.20,000,000 (£9,900)

GIAN LORENZO BERNINI: *David*
74 x 65.5 cm
Sold 24.11.81 in Rome for L.291,200,000 (£124,444)

FILIPPO PALIZZI: *Setter and Pointer flushing a Quail*
115 x 186 cm
Sold 18.5.82 in Rome for L.56,000,000 (£24,003)

Pair of creamware neoclassical vases
46.5 cm high
Sold 30.4.82 in Rome for
L.16,800,000 (£7,179)

Far right

Meissen teapot with Augsburg
goldmalerei
*c.*1725
13 cm high
Sold 30.4.82 in Rome for
L.16,800,000 (£7,179)

Right

Meissen covered jug with Augsburg
goldmalerei, and silver-gilt mounts
By Paul Solanier, 1722-4
20 cm high
Sold 30.4.82 in Rome for
L.21,280,000 (£9,094)

JAN GOSSAERT VAN MABUSE:
Portrait of a Young Gentleman
Oil on panel
38 x 28 cm
Sold 1.10.81 in
Amsterdam for
D.fl.855,000 (£180,370)

CORNELIS SPRINGER: *The Lombard on the Oude Zijds Voorburgwal, Amsterdam*
Oil on panel
Signed and dated 1884
65.8 x 85 cm
Sold 6.4.82 in Amsterdam for D.fl.250,800 (£54,521)

Gold standing cup and
cover
Signed P. Metayer
1754
24.5 cm high
Sold 6.10.81 in
Amsterdam for
D.fl.524,000 (£114,000)

Part of a collection of
400 polychrome, blue
and white tiles
Sold 13.10.81 in
Amsterdam
The tile of the three-
masted ship fetched
D.fl.27,360 (£5,984)
Record auction price
for a Dutch tile

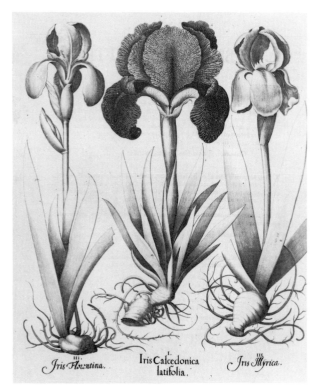

Seba (Albert):
Locupletissimi Rerum
Naturalium Thesauri
Accurata Descriptio
First edition, 4 vols.; 449
engraved plates, 175 of
them double-page, all of
them finely hand-
coloured by a
contemporary hand
Text in Latin and French
Large folio:
50.8 x 33.7 cm
Amsterdam, 1734-65
Sold 17.6.82 in
Amsterdam for
D.fl.51,300 (£10,940)

Besler (Basilius): Hortus Eystettensis
3 vols.; 367 engraved plates with 1084 figures
Large folio: 50.4 x 40.4 cm
1713
Sold 17.6.82 in Amsterdam for D.fl.104,880
(£22,360)

Weinmann (Johann
Wilhelm): Duidelyke
Vertoning
8 vols.; 1025 fine
botanical plates, printed
in colour and finished by
hand
Folio, Amsterdam, Zach.
Robberg
1736-48
Sold 17.6.82 in
Amsterdam for
D.fl.51,300 (£10,940)

Louis XVI silver tureen on stand
By Philippus Priée
Middleburg, 1773
Tureen 30 cm wide
Sold 20.4.82 in Amsterdam for D.fl.34,200 (£7,435)

Walnut group of the
Virgin and Child
Probably Normandy,
14th century
73 cm high
Sold 21.10.81 in
Amsterdam for
D.fl.47,880 (£10,408)

Blue and white Delft tulip vase
117 cm high
Sold 14.10.81 in Amsterdam for
D.fl.22,800 (£4,956)

Dutch bronze sixteen-branch chandelier
17th century
110 cm high
Sold 16.12.81 in Amsterdam for D.fl.57,000 (£12,127)

431

HUGO SALMSON: *Afternoon in the Garden*
Signed and dated 1875
On panel
26.6 x 20.3 cm
Sold 24.2.82 for $8,250 (£4,388)

EDWARD SEAGO: *In the Tuileries*
Signed
45.7 x 60.9 cm
Sold 27.10.81 for $11,550 (£5,923)

Above

Ebony burr-walnut and ivory Renaissance style writing cabinet
146 cm wide; 184 cm high
Sold 16.3.82 for $49,500 (£26,612)

Above right

Two from a set of 10 George I style walnut dining chairs
Sold 26.1.81 for $12,650 (£6,801)

Right

Federal mahogany console table
New York
101.6 cm long
Sold 27.10.81 for $15,400 (£7,897)

Far left

Mid-19th century
pitcher and matching
goblet, in the Gothic
taste
By Zalmon Bostick
New York, 1845
27.9 cm and
19.5 cm high
Sold 10.2.82 for $9,350
(£5,026)
Acquired by the
Brooklyn Museum,
New York

Left

Monumental 19th
century French bronze
figure of a Nubian
maiden playing a harp
Paris
189.1 cm high
Sold 13.5.82 for
$20,000 (£11,111)

Far left

Berlin KMP plaque
painted with Hagar
and Ishmael
Signed Links
19th century
48.2 x 13.9 cm
Sold 17.11.81 for
$15,400 (£8,105)

Left

Ormolu-mounted
marquetry, bronze,
marble and tulipwood
Psyche mirror from
the 1900 Exposition
Universelle
264 cm high;
169 cm wide
Sold 18.5.82 for
$50,600 (£28,111)

Right

F.C. Lecoultre bells in sight interchangeable cylinder music box on stand
Geneva, *c*.1860
Sold 8.12.81 for $8,800 (£4,631)

Pair of "ruby slippers" from the 1939 film *The Wizard of Oz*
Sold 1.10.81 for $13,200 (£6,947)

Far left

Camel Corps Figure from a set of 131 lead soldiers made by Britains
1910
9 cm high
The trooper belongs to one of the camel mounted detachments of British cavalry formed during the late 19th century
Sold 1.10.81 for $616 (£324)
Record auction price for a single lead soldier

Left

Deep green velvet coat by Mariano Fortuny
Round label, *Mariano Fortuny, Venise*
Sold 14.10.81 for $8,500 (£4,473)
Record auction price for a Fortuny dress

435

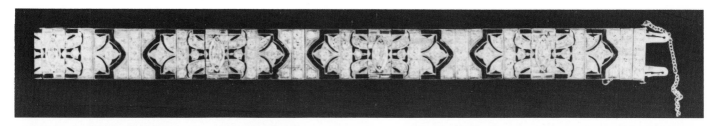

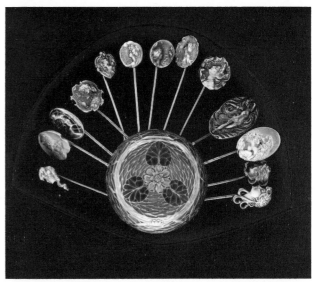

Top

Art Deco sapphire and diamond bracelet
Sold 19.10.81 for $7,700 (£4,052)

Above

Art Deco jewelled and enamelled evening bag
Sold 25.2.82 for $2,200 (£1,222)

Above right

Gold and plique-à-jour enamel box
French
Third quarter of 19th century
Sold 25.2.82 for $5,500 (£3,055) and a group of gold
stick pins which sold for a total of $3,575 (£1,986)

Diamond brooch, designed as a pavé-set diamond and
platinum bow with circular-cut diamond knot
Signed Webb
Three largest diamonds approx 6.65 carats
Sold 19.10.81 for $16,500 (£8,684)

EDWARD ATKINSON
HORNEL: *Water Nymphs*
Signed and dated
1904
91.5 x 76 cm
Sold 8.7.82
in Glasgow
for £15,500 ($26,350)
Record auction
price for a
work by the
artist

Far left

Life-sized model of a
capercaillie
London hallmark for 1900
Sold 30.3.82 for £1,500
($2,655)

Left

Pair of Bohemian blue-flash
and blue overlay cylindrical
vases
31.8 cm high
Sold 18.3.81 for £650 ($1,183)

Edwardian pendant, composed of 16
diamonds enclosing a rectangular pink
tourmaline
Sold 16.3.82 for £4,600 ($8,464)

Victorian gilt-mounted flagon,
the ivory body carved with
scenes from a lion hunt
By E & Co., Birmingham,
1858
36 cm high
Sold 30.3.82 for £2,500
($4,475)

JAMES ARCHER, R.S.A.:
Hearts are Trumps
Signed with monogram and
dated 1872
79 x 108 cm
Sold 1.10.81 for £8,000
($14,400)

CHARLÈS MARTIN HARDIE:
An Unrecorded Coronation
Signed and dated 1888
106 x 155 cm
Sold 1.10.81 for £12,000
($21,600)
The subject represents
Mary Stuart and her "Four
Marys" at Inchmaholm
Priory in 1508

Regency rosewood and satinwood crossband sofa table
193 cm wide, open
Sold 24.2.82 for £6,500 ($11,960)

One from a set of 14
Regency mahogany
dining chairs
including four open
armchairs
Sold 24.2.82 for £6,800
($12,580)

Late 17th century oak
court cupboard carved
with the initials L.H.
and the date 1694
Sold 24.2.82 for £3,200
($5,888)
Removed from the Palace
of Holyroodhouse

PHOTOGRAPHS
CHRISTIE'S SOUTH KENSINGTON
AND CHRISTIE'S EAST, NEW YORK

Wooded scene: large waxed-paper
negative by George Shaw,
Birmingham, from a group of 20,
early 1850s
Sold 29.10.81 in London for
£3,800 ($6,954)

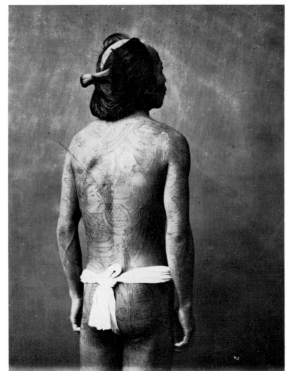

Above left

Portrait of Alexander Dumas
Albumen print, from an important portrait
album: Photographs by Herbert Watkins,
Regent Street
*c.*1860
Sold in London 11.3.82 for £750 ($1,365)

Above

Whitby and Environs, an album including 35
photographs by F.M. Sutcliffe
Sold 11.3.82 in London for £1,400 ($2,548)

Left

Views and Costumes of Japan by Stillfried & Anderson
Yokohama: a good album of 100 photographs
Sold 11.3.82 in London for £1,200 ($2,184)

Right

Monseratt
Albumen print, from an
album of 56 photographs by
Charles Clifford recording
the 1860 royal journey of
Her Majesty Queen
Isabel II of Spain to
Eastern Spain
Sold 29.10.81 in London
for £3,800 ($6,954)

Far right

Tintern Abbey with girl
seated in portico reading a
book, by Roger Fenton
Salt print, 1850s
23.4 x 20 cm
Sold 11.3.82 in London for
£2,000 ($3,640)

Cemetery, Agra, with figure
seated in foreground, by
Dr John Murray
Albumen print
45 x 39.3 cm
Sold 11.3.82 in London
for £1,200 ($2,184)

443

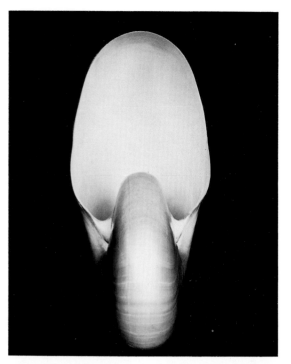

Far left

Edward Weston:
Nautilus
Gelatin silver print
March, 1927
Sold 10.11.81 in New York
for $28,600 (£15,052)
Record auction price
for a 20th century
photograph and for a
photograph by
Weston

Left

Edward Steichen:
Gloria Swanson (1924)
Toned gelatin silver
print
Sold 25.6.82 in New York
for $7,700 (£4,277)

Edward Steichen:
Solitude –
F. Holland Day
Platinum print, 1901
Sold 10.11.81 in New York
for $19,800 (£10,421)

Gertrude Käsebier: *Blessed art thou among women*
Platinum print
1899
Sold 10.11.81 in New York for
$20,900 (£11,000)

E.J. Bellocq: *Prostitute, Storyville District, New Orleans*
Gelatin silver contact print
c.1912
Sold 26.5.82 in New York for $8,800 (£4,888)
Record auction price for a photograph by Bellocq

Andrew Joseph Russell: *The Great West*
illustrated in a series of views across the
continent; taken along the line of the Union
Pacific Railroad, West from Omaha, Nebraska
Oblong quarto
London, 1869
50 albumen prints
Sold 26.5.82 in New York for
$41,800 (£23,222)

Edward Weston: *Wind Erosion – Dunes*
at Oceano, California
Gelatin silver print
1936
Sold 10.11.81 in New York
for $12,100 (£6,368)

CHRISTIE'S SOUTH KENSINGTON AND MODELS AT THE BRITISH ENGINEERIUM

The sale of the Wardrobe of The Old Vic Company on the evening of 3.12.81 took place on the stage of the actual theatre and totalled £24,500 ($48,020)

Christie's South Kensington

WILLIAM BROOKS

Over the past few years Christie's South Kensington has seen a continuous expansion into new areas of collecting, and within these fields we have seen articles undergo a metamorphosis from chattels through collectables to Fine Art. This expansion is both a cause and an effect of a widening of interests, expanding in turn the potential market for the auction rooms.

Christie's South Kensington has broken new ground by inaugurating auctions catering for new areas of specialist collecting, including the highly successful Topographical sales, which have been instrumental in setting world record prices as shown by the £85,000 ($154,700) achieved for a work by Krieghoff. It has also enhanced its reputation for such unique sales as the British Racing Motors (B.R.M.) Collection, which achieved in excess of £500,000 ($920,000), and the sale of the contents of the Bath Club, which lamentably signified the end of an era of London club history.

The sale of the wardrobe of the Old Vic Company, attended with great interest by the public, press and television, was held in the renowned theatre, in an atmosphere reminiscent of a Gala performance; while pupils from the Webber Douglas Academy of Dramatic Art performed vignettes from relevant plays, the auctioneer conducted the sale from the front of the stage, indicating perhaps that all auctioneers are ham actors at heart! At South Kensington another theatrical sale, including costumes worn by such legendary figures as Rudolph Valentino and Lord Olivier and the costumes from the stage play of *My Fair Lady* also attracted considerably publicity along with enthusiastic attendance.

The field of studio sales has become increasingly associated with Christie's South Kensington, the contents of the studio of K. Nixon, illustrator of such classic children's books as *Brer Rabbit* and works by Enid Blyton, was a particular success. Another unusual sale held here was that of the renowned Hart/Hall Bird Collection sold on behalf of Stowe School, consisting of over 30 examples of beautifully mounted birds, all of whom had been sighted in the British Isles.

The sale of the Friberg collection of mechanical music attracted international interest, and grossed over £300,000 ($567,000): a unique sale of an unequalled private collection requiring the transportation of over 500 items, many of them of enormous weight and fragility from Denmark, to form a one-day sale held at South Kensington. While this was a record sale, we were also delighted to entertain and be entertained by the whole Friberg family during the run up to the sale. Through the view days and the actual sale, their enthusiasm and expertise were appreciated by us all, including our buyers.

To conclude this year's report, I would like to thank all the staff for their continued enthusiasm and hard work, and in particular to thank them for the efforts they have put in to over 20 Charity Auctions and Valuations that South Kensington have held during the past year, including among others the Royal Institute for the Blind, The National Trust, N.S.P.C.C., R.N.I.B., Imperial Cancer Research, British Sailors Society, and The Artists Benevolent Fund.

PIETER CORNELIS DOMMERSEN:
On the Znider Estuary
Signed and dated 1884
On panel
39 x 59 cm
Sold 16.9.81 for £3,600
($6,444)

ALFONS WALDE: *Figures by an*
Alpine Chalet
Signed
42 x 58 cm
Sold 20.1.82 for £4,500
($8,460)

449

HELEN ALLINGHAM: *Reaping Corn*
Signed and dated 1878
Watercolour
11.5 x 19 cm
Sold 9.11.81 for £2,200 ($4,136)

HELEN ALLINGHAM: *The Cottage Garden*
Signed
Watercolour heightened with body colour
and white
23 x 25.5 cm
Sold 5.4.82 for £3,000 ($5,400)

Pair of George I style
silver double-lipped
sauce boats
Crichton Bros.
London, 1910
20 cm wide

Pair of dog-nose
sauce ladles
London, 1912
Sold 17.5.82 for
£450 ($823)

Continental model of
a knight in armour
with carved ivory
face
Import marks
23 cm high
Sold 22.3.82 for
£420 ($760)

Silver-mounted
wooden mazer-bowl
By Omar Ramsden
London, 1938
26 cm diam.
Sold 1.6.82 for £1,800
($3,276)

451

A Suite of Embroidered Hangings

SUSAN MAYOR

On the 14th and 15th June the Hangar saleroom at Christie's South Kensington was momentarily transformed into a palace: one of its aisles had been hung as a room with a magnificent suite of embroideries.

These hangings are not only dazzlingly beautiful, they are also a remarkable survival. Hangings of this quality are rare. Hangings for a complete room are rarer still. Their condition was certainly extraordinary; they had been hanging unprotected by glass for over 160 years, first in the Comtess de Flahaut's Paris house, later at Meikleour in Perthshire. Half of them had been simply nailed to the wall without a protective linen backing. They retain their fresh sheen as if brand new, but inevitably they have faded from very bright clear colours to pretty pastel shades. Even so, the present colours are in many ways more attractive and practical as interior decoration.

The set comprises nine satin panels of various widths and two pairs of curtains embroidered in Canton with a panorama of exotic flowering trees fluttering with colourful birds and butterflies. The tree trunks and the landscapes are worked in chenille. The suite originally formed part of the celebrated collection of furniture, furnishings and *objets d'art* formed by Margaret, Baroness Nairne and Keith (1788-1867) and her husband Auguste-Charles-Joseph, Comte de Flahaut (1785-1870), natural son of Talleyrand and nephew of the Comte d'Angivillier, Marigny's nephew and successor as *Directeur-général des Bâtiments du Roi*. These hangings are traditionally associated with Marie Antoinette, but it seems more likely that they were commissioned by the Flahauts for their house in Paris, the Hôtel de Massa, following their marriage in 1817. The Flahaut's daughter, Emily, heiress of Meikleour, married the 4th Marquess of Lansdowne in 1843 and it was her great-grandson, the 8th Marquis, who sold the hangings at Christie's South Kensington for £19,000 ($32,300).

Right
One from a suite of embroidered wall hangings
comprising 11 panels and two pairs of curtains
Canton
Early 19th century
Sold for a total of £19,000 ($32,300) on behalf of
The Marquis of Lansdowne

Below
One of a pair of four pairs of chintz curtains
Indian, 18th century, the borders French
426 x 137 cm approx.
Sold for a total of £6,000 ($10,200)

Below right

Detail from a set of crewelwork bed hangings,
comprising four curtains and two valances
English, mid-18th century
Sold for £6,500 ($11,050)

All sold 14 and 15.6.82 at Christie's
South Kensington

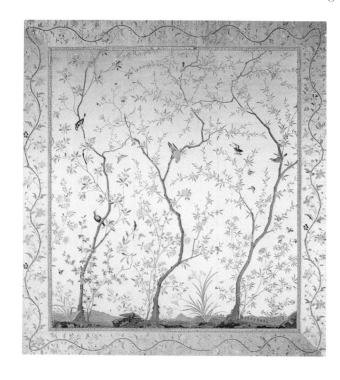

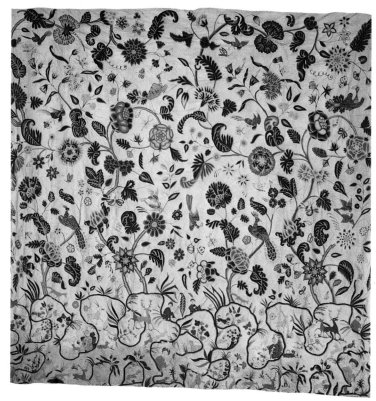

Edwardian rosewood Carlton
House style desk
121 cm wide
Sold 2.9.81 for £720 ($1,288)

Regency style mahogany
Carlton House writing table
19th century
99 cm long
Sold 24.2.82 for £2,600
($4,810)

Victorian burr-walnut dining table
126 cm long
Sold 28.4.82 for £800 ($1,432)

Pair of Regency simulated dwarf
cabinets with marble tops with
painted decoration
86 cm wide
Sold 3.3.82 for £2,400 ($4,344)

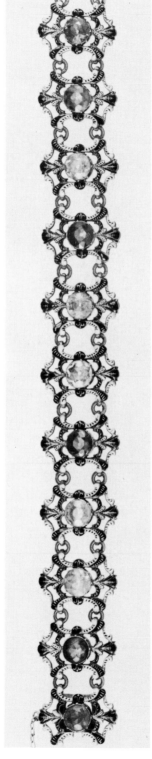

Bracelet of 11 openwork links decorated with black and white enamel, each link set with a zircon, bearing the mark C & AG for Carlo and Arthur Guiliano
Sold 15.5.82 for £4,000 ($7,400)

Art Deco design opal mosaic plaque pendant with diamond and sapphire mounts
Sold 16.2.82 for £2,400 ($4,440)

Antique carved coral brooch of child's head bordered by a fruiting vine and two masks with three urn drops attached
Sold 3.11.81 for £720 ($1,360)

Silver open-face keyless pocket watch with six subsidiary dials for the Far East
Sold 26.1.81 for £620 ($1,159)

One of a pair of 19th century Imari jars
and covers
107 cm high
Sold 3.11.81 for £4,200 ($7,938)

One of a pair of late 18th century Chinese
blue and white soup-tureens
33 cm wide
Sold 23.11.81 for £700 ($1,344)

Japanese cloisonné vase decorated in
the style of Namikawa
45.7 cm high
Sold 11.3.82 for £1,100 ($2,002)

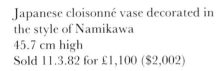

Early 18th century Japanese Imari
barber's bowl
25 cm diam.
Sold 8.3.82 for £450 ($828)

Theatre Sales

EMMA CLARK

Of the two sales of Theatrical Costume and Memorabilia held by Christie's South Kensington in the last season there is no doubt that the most exciting was the sale of the Wardrobe of the Old Vic Company. On the evening of December 3rd, 1981, crowds packed into the Old Vic Theatre to see the wonderful collection of costumes and props on this stage for the last time. With Christopher Elwes conducting the auction from the rostrum at one side of the stage, the costumes hanging on the "fly-bars" above, and students from the Webber Douglas Academy of Dramatic Art modelling the lots as they came up for sale – often reciting witty lines from the relevant plays – it was a stunning spectacle and as smooth and professional a performance as London's most famous theatre could wish for.

The Old Vic Company was originally called Prospect Productions Ltd, and was formed at the Oxford Playhouse in 1961. In the 1970s it became the leading national touring company, Sheridan Morley writing in Punch in 1977: "With the one obvious exception of the RSC, no theatre company formed outside London since the war has equalled the distinction and range of work that has been Prospect's achievement over the last decade." Because of its excellent reputation, Prospect was offered the Old Vic as its permanent home when the National Theatre Company left it in 1976. From 1977 to 1978 they presented 10 major productions, including *Hamlet, Anthony and Cleopatra* and *Twelfth Night*: and of the 1,000 or so costumes and props that were offered for sale, most came from these productions.

Among the designers represented, the most well known were Nicholas Georgiadis and Robin Archer. In *All for Love* by John Dryden and *Anthony and Cleopatra*, Nicholas Georgiadis's taste for the lavish and extravagant was evident in his elaborately styled robes made from rich coloured velvets, soft leather and glittering imitation silks: two cloaks worn by Alec McCowan as Anthony fetched £120 ($235) and two sparkling dresses worn by Dorothy Tutin as Cleopatra made £70 ($137). In contrast, Robin Archer's costumes in, for instance, Cottrell's *A Room with a View* were gentle and understated, many made from the finest wool and tweed, and beautifully tailored in Edwardian style – Mr Emerson's suit worn by Timothy West realized £75 ($147). However, most excitement was probably aroused when the bidding for Macbeth's leather tunic and velvet robe worn by Peter O'Toole reached £440 ($862). The highest price, £500 ($980) was paid for the exotic Players' costumes from *Hamlet* by a costumier from America, and the Theatre Museum at the Victoria and Albert bid £180 ($352) for *Richard II*'s richly decorated court tabard worn by Ian McKellan in the 1969 production.

With various television networks filming during the auction, the champagne and smoked salmon in the Dress Circle, Christie's South Kensington's first ever Theatre Sale went off in splendid style. The sale was an outstanding success totalling £24,500 ($48,020) with no lot left unsold.

458

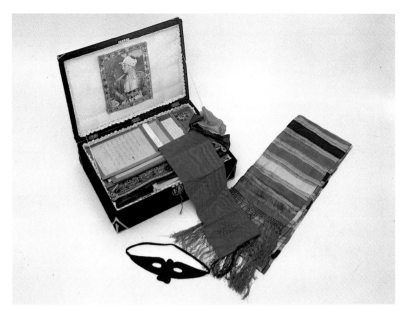

Above Part of a large collection of memorabilia relating to Rudolph Valentino.
Sold 20.4.82 for a total of £8,445 ($14,863)

Right A dress of black imitation watered silk worn by Joan Sutherland in *Don Giovannni* at Glyndebourne in the 1960s.
It sold for £350 ($619)

Although difficult to recapture the atmosphere of that evening at the Old Vic in the Hangar saleroom at Christie's South Kensington, there was, nevertheless, a feeling of great excitement and anticipation on April 20 when the "Opera, Cinema and Stage" sale took place. This sale of Costume and Memorabilia included many costumes worn by stars, mainly in the 1940s and 1950s. Museums, collectors, theatre companies and costumiers bid fiercely for mementoes of theatrical history such as the scarlet cloak worn by Lord Olivier as *Henry V* in the 1944 film he also directed, which fetched £300 ($531), and Julie Andrews's stunning strapless satin evening dress, richly embroidered with diamanté, designed by Sir Cecil Beaton for the Ball Scene in *My Fair Lady*: this went to the Theatre Museum at the Victoria and Albert for £500 ($885).

A collection of beautiful and unusual costumes originally from the Monte Carlo opera house also attracted much interest, mainly from abroad, particularly Italy, where most of the costumes were made.

There is no doubt, however, that the biggest attraction of the sale was the large collection of memorabilia relating to one of the cinema's greatest stars, Rudolph Valentino. Almost all the lots made well over their upper estimates – the eagle-shaped black mask he wore in the film *The Eagle* in 1924 made £450 ($796) and the two signed stills from the same film fetched £170 ($301) and £220 ($389). The sale totalled £28,532 ($50,502) with less than 10 per cent unsold.

These two sales reflect the increasing interest in anything related to theatre and film history. Christie's South Kensington looks forward to holding more sales of this kind in the future.

Pair of rare Obadiah Sherratt busts of King
William IV and Queen Adelaide
26 cm high
Sold 8.6.82 for £2,100 ($3,780)

Berlin plaque painted with a girl and a
parakeet, after Kiefel
33 cm high
Sold 15.10.81 for £1,880 ($3,515)

After Reading, an Art
Nouveau parcel-gilt and
cold painted bronze and
ivory figure of a young
woman, cast and carved
from a model by Demêtre
Chiparus. Inscribed
Chiparus
37.5 cm high
Sold 26.2.82 for £1,200
($2,208)

Butler's half-plate one-shot
three-colour camera
Sold 26.11.81 for £1,800
($3,492)

Postcard-size Soho tropical
stereoscopic reflex camera by
Marion & Co., London
Sold 8.4.82 for £3,700 ($6,549)

Postcards of Nijinsky signed by the subject and another
with manuscript musical score
Signed V. Nijinsky and dated 1913
Sold 22.1.82 for £600 ($1,134)

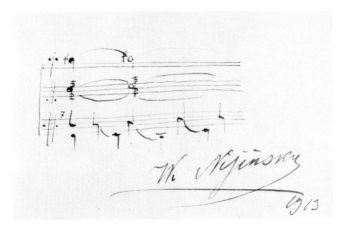

Bing 1902 "Phaeton", the tinplate open body with padded
and railed seats, finished in yellow with red lining, the
clockwork motor also operating a horn through bellows
(inoperative)
34.2 cm long; 19 cm wide
Sold 17.2.82 for £3,600 ($6,876)

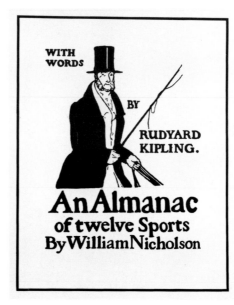

Nicholson (Sir
William) and Kipling
(Rudyard): An
Almanac of Twelve
Sports
De Luxe edition with
20 hand-coloured
woodcuts by
Nicholson, folio, 1898
Sold 26.2.82 for £3,200
($5,888)

Far right

Bisque-headed bébé with
fixed blue eyes, pierced ears
and blonde wig, marked
BRU JNE 9 and on the body
BEBE BRU No.9
50 cm high
Sold 13.11.81 for £2,200
($4,202)

Right

Bisque-headed bébé with
pierced ears, fixed blue eyes,
blonde wig, in contemporary
pink satin dress, marked 16
and stamped on the body
JUMEAU MEDAILLE
D'OR
*c.*1890
83.8 cm high
Sold 15.1.82 for £5,800
($10,962)

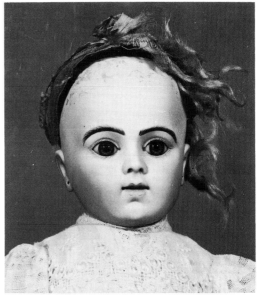

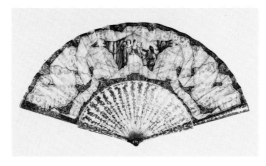

Fan, the leaf painted with a *trompe-l'oeil* of
lace with a troupe of pierrots and pierettes
peering through a curtain in the centre
After Watteau, *c.*1730
Sold 25.5.82 for £800 ($1,424)

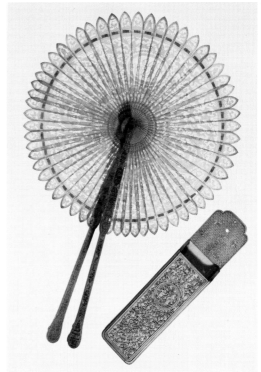

Pierced ivory Canton parasol cockade fan
*c.*1820
Sold 4.8.81 for £1,100 ($2,013)

The Copenhagen Mekanisk Musik Museum Sale

CHRISTOPHER PROUDFOOT

After the highly successful sale of the E.M.I. collection of phonographs and gramophones at South Kensington in the autumn of 1980, it was a natural progression to the even larger and more comprehensive sale of the Mekanisk Musik Museum from Copenhagen in 1981. Phonographs and gramophones there were again, but these were but a minor part of this collection. The sheer size of many of the instruments distinguished this from previous British auctions; the largest, a Weber Maesto orchestrion of the 1920s, had to be brought in in two parts and assembled with the aid of a fork-lift truck. The entire Hangar saleroom at South Kensington was filled with musical machines on the view days, the collection having been shipped from Denmark in five containers.

The Mekanisk Musik Museum was founded by its owner, Claes O. Friberg, some 10 years previously, and had been a major tourist attraction in Copenhagen. However, Mr Friberg had come to feel, like so many other private museum owners, that without support from the state or city authorities (which was not forthcoming) he could not continue indefinitely as a museum curator, and the time had come to sell.

There were over 500 lots in the sale, ranging from large orchestrions down to miscellaneous lots of piano and organ rolls, musical box discs, spare parts and incomplete gramophones and musical boxes. Not only the contents of the Museum as displayed to the public were being sold, but also the vast quantity of secondary material from the back rooms and basement.

The sale totalled £341,050 ($644,580) with only 2.2 per cent unsold. Much of the total was accounted for by the Weber Maesto at £58,000 ($109,620), a rare Phonoliszt Violina (with three self-playing violins) at £35,000 ($66,150), and an Imhof & Mukle orchestrion at £27,000 ($51,030). Other, lesser barrel organs and orchestrions were mainly in the £2,000 ($3,780) to £5,000 ($9,450) bracket, as expected, but what was not anticipated was the abnormal demand for what can best be described as "bits and pieces" – orchestrion and piano rolls, musical box discs, and gramophones in less than perfect condition, most of which, despite their quantity, sold well over their pre-sale estimates.

Above left

Rare Weber "Maestro" Orchestrion
Sold for £58,000 ($109,620)

Above

Imhof and Muckle barrel Orchestrion
Sold for £27,000 ($51,030)

Left

Rare Hupfeld Model C Phonoliszt Violina:
automatic violin and piano
Sold for £35,000 ($66,150)

All sold 14.11.81 at Christie's South Kensington

The B.R.M. Collection

ROBERT BROOKS

Christie's South Kensington's sale of the British Racing Motors Collection at Earls Court on October 22nd 1981, was a unique occasion. Not only was this the first time that an entire Grand Prix stable had come on the market, but it was undoubtedly the most important collection of one-make Formula One machines in existence.

The story of British Racing Motors began in 1946. Raymond Mays, a well known pre-war racing motorist, held a dream that an all-British Grand Prix car should be built to take on and beat the world. Due partly to the great political capital that had been made by the Germans and the Italians before the outbreak of hostilities, feelings ran high within the British Automotive industry in favour of such a project, and Mays soon had the financial and material support necessary to turn his dream into reality. The new car, first raced in 1950, was a complicated V16 cylinder design with an enormous power potential. Its complexity, however, proved to be its downfall. In their very first race, following an enormous press build-up, B.R.M. were struck by disaster when the car failed on the starting grid, setting a pattern that was to be repeated throughout their early years.

At that time, the team were the only serious British Formula One contenders and it was as a direct result of their involvement that other British teams sprang up and were soon dominating the motor racing world, a position they still occupy today. Although it was not until 1962 that B.R.M. won their first World Championship with Graham Hill, over the years they designed and built some of the most exciting Formula One machines and employed the world's best drivers to campaign them.

The *marque's* owners Rubery Owen Holdings, the automotive component giants, adopted a policy of retaining the more important cars from the very earliest days. Thus undoubtedly the most important collection of its kind evolved from the first V16; via the 1959 2½ litre (in which Jo Bonnier scored B.R.M.'s first Grand Prix win); to the 1962 championship winner.

The sale of the collection at the Motorfair, (London's Motor Show), was an unprecedented occasion. A crowd of over 1,500 packed Earls Court's Warwick room, which had been specially adapted, and witnessed the 11 cars and associated items (including engines, films, design drawings and a multitude of material gathered over 25 years of Grand Prix competition), sell for a total of £569,115 ($1,047,170). One of the three V16 cars on offer realized £160,000 ($294,400), the highest price ever paid for a motor car at auction in Europe. Hill's World Championship car sold for £50,000 ($92,000) and the 1959 front engined 2½ litre for £85,000 ($156,400). Despite great interest from overseas, it seems likely that all of the cars will remain in the United Kingdom. Mr Tom Wheatcroft, owner of the world's finest collection of single seater racers, purchased five of the cars and all of the engines for his museum at Donington Park.

1950 B.R.M. Type 15 (Mark I) 1½ litre V16 Grand Prix Single Seater
Juan Manuel Fangio in B.R.M. Mark 1/01 at Silverstone, 1953
Photo: Tom March
Sold 22.10.81 in London for £100,000 ($184,000)

1954 B.R.M. P30 1½ litre V16 Single Seater ("Mark II")
Chassis no: 2/01
Engine no: 20/2
Gearbox no.: 002
Sold 22.10.81 for £160,000 ($294,400)

1961 B.R.M. P578 1½ litre V8 Grand Prix Single Seater
Graham Hill in B.R.M. P578/1 at the British Grand Prix, Aintree 1962
Photo: Tom March
Sold 22.10.81 for £50,000 ($95,000)

Wings and Wheels

ROBERT BROOKS

The Wings and Wheels Museum of historic aircraft and collectors' motor cars in Orlando, Florida, was the third major collection in these fields to have been secured by Christie's for sale during 1981. The success there, on December 6th, contributed to a worldwide total for motor car and aeroplane sales (of which there have been seven) of over £2.5 million ($4.7 million) representing a four-fold increase on last year's figure.

The Wings and Wheels Museum was made up, in the main, of three major collections and included some of the finest early aircraft in existence. There was a strong element of World War I fighter machinery, including examples of the legendary Sopwith Camel, Spad and Fokker DVII. Earlier still were fine representations, albeit reproductions, of the Wright brothers' Glider and Flyer. The majority of the motor cars fell in the medium price range, such as pre-war Fords, including a number of model A's. Two vehicles in particular, however, were of an exceptional nature. The 1934 Duesenberg sedan by Judkins and the 1934 Packard V12 dual-cowl Phaeton by Le Baron – the car produced for the Worlds Fair of 1934.

The motor cars, offered first, immediately set the pace with exceptionally good prices for the more commonly encountered of collectables. Few were surprised at the $121,000 (£61,735) paid for the Duesenberg although this represented a respectable price in the present market. The Packard however, astonished many, reaching the record auction price for an American automobile of $385,000 (£196,428). The aircraft, which made up the larger part of the sale, continued the trend of high prices. $110,000 (£56,122) was paid for an example of the famous German World War II Heinkel HE III bomber. The classic De Havilland DH 4 bi-plane realized $93,500 (£47,704) as did the Curtiss JN4D (the ubiquitous Jenny). Not surprisingly the highest price of the aircraft section, $132,000 (£67,347), was paid for the Sopwith Camel, one of the many aircraft to be acquired by British collectors.

1917-18 Sopwith Camel
Max speed 113 m.p.h.
Sold 6.12.81 in Florida for $100,000 (£52,630)
This compact single-seater fighter biplane with equal-span wings has the distinction of having scored more victories than any other Allied airplanes during World War I. An enlarged and improved version of the successful Sopwith Pup it earned its nickname from the characteristic hump in the top cowling, covering the machine-guns.

Camels were supplied to American units for service in France, and a number of the type were brought back to the USA after the Armistice for test and training purposes. Sea trials were conducted, in the course of which aircraft were flown off platforms constructed on the forward turrets of battleships

1934 Packard Twelve model-1108 five passenger dual-cowl sport phaeton
Body by Le Baron, Detroit
Sold 6.12.81 in Florida for $350,000 (£184,210)

1963 Ferrari 250 GT short-wheelbase two-seater Berlinetta
Coachwork by Scaglietti, Milan
Sold 29.10.81 in London for £40,000 ($73,200)

Well presented 1½ in scale model of an Aveling & Porter twin cylinder two-speed four-shaft convertible road engine
35.5 x 65 cm
Sold 12.10.81 for £2,640 ($5,095)

Contemporary hand-operated detailed wooden display model of Carisbrook Sawmill c.1900
63.5 x 122 cm
Sold 26.4.82 for £1,188 ($2,292)

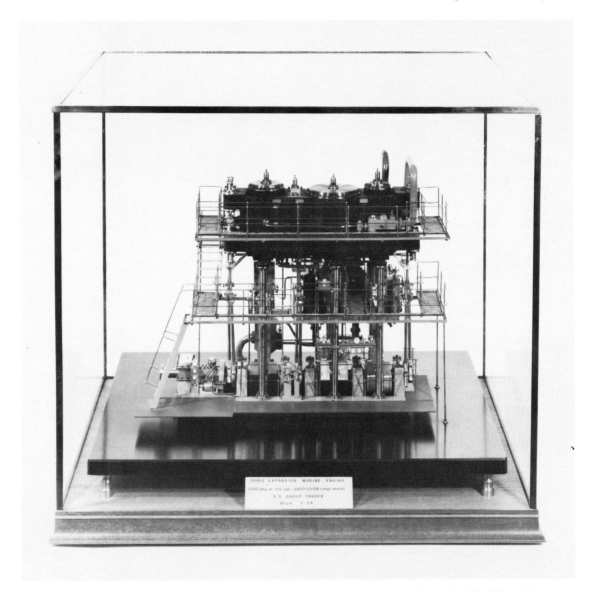

Highly detailed and well presented 1:24 scale display model of the three pillar 1200 B.H.P. triple expansion reversing marine engine, fitted to the cargo vessel S.S. "Group Trader"
*c.*1935
29 x 35.5 cm
Fitted glazed case 47.5 x 54.5 cm
Sold 26.4.82 for £1,728 ($3,335)

Live steam spirit-fired gauge "1" model of the London and North Western Railway 4-4-0 locomotive and tender No.2663 "George the Fifth" By Marklin for Gamages c.1913 Sold 26.4.82 for £3,240 ($6,253)

Exhibition standard 5 in gauge model of the Great Western Railway 4-6-0 locomotive and tender No.6206 "King John", built by J. Perrier, Ringwood Rebuilt by J.F. Adams, Poole 37 x 185.5 cm Sold 12.10.81 for £8,250 ($15,922)

Exceptionally fine 1:22 scale (metric) oak model of the 62-gun man-of-war "Wasa" built to plans made available by the "Wasavarvet" Museum in Stockholm
183 x 234 cm
Sold 26.4.82 for £9,720 ($17,301)
Complete with individually made running and standing rigging with hardwood block with brass sheaves, oak main lower masts built in eight pieces, pitchpine topmasts, bowsprit and spars and hammered ironwork, pins, etc. The hull is of fully pinned and rivetted oak planking of exactly researched lengths with the same jointing as on "Wasa" over oak frames, complete in every minute detail including extremely well observed and executed carvings numbering over 400 and including the lion figurehead, hair rails with tracery and figurines and full stern gallery details, Royal coat-of-arms and individually carved lions' heads on each gun port cover.

477

Exhibition standard boxwood and pine model of a simple screw yacht of *c.*1870
Built by W. Morrison
Saltcoats, *c.*1900
45.5 x 109 cm
Sold 12.10.81 for £4,400 ($8,492)

CHRISTIE'S INAUGURAL AND CHRISTIE'S FINE ARTS COURSE

Nicola Hicks of the Chelsea School of Art standing by her sculpture "Celeste"

Christie's Inaugural: The pick of new graduate art 1982

RICHARD CORK of *The Standard*

Christie's has never seen anything like it. Visitors walking up the dignified main staircase towards the Great Rooms where Rembrandts and Titians are normally sold, now find themselves assailed by a bilious yellow-green female nude dancing on the wall.

It is the work of Jane Burgess, a graduate of St Martin's School of Art and one of 230 young artists who have transformed Christie's with a startling uninhibited exhibition.

They are all degree-level students who have trained at London's seven State art colleges, and their chances of finding space to show their work in the West End would usually be minimal.

But Christie's, inspired by its founder's willingness in the 18th century to show contemporary artists like Gainsborough and Reynolds, has decided to help new graduates by staging an annual survey of their best work.

The result allays the suspicion of anyone who might have imagined that only the most safe and traditional art would be selected. An exhilarating variety of styles has been included, and the emphasis is placed on brash vitality rather than dull conformity.

The orthodox pleasures of drawing from a posed model can be found at their best in Neil Harvey's quiet, observant study of a middle-aged woman.

But most of the paintings trample on the boundaries of good taste as gleefully as Erica Lansley's rogue elephant, which charges across the canvas in a flurry of smeared, excitable pigment.

Among the sculptures Stephanie Wolfe's outrageously kitsch mosaic *Fruit Bowl* also revels in its own vulgarity, making most of the nearby abstract work look discreet by comparison.

Throughout the show, in fact, representational art in a variety of styles provides the most arresting moments. Much is violent and disturbing, like the society which produces it.

Fergus Goodman's *Reclining Nude* cowers on her bed, as if horrified by the sinister brown sores which disfigure her body.

Not all the exhibits investigate such alarming themes. Antoni Trzebiski's assured painting of Elizabeth Reading is as well mannered as a typical exhibit in the Royal Academy Summer Show.

I hope it receives the success it deserves, and Christie's should be congratulated for giving so many young artists at the beginning of their career an opportunity to show us their work.

Christie's are indebted to The Standard for permission to reproduce this article

Sir Hugh Casson, K.C.V.O., P.R.A., opening the Christie's Inaugural Exhibition

Graduates from London's seven State art colleges at the opening reception

Sculpture and pictures on view in the main saleroom

Christie's Fine Arts Course

ROBERT CUMMING

The provenance of a work of art is of the greatest interest and importance, and Christie's muniment room, with records of sales going back to the firm's foundation in 1766, is a unique mine of information. The label "Sold at Christie's" is an important one. At Christie's Fine Arts Course we are, after four years, beginning to establish another provenance, for our students have gone away from London with the status "educated at Christie's", and in a gratifying number of cases established themselves with success in the art world.

Between 1978 and 1981 – three academic years – we guided a total of 238 students, 172 Full Time and 66 Part Time. Our youngest Full Time student was 18, the oldest over 50, and the majority of Full Time students, 41 per cent, were in the 21-25 age group. The group of Part Time students have a different identity, for over 63 per cent were over 30, and each year we welcomed at least one old age pensioner. We encourage all our students to mix and share their knowledge, but we separate them into Full and Part Time since there are those who are looking for, and require, continuous supervision of their studies, and those who, because of previous study or because of outside demands and commitments, prefer a less intensive and more flexible working week. Women outnumber men in the ratio 2:1.

Students have come from all over the world, and in a quiet way we have become our own United Nations. If we flew all the flags there would be 37 in all, and they would range from Japan and the Philippines in the East, to Peru and Mexico in the West; from Norway in the North, to South Africa and Australia in the South. We have taken more Britons than any other nation (35 per cent), followed by Europe (29 per cent) and USA (23 per cent). Of the European nations the Germans are the front runners.

Of the 238 students 34 have been taken on by Christie's offices round the world, nearly all of them Full Time students. Twenty-five are currently working in our offices in London, Glasgow, New York, Geneva, Amsterdam, Rome, Milan and Hamburg. Two of them regularly take auctions. Nineteen other students have gone to work in other auction houses in the UK, USA and Europe. But not all our students have ambitions to work in auction houses. A significant proportion go on to further education, a total of 32 (13.5 per cent) in all, and we are gradually building contacts with universities and art schools round the world. Some of our students are already graduates when they come to Christie's. Fifty-three students – nearly a quarter – have found employment with dealers and commercial galleries, or have established businesses of their own. Twelve have gone to work in Museums. Some students have returned to their own business enterprises having used their year at Christie's as a sabbatical. Others have returned to their demanding families – refreshed we hope, by their year's education in the arts; others still can assume or continue the happy and important role of collectors and connoisseurs, with a

Robert Cumming, Director of the Christie's Fine Arts Course, lecturing to his students

better eye and the prospect of new fields to explore. And we have those who have found a special niche: working for the Arts Council; for the Fine Art Department of an insurance company; a career in films; another in television setting up a new art journal; cabinet making. We have inspired one student to seek to establish himself as a practising artist in the Virgin Islands. Unpredictably one student became a strawberry farmer, and another a bouncer in a night club! And there are those who have flown our nest for destinations unknown, whom our statistics cannot allow for. Several have taken the matrimonial plunge, but we can report only one marriage where both partners met on the Fine Arts Course.

The Guggenheim Museum in Venice will have taken five of our students to work as apprentices in the running of the museum, and we are proud and honoured to have established this link with them. We regularly take our students to country houses within reach of London, and can now claim knowledge of 27. We have also introduced them to Edinburgh, Glasgow, Stoke-on-Trent, Paris, Florence, Amsterdam and Madrid. Many of the words spoken in our lecture theatre have come from distinguished members of universities, museums and art colleges, and from restorers, authors, collectors and gallery owners, who have been willing to share their experience and enthusiasm.

Nothing in the world stands still, and after four years we have plans to build on our success. During the coming year we are starting a wine course, and have plans for evening classes and a summer school. Do not be surprised, therefore, if you see, anywhere in the world, people young and old wearing a T-shirt or pullover which carries the Christie's emblem and the words Christie's Fine Arts Course. They are like works of art they have learned about, declaring that they have a provenance to be proud of.

WINE

White metal decanting cradle
Sold 25.2.82 in London for £620 ($1,116)

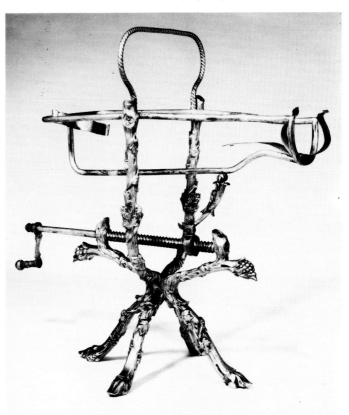

A Record Wine Season

MICHAEL BROADBENT, M.W.

Despite all the signs of recession that surround us, I am happy to report that the Wine Department's sales increased by a healthy 21 per cent to a net figure only a fraction short of £3.5 million ($6.3 million), whilst the number of sales has increased from 45 to 50.

It is perhaps not realized that the relatively small department based in King Street organizes, catalogues and conducts not only the major Fine Wine and specialized sales in the Great Rooms but also the monthly mixed wine sales at Christie's South Kensington and elsewhere in London, the Christie Fine and Rare wine sales on the Continent and in the United States. During the period we have also conducted charity wine auctions and lecture/tastings in the United Kingdom and overseas. The Wine Department also publishes and sells books. In fact the total volume generated or handled by the department now exceeds £4 million ($7.2 million).

KING STREET FINE WINE AND SPECIALIZED SALES

Our main sales are, and doubtless will continue to be, held in our Great Rooms. The "Finest and Rarest" category is still unsurpassed although it is noticeable that fewer really great private cellars emanate from the United Kingdom: it seems as though the remarkable accumulations of old wines which passed through our hands between 1967 and 1976 – the roll-call includes Rosebery, Linlithgow, Sir George Meyrick, Sir John Thomson and Fasque – have dwindled. Their place is taken by solid collections of less venerable but high-value claret, and cellars from France – a country still replete with stock, yet lacking a mature wine market like ours.

Claret dominates our sales and there has been a remarkable surge in price, particularly for the best vintages, notably 1961, 1966 and 1970, of the better-known châteaux. In fact our specialized claret sales alone account for exactly half the King Street turnover, the average lot size having increased from £228 last season to £277 in 1981/2. But claret also appears in the eight major mixed sales, from Fine Wine to Finest and Rarest. It is fair to say that Bordeaux dominates the market.

Before leaving the King Street sales I should like to pay tribute to Alan Taylor-Restell, the principal auctioneer. For speed, accuracy and authority he is without equal.

THE SANDEMAN SHERRY SALE

Undoubtedly the most unusual and certainly the most challenging sale of the season was *A Highly Important Sale of Finest Old Sherry* for the very old established firm of Sandeman. The date, June 24, coincided neatly with an identical size of sale held by Christie's in 1901: '*Five thousand dozens of Fine Old Bottled Sherries, the Property of her late Majesty Queen Victoria and his Majesty the King*'

(Edward VII). This clearout of the five Royal Cellars caused a sensation and was a great success. The Sandeman sherry sale had two purposes: to draw attention to an underrated style of wine and to clear a substantial stock. The excellent catalogue and subsequent tastings accomplished the first aim but though we could not claim 100 per cent sold, 3,000 dozen found appreciative buyers not only in this country (all the London-based stock sold out) but in America, Australia and even in France during a period of marked recession in the sherry market.

CHRISTIE'S SOUTH KENSINGTON AND OTHER LONDON SALES

In addition to the monthly mixed sales of mainly inexpensive wines at South Kensington, the Wine Department has continued Christie-Restell City sales at Beaver Hall; and in place of the mini Fine Wine sale at last year's World Wine Fair in Bristol, we mounted a similar wine auction on June 3 at the International Wine & Spirit Trade Fair at Olympia.

The 24 King Street wine sales, eight being two-part all-day sessions, plus the extra-mural auctions mentioned above, bring the London total up to 41 sales with in excess of £2.8 million sold, an increase of 15 per cent on the previous season.

SWITZERLAND AND THE NETHERLANDS

Duncan McEuen, now responsible for our sales on the Continent, organized our first wine auction in Zürich on March 13. There were the usual autumn and spring sales in Geneva.

Despite an additional two sales in Amsterdam, the market there has been a little lack-lustre and we will, next season, revert to two annual sales, keeping our options open in case another major collection comes along.

The seven wine auctions in Europe totalled just under £300,000 ($540,000) at the rates of exchange prevailing at the time of the sale.

From left to right

Grande Chartreuse
1878-1903
£115 ($207)

Constantia 1791
£90 ($162) ½ bottle

Fromy
Gr. Fine Champ
1815
£82 ($147) ½ bottle

Briand Cognac
1893
£82 ($147) ½ bottle

Marc de Bourgogne
1895
£95 ($171)

All sold 8.10.81
in London

WINE SALES IN THE UNITED STATES

Without any doubt the most exciting developments have been in America. Because of what we consider quite unreasonable opposition initiated by one or two leading retailers and supported by a mass of irrelevant, misleading and some totally false evidence, we have not yet succeeded in obtaining permits to auction wine in New York. However this has not stopped us from holding sales elsewhere and after our first most successful sale in Chicago in the spring of 1981, enough solid interest was shown – and instructions to sell received – to encourage us to continue.

The first sale of the current season was held in Washington on October 31 1981, and the second, back again in Chicago, on April 17 1982. Notable features of both sales were the enthusiastic attendance, the extraordinary number of commissions to bid, the encouraging percentage sold and the high average lot value (the equivalent of £372 per lot, compared with an average of £277 per lot at our claret sales in King Street).

The Chicago sale was dominated by a remarkable cellar of wine belonging to the family of the late Dr George H. Rezek, for long one of the most noted gourmets and connoisseurs in North America.

Prices are undoubtedly high at these sales, reflecting the demand for mature wines of high quality and rarity which are less familiar and certainly less readily available in America than in the United Kingdom.

From left to right

Mouton-Rothschild
1873
£145 ($261)

Tokay Essence
1896
£210 ($378) ½ litre

Tokay Essence
1880
£145 ($261) ½ litre

A de Luze Cognac
1848
£110 ($198)

Napoleon Cognac
Age inconnu
£75 ($135)

All sold 25.2.82
in London

The second annual Napa Valley Wine Auction was held on a perfect June day – as opposed to 110°F in the shade last year. A colourful and well organized occasion, the auction raised some $250,000 (£140,450) in aid of two hospitals in the valley.

After 13 years' association with the Heublein Group of Wine Companies, we have severed our connection, mainly due to growing conflict of interests, although we did participate in the 1982 Wine Auction at Sakowitz in Houston, Texas, which is a more low-keyed and local event.

The American wine scene is lively and the potential for our style of wine auctions immense. I think we can expect worthwhile developments in this area.

COLLECTORS' PIECES

Pictures of ingenious Victorian corkscrews and decanting cradles, old sealed bottles and silver labels garnish our Finest and Rarest catalogues. They are appealing and attractive but, with a low average lot value, hardly economic to handle. Moreover the market is very erratic. Nevertheless, some outstanding items fetched substantial prices.

Whether the Silver Department realized it or not, the world record price for a corkscrew was achieved at one of their sales in July: £2,700 ($4,590) for a most unusual 17th century silver corkscrew "the handle formed as a ring surmounted with plain tapering screw cover".

Decorative brass corkscrew,
probably German, *c*.1900, 25.5 cm long
Sold 25.2.82 in London for £500 ($900)

CHRISTIE'S WINE PUBLICATIONS

For just over 10 years the Wine Department has been publishing books on wine for the specialist including nine editions of Christie's Wine Review, now divided into two sections: Christie's Wine Companion, published last autumn, and the Price Index pocket book just out. There have been monographs on Châteaux Lafite, Mouton-Rothschild and Margaux, three editions of Harry Waugh's *Wine Diaries*, several editions of *Wine Tasting*, now a pocket book in association with Mitchell Beazley, with whom we also published the astonishingly successful *Great Vintage Wine Book*. Smaller works include the only book on Armagnac and The Factory House at Oporto.

Sales of the 10 titles currently in print have totalled 11,000 copies this season. Further new books are planned.

All in all, it has been an abundantly active season handled by a small but highly experienced team. A complete list of the wines and vintages handled, and the prices obtained, appears in the annual Christie's *Price Index of Vintage Wines*, to be distributed by Phaidon Press.

STAMPS

A £15,000 Colour Problem

Rhodesia 1910 5d. lake-brown and yellow-green
Sold 18.11.81 in London for £15,000 ($28,800)
This was one of the seven known unused examples of
this rare colour, two of which were found at different
times in small collections sent in for sale. The
normal shades, purple-brown and olive, are worth
about £5 ($9.6).
Philatelists, too, can have a colour problem

Stamp Sales during 1981-2

PETER COLLINS

With less interest in the stamp market than there has been for many years, it was again items of visual beauty, the unexpected and the unusual which caused excitement. Rarity is something which is quantitively definable; character is more elusive.

Perhaps the romantic appeal of the Greek nation (Byron was besotted by the glamour of its struggle against the Ottomans) and the classical allusion of its first stamp depicting Hermes's Head, attracted collectors to its early stamps. From the 1860s there has been competition for fine Greek stamps, and the striking strip of five 1 lepta and three 5 lepta of the Paris printing used on an entire letter from Karaetena to Kalmata on 14th October 1861, persuaded a connoisseur to pay Sw.fr.11,500 (£3,230) to possess it at the Zürich 18th May, 1982 sale. The first issue of Greek stamps only appeared on 1st October, 1861 so the early date of use and the unusual route added enhancement to the striking appearance of the stamps.

The handsome envelope addressed to Manila originated in Malaga, Spain. In passing in transit through the Gibraltar Post Office, it had 4d., 6d. and 1/- stamps of Great Britain (which were held in stock at Gibraltar) applied to pay the postage onwards. The "G" cancellation supplied to Gibraltar by the G.P.O. London, has been neatly struck, producing an unusually attractive cover which realized £3,800 ($6,992) in London on 23rd February, 1982. British stamps used in Gibraltar at this period are not scarce. It was the brilliant appearance of the envelope and its unusual usage that attracted the high price against a valuation of £800 ($1,472). The buyer was an airport controller at an important aerial crossroads, which shows the range of collectors who find their pleasure and relaxation in the hobby.

The New York April 1/2 1982 sale was full of good things, but of great note was the Waterbury Running Chicken. Until the 1860s, U.S. postmasters had to provide their own cancellations and, in order to save their money and exercise their artistic ingenuity, many bucolic craftsmen carved their own original fanciful designs in wood or cork. A great favourite is the Running Chicken from Waterbury, Connecticut. The postmaster there, John W. Hill, was a humourist with a natural artistic flair. He carved woodblocks by hand in many different designs, the most popular of which is a caricature chicken with wings outstretched and legs astraddle so that it became a highly prized collector's item in its own right. An example sold on 1st April 1982 in New York for $3,740 (£2,113). It was struck clearly and centrally on a most ordinary stamp that normally would sell for coppers. The appeal of the Running Chicken is inexplicable: perhaps every motorist in a rural area has seen such a squawking bird with its beak open and wings flapping! Two equally distinctive, clear and attractive carved fancy cancellations depicting soldier's heads, again on stamps of no consequence, realized $264 (£467) and $220 (£389) in the same sale.

1861 letter from Karytaena to Kalmata bearing the Paris printing of the Greek I
lepta, strip of five, and five lepton, strip of three
Sold 17.5.82 in Zurich for Sw.fr.12,937 (£3,696)

1858 letter from Malaga in Spain to Manilla via Hong Kong bearing a complete set of the first
British stamps printed by De La Rue applied and cancelled 'G' at Gibraltar
Sold 23.2.82 in London for £3,800 ($6,840)

1871 letter from Grasse to Paris sent during the siege by the Germans. The stamps are the 20c. provisional printed in Bordeaux and the Napoleon lauré 40c. The letter was endorsed 'Par Moulins (Allier)' and enclosed in a steel ball and floated down the Seine, remaining undiscovered for ninety years. The letter is still sealed
Sold 17.5.82 in Zurich for Sw.fr.1,237 (£350)

Following an "open day" by Christie's in Nairn, Scotland, a package was received by Robson Lowe containing a series of colourful stamp-like reproductions of Great Britain Queen Victoria stamps on card. Unbelievably they proved to be official prints from the original dies, prepared for the London Exhibition of 1871. They were in small Victorian-type envelopes so, we wrote asking the owner if they could have been in his family since they were first printed, also taking the opportunity to point out various faults in their general condition. The owner replied that they had been regarded as family heirlooms of interest though probably of little worth, and had been kept in the box of the family sewing machine and used from time to time as bookmarks, playthings and for other casual domestic purposes. This accounted for their indifferent condition; the owner was surprised and delighted that we broke them into 28 lots with a valuation of over £6,000 ($10,620).

During the siege of Paris in the Franco-Prussian War, 1870-1, experiments were made at floating letters sealed in lead balls (Boules de Moulin) down the Seine into the City, to which access was barred by the Prussian army. Unfortunately the experiment was not a success. The Prussians fished some of the boules from the river; some stuck in the reeds, some sank. Over 60 years later, in the 1930s, during dredging operations, some were pulled up. So conservative are the Parisians that many families still occupied the same residence and some of the letters were delivered to the descendants of the original addresses. This charming cover from Grasse was seemingly one which could not be delivered, for it had never been opened, so the privilege of reading the contents for the first time falls to the purchaser. He has bought a piece of history for Sw.fr.1,100 (£309) (Zurich 17th May 1982).

Such touches of romance stir the mind of any imaginative person and perhaps revelations of this kind go some way to explaining the appeal of collecting these little bits of waste paper which have fascinated us for almost 150 years.

Fiji: two 1d. and 6d.
cancelled with the sunburst
of Levuka on an 1879
envelope to California. The
U.S. 5c. postage due added
at San Francisco.
Sold 21.4.82 in London
for £1,700 ($3,036)

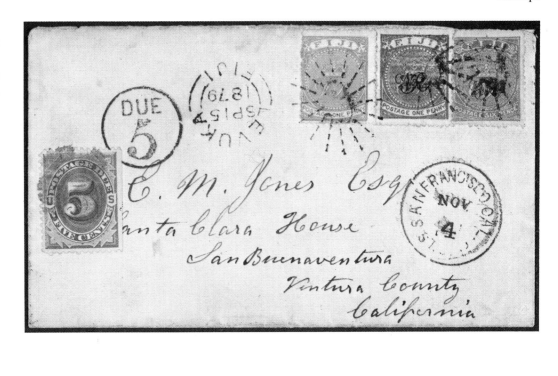

Victoria: Ham's engraved 2d.
– a strip of six and three singles
used on an 1854 letter from
Hamilton to Glasgow.
Sold 4.11.81 in Basle for
SF.7,500 (£1,242)

Christie, Manson & Woods Ltd

LONDON
8 King Street, St James's, London SW1Y 6QT
Telephone (01) 839 9060   *Telex* 916429
Cables Christiart London SW1

SOUTH KENSINGTON
Christie's South Kensington Ltd
85 Old Brompton Road, London SW7 3JS
Telephone (01) 581 2231   *Telex* 922061
Cables Viewing London SW7 England

GLASGOW
Christie's & Edmiston's Ltd
164-166 Bath Street, Glasgow G2 4TG
Telephone (041) 332 8134/7 *Telex* 779901

Agents in Great Britain and Ireland

INVERNESS
Jack Buchanan
111 Church Street, Inverness
Telephone (0463) 34603

PERTH
Sebastian Thewes
Strathgarry House, Killiecrankie
by Pitlochry
Perthshire
Telephone (079681) 216

ARGYLL
Sir Ilay Campbell, Bt.
Cumlodden Estate Office
Furnace by Inveraray, Argyll
Telephone (04995) 286

EDINBURGH
Michael Clayton
5 Wemyss Place, Edinburgh
Telephone (031) 225 4757

NORTHUMBRIA
Aidan Cuthbert
Eastfield House, Main Street
Corbridge, Northumberland
Telephone (043471) 3181

NORTH-WEST
Victor Gubbins
St. Andrew's Place, Penrith, Cumbria
Telephone (0768) 66766

YORKSHIRE
Nicholas Brooksbank
46 Bootham, York
Telephone (0904) 30911

WEST MIDLANDS
Michael Thompson
Stanley Hall, Bridgnorth, Shropshire
Telephone (07462) 61891

EAST ANGLIA
Veronica Bowring
Davey House
Castle Meadow
Norwich NR1 3DE
Telephone (0603) 614546

CHELTENHAM
Philip Leatham
111 The Promenade, Cheltenham, Glos.
Telephone (0242) 518999
Rupert de Zoete *Consultant*

MID-WALES
Sir Andrew Duff Gordon, Bt.
Downton House, New Radnor,
Presteigne, Powys
Telephone (0242) 518999

WEST COUNTRY
Richard de Pelet
Monmouth Lodge, Yenston
Templecombe, Somerset
Telephone (0963) 70518

Nigel Thimbleby
Wolfeton House, Dorchester, Dorset
Telephone (0305) 68748
and at
Christie's at Robson Lowe
39 Poole Hill, Bournemouth, Dorset
Telephone (0202) 292740

HAMPSHIRE
Denys Wrey
The Common, Smannell, Andover, Hants.
Telephone (0264) 3750

DEVON AND CORNWALL
Christopher Petherick
Tredeague, Porthpean
St. Austell, Cornwall
Telephone (0726) 64672

KENT AND SUSSEX
Kim North
York House, 58 Grosvenor Road,
Tunbridge Wells, Kent
Telephone (0892) 31122/26

IRELAND
Desmond Fitz-Gerald, Knight of Glin
Glin Castle, Glin, Co. Limerick
Private Residence: 52 Waterloo Road, Dublin 2
Telephone (0001) 68 05 85

NORTHERN IRELAND
John Lewis-Crosby
Marybrook House, Raleagh Road
Crossgar, Downpatrick, Co. Down
Telephone (0396) 830574

CHANNEL ISLANDS
Richard de La Hey
8 David Place, St. Helier, Jersey
Telephone (0534) 77582

Companies and Agents Overseas

Argentina
Cesar Feldman *Consultant*
Libertad 1269, 1012 Buenos Aires
Telephone (541) 41 1616 or 42 2046
Cables Tweba, Buenos Aires

Australia
Sue Hewitt
298 New South Head Road
Double Bay, Sydney 2028
Telephone (612) 326 1422   *Telex* AA 26343
Cables Christiart Sydney

Austria
Vincent Windisch-Graetz
Ziehrerplatz 4/22, 1030 Vienna
Telephone (43222) 73 26 44

Belgium
Richard Stern   Janine Duesberg
Christie, Manson & Woods (Belgium) Ltd
33 Boulevard de Waterloo
1000 Brussels
Telephone (322) 512 8765 or 8830
Telex Brussels 62042

Brazil
Vera Duvernoy *Consultant*
Marques de São Vincente 512, No. 303
Rio de Janeiro
Telephone (5521) 274 4265
Cables Christiart Rio de Janeiro

Canada
Murray Mackay
Christie, Manson & Woods International, Inc.
Suite 803, 94 Cumberland Street,
Toronto, Ontario M5R 1A3
Telephone (416) 960 2063   *Telex* 065 23907

Denmark
Birgitta Hillingso
20 Parkvaenget, 2920 Charlottenlund
Telephone (451) 62 23 77

France
Princesse Jeanne-Marie de Broglie
Christie's France SARL
17 rue de Lille, 75007 Paris
Telephone (331) 261 12 47   *Telex* 213468

**Monsieur Gérald Van der Kemp,
President d'Honneur of Christie's Europe**
is based in our Paris Office

Italy
Christie's (International) S.A.
Palazzo Massimo Lancellotti
Piazza Navona 114, Rome 00186
Telephone (396) 654 1217   *Telex* Rome 611524
Maurizio Lodi-Fè   Tom Milnes-Gaskell
d.ssa. Luisa Vertova Nicolson *Consultant*

MILAN
Giorgina Venosta
Christie's Italy S.r.l.,
9 via Borgogna
20144 Milan
Telephone (392) 794 712

TURIN
Sandro Perrone di San Martino
Corso Vittorio 86, 10121 Turin
Telephone (3911) 548 819

Japan
Toshihiko Hatanaka
c/o Dodwell Marketing Consultants
Kowa Building No. 35, 14-14 Akasaka,
1-chome, Minato-ku, Tokyo 107
Telephone (03) 584 2351   *Telex* J23790

Mexico
Ana Maria de Icaza de Xirau *Consultant*
Callejon de San Antonio 64
San Angel, Mexico 20 D.F.
Telephone (905) 548 5946

The Netherlands
Christie, Manson & Woods Ltd
Cornelis Schuytstraat 57
1071 JG Amsterdam
Telephone (3120) 64 20 11
Telex Amsterdam 15758
Harts Nystad

Norway
Ulla Klaveness
Riddervoldsgt 10 B
Oslo 2
Telephone (472) 44 12 42

Spain
Casilda Fz-Villaverde de Eraso, Carlos Porras
Edifico Propac
Casado del Alisal 5, Madrid 14
Telephone (341) 228 39 00   *Telex* 43889
Cables Christiart Madrid

Sweden
Lillemor Malmström
Hildingavägen 19
182 62 Djursholm, Stockholm
Telephone (468) 755 10 92
Telex Stockholm 12916

Switzerland
Christie's (International) S.A.
8 Place de la Taconnerie, 1204 Geneva
Telephone (4122) 28 25 44
Telex Geneva 423634
Cables Chrisauction Geneva
Dr Geza von Habsburg
Richard Stern

ZÜRICH
Maria Reinshagen
Christie's (International) A.G.
Steinwiesplatz, 8032 Zürich
Telephone (411) 69 05 05
Telex Zürich 56093

West Germany
Jörg-Michael Bertz
Alt Pempelfort 11a, 4000 Düsseldorf
Telephone (49211) 35 05 77   *Telex* 8587599
Cables Chriskunst Düsseldorf

Isabella von Bethmann Hollweg
Wentzelstrasse 21, D-2000 Hamburg 60
Telephone (4940) 279 0866

Maximilianstrasse 20, 8000 Munich 22
Telephone (4989) 22 95 39

Charlotte Fürstin zu Hohenlohe-Langenburg
Schloss Langenburg
7183 Langenburg, Württemberg

United States of America
Christie, Manson & Woods International, Inc.
502 Park Avenue, New York, N.Y. 10022
Telephone (212) 546 1000
Cables Chriswoods, New York
Telex (International) New York 620721
(Domestic) 710 5812325
President David Bathurst

CHRISTIE'S EAST
219 East 67th Street, New York, N.Y. 10021
Telephone (212) 570 4141   *Telex* 710-581 4211
President J. Brian Cole

CALIFORNIA
Christie, Manson & Woods International, Inc.
342 North Rodeo Drive
Beverley Hills, California 90212
Telephone (213) 275 5534   *Telex* 910 490 4652
Russell Fogarty   Christine Eisenberg

SAN FRANCISCO
Ellanor Notides
125 Lake Street, San Francisco, California 94118
Telephone (415) 751 2501

FLORIDA
Helen Cluett
225 Fern Street, West Palm Beach, Fla. 33401
Telephone (305) 833 6952

MID-ATLANTIC
Paul Ingersoll
P.O. Box 1112, Bryn Mawr, Pa. 19010
Telephone (215) 525 5493

David Ober
2935 Garfield Street, N.W.
Washington D.C. 20008
Telephone (202) 387 8722
Nuala Pell *Consultant*
Joan Gardner *Consultant*

MID-WEST
Frances Blair
46 East Elm Street, Chicago, Illinois 60611
Telephone (312) 787 2765

TEXAS
Linda N. Letzerich
2504 Avalon Place
Houston, Texas 77019
Telephone (713) 529 7777

ACKNOWLEDGEMENTS

Christie's are indebted to the following who have allowed their names to be published as purchasers of works of art illustrated in the preceding pages. The figures refer to the page numbers on which the illustrations appear.

Gunther Abels, Germalde-Galerie Abels, 116
Aquavella Galleries Inc, 119
Alice Adam Ltd., 99
Thomas Agnew & Sons., 43, 44, 88, 91, 310 (above right)
Ahuan UK Ltd., 380, 388, 390
Albert Amor Ltd., 344
W. Graham Arader III, 169
Armin B. Allen Inc., 333
Asprey & Co. Ltd., 194, 232, 279, 282, 350 (above centre)
Maurice Asprey Ltd., 305 (above right)

Hadji Baba, 396 (above, lower left, upper bracelet)
Mrs. H. Baer, 12 (above right), 226
Banca S. Paolo-Brescia, 16
J.P. Barbier-Muller, 166 (below left)
Gregory Baron, Esq., 241
S. Berger, 311 (above left)
Raymond Benardout Ltd., 381
Galerie Beyeler, 125
P. Biddulph, 242 (left and right)
Boss & Gopfert, 339
Bobinet Ltd., 239 (above right)
D.F. Brooke-Hitching, 166 (below right)

M. Carr, 315
David Carritt Ltd., 35
Dr. Chiavelli, 20,21
J.G. Cluff, Esq., 155
Colefax and Fowler, 344 (above)
Colt Industries, 412 (above)

Mr. D. Dillon, 336
Anthony D'Offay, 156, 158 (right), 159 (below)

Eaton's of Canada, 53
Antiquariaat Meÿer Elte, B.V., 430 (left)
Emanouel Antiques Ltd., 389
Eskenazi Ltd., 352, 354
Essoldo Fine Arts Ltd., 24

Mr. Fernstrom, 134
Fine Art Society Ltd., 160 (left and right)
Fischer Fine Arts, 270 (centre left), 270 (below right, centre and below left)
John Fleming Inc., 177, 179
Forbes Magazine Collection, New York, 175
Frost & Reed, 51

Gammon Art Gallery Ltd., 360
Gemcut S.A., 253

J. Gismondi, 210
Graff Diamonds Ltd., 245, 248 (necklace)
Groves Foundation, 205

Frank Hammond Bookseller, 164 (below)
Joseph Hajec, 411
Julian Hartnoll, 285
Hazlitt, Gooden & Fox, 28, 84 (left)
Hennell Ltd., 304 (line 4, left)
Mr. Hirano, 353

Yoshihiro Imura, 367 (above left, above right, below left)
H. Ismail, 386 (below right)

Japan Sword Co. Ltd., 378
J.P.L. Fine Art, 121
Jellinek & Sampson, 196, 342 (above left, below right, above right)
Samuel Josefowitz, 104

Nevill Keating Pictures Ltd., 114
Kennedy Galleries, 56
James H. Kirkman, 152
E. & C.T. Koopman & Sons., 278, 280, 281, 283, 284, 297, 298, 306
H.P. Kraus, 163

Galerie du Lac, 304 (line 1, right; line 2, left and second left)
Mr. Arne Larsson, 141
A. Laube & Sons., 94 (above)
Ronald A. Lee, 189, 191, 233, 314
Leggatt Bros., 41, 154 (above)
R.E. Lewis Inc., 98 (below right)
Collections of the Reigning Prince of Liechtenstein, Vaduz, 85 (below left and right)

MacConnal Mason Gallery, 52
Maclean Gallery, 157
Edgar Mannheimer, 239 (left)
Mansour Gallery, 386 (below left)
Matsuoka Jisho Co. Ltd., 355, 357, 361
H. McKay, 366 (lower right)
Christopher Mendez, 95 (above left)
Metna S.A., Masis Jouaillier Antiquaire, 273 (above right)
Franz A. Morat, 136
Nicholas Morley, 304 (line 1, 2nd right; line 2, 2nd left)
Sydney L. Moss Ltd., 369 (lower left)
Frederick Mulder, 112 (below)
Museum of Mankind, 398
Mr. Albrecht Neuhaus, 19
Lady Newman, 276

INDEX

A DIP INTO THE BATH CLUB.